The Residence

The Residence

Inside the Private World of The White House

Kate Andersen Brower

HARPER

An Imprint of HarperCollins*Publishers*

PORTRAITS ON PP. 82, 95, 119, 157, 216, 260: TINA HAGER/WHITE HOUSE, COURTESY GEORGE W. BUSH PRESIDENTIAL LIBRARY AND MUSEUM

HarperCollins books may be purchased for educational, business, or sales promotional use. For information, please e-mail the Special Markets Department at SPsales@harpercollins.com.

FIRST EDITION

Designed by Renato Stanisic

Library of Congress Cataloging-in-Publication Data has been applied for.

ISBN: 978-0-06-230519-0

15 16 17 18 19   OV/RRD   10 9 8 7

For Brooke Brower, my husband, and the one who makes me believe that anything is possible.

And for our joyous babies, Graham and Charlotte.

Contents

★

Main Cast of Characters

★

James W. F. "Skip" Allen	Usher, 1979–2004
Reds Arrington	Plumber, Plumbing Foreman, 1946–1979
Preston Bruce	Doorman, 1953–1977
Traphes Bryant	Electrician, Dog Keeper, 1951–1973
Cletus Clark	Painter, 1969–2008
William "Bill" Cliber	Electrician, 1963–1990; Chief Electrician, 1990–2004
Wendy Elsasser	Florist, 1985–2007
Chris Emery	Usher, 1987–1994
Betty Finney	Maid, 1993–2007
James Hall	Part-time Butler, 1963–2007
William "Bill" Hamilton	Houseman, Head of the Storeroom, 1958–2013
James Jeffries	Kitchen Worker, Part-time Butler, 1959–Current
Wilson Jerman	Houseman, Butler, 1957–1993; Part-time Doorman, 2003–2010

Jim Ketchum	Curator, 1961–1963; Chief Curator, 1963–1970
Christine Limerick	Executive Housekeeper, 1979–2008 (hiatus between 1986 and 1991)
Linsey Little	Houseman, 1979 –2005
Roland Mesnier	Executive Pastry Chef, 1979–2006
Betty Monkman	Curator, 1967–1997; Chief Curator, 1997–2002
Ronn Payne	Florist, 1973–1996
Nelson Pierce	Usher, 1961–1987
Mary Prince	Amy Carter's Nanny
James Ramsey	Butler, end of Carter Administration–2010
Stephen Rochon	Chief Usher, 2007–2011
Frank Ruta	Chef, 1979–1991 (hiatus between 1987 and 1988)
Tony Savoy	Operations Department Staffer/Supervisor, 1984–2013
Bob Scanlan	Florist, 1998–2010
Walter Scheib	Executive Chef, 1994–2005
Rex Scouten	Usher, 1957–1969; Chief Usher, 1969–1986, Chief Curator, 1986–1997
Ivaniz Silva	Maid, 1985–2008
Herman Thompson	Part-time Butler, 1960 –1993
Gary Walters	Usher, 1976–1986; Chief Usher 1986–2007
J. B. West	Usher, 1941–1957; Chief Usher, 1957–1969
Lynwood Westray	Part-time Butler, 1962–1994
Worthington White	Usher, 1980–2012
Zephyr Wright	The Johnsons' Family Cook

Introduction

Living in the White House is like being on the stage,
where tragedies and comedies play alternately. And we, the servants
of the White House, are the supporting cast.

—Lillian Rogers Parks, White House maid and seamstress,
1929–1961, *My Thirty Years Backstairs at the White House*

Preston Bruce was sitting in his Washington, D.C., kitchen with his wife, listening to the radio and having lunch—the one meal they ate together every day—when an announcer interrupted with an urgent message: *the president has been shot.*

He jumped up from his chair, cracking his knee on the table and sending dishes crashing to the floor. A minute or so later came another announcement, the voice even shriller: *The president has been shot. It has been verified that he has been shot. His condition is unknown.*

This can't be happening, thought Bruce. He threw on his coat, forgetting his hat on the brisk November day, and jumped in his car, tearing out of the driveway. His wife, Virginia, was left behind standing in their kitchen, shell-shocked amid the shards of broken dishes lying on the floor.

The normally unflappable Bruce was weaving through downtown traffic at fifty-five miles an hour—"I didn't realize how fast I was going," he would say later—when he suddenly heard a police siren blaring behind him. An officer on a motorcycle pulled up alongside him at Sixteenth Street and Columbia Road, jumped off his bike, and walked over to the driver's door.

"What's the hurry?" He was in no mood for excuses.

"Officer, I work at the White House," Bruce said breathlessly. "The president has been shot."

A stunned pause followed. Not everyone had heard the devastating news. "C'mon," the startled officer said, jumping back onto his motorcycle. "Follow me!" Bruce got his own police escort to the southwest gate of the White House that day.

Most Americans who were alive in 1963 remember exactly where they were when they learned that President Kennedy had been shot. For Bruce, though, the news had a special impact: Kennedy wasn't only the president, but he was also his boss, and—more important—his friend. Preston Bruce was the doorman at the White House, and a beloved member of the staff. Just the morning before, he had escorted the president, the first lady, and their son, John-John, to the marine helicopter on the South Lawn, which would carry them to Air Force One at Andrews Air Force Base. From there the Kennedys would leave for their fateful two-day, five-city campaign tour of Texas. (John-John, who was just four days shy of his third birthday, loved helicopter rides with his parents. He went only as far as Andrews; when he was told he couldn't accompany his mother and father all the way to Dallas, he sobbed. It was the last time he would ever see his father.)

"I'm leaving you in charge of everything here," President Kennedy shouted to Bruce, above the whir of the helicopter's engines on the South Lawn. "You run things to suit yourself."

A descendant of slaves and the son of a South Carolina sharecropper, Bruce had become an honorary member of the Kennedy

family. He watched movies with them in the White House theater and looked on as the president played happily with his children.
He winced when Kennedy bumped his head on a table while chas-
ing John-John, a rambunctious toddler, around the Oval Office.
(JFK's desk was one of John-John's favorite hiding places. Bruce
would sometimes have to fish him out from underneath before important meetings.) Tall and thin in his midfifties, with a shock of
white hair and a bright white mustache, Bruce wore a black suit
and white bow tie to work every day. He was so devoted to his job,
which included the delicate assignment of seating nervous guests at
state dinners, that he designed a table nicknamed the "Bruce Table,"
with a slanted top that made it easier to arrange table place cards. His
invention would be used for decades.

On November 22, as he raced toward the White House, Bruce
was in disbelief. "To this day I can still feel the shock that ran
through my whole body," he later recalled.

After arriving at the executive mansion, he had only one thing
on his mind. "I would wait for Mrs. Kennedy." He huddled around
the TV with other workers in the crowded Usher's Office. The news
confirmed fears shared by every White House staffer. "In most of
our minds," he wrote years later, "you're always aware that it was
completely possible that any president that ever left that eighteen
acres could come back just like President Kennedy."

When Jackie Kennedy finally returned to the White House
at 4:00 A.M. wearing the iconic bloodstained pink wool suit and
clutching the arm of her brother-in-law Robert F. Kennedy, she was
ghostly white and eerily calm. "Bruce, you waited until we came,"
she said softly, as though she was trying to comfort him. "Yes, you
knew I was going to be here, Mrs. Kennedy," he replied.

After a short service in the East Room, he led the first lady and the
attorney general up to the private residence on the second floor. In that
quiet moment in the elevator, standing next to the two people who

had been closest to JFK, Bruce finally broke down sobbing. Jackie and Robert joined him, folding their arms around one another, they cried together until they reached the second floor. When Jackie got to her bedroom she told her personal maid and confidante, Providencia Paredes, "I thought they might kill me too." Then she finally took off the suit caked in her husband's blood and bathed.

Exhausted, Bruce spent what was left of that night sitting upright in a chair in a tiny bedroom on the third floor. He took off his jacket and bow tie and unbuttoned the collar of his stiff white shirt, but he wouldn't let himself give into exhaustion. "I didn't want to lie down, in case Mrs. Kennedy needed me." His allegiance was reciprocated. Shortly after the funeral, the first lady gave him the tie her husband had worn on the flight to Dallas. "The president would have wanted you to have this," she told him. (JFK had switched ties just before getting into the motorcade, and had the old one in his jacket pocket when he was shot.) Robert Kennedy pulled off his gloves and handed them to his stricken friend: "Keep these gloves," he told Bruce, "and remember always that I wore them to my brother's funeral."

The White House doorman refused to leave his post to return home to his wife until November 26, four days after the assassination. Bruce's devotion to his job, and to the first family, may seem remarkable, but nothing less is expected from those who work in the residence.

———

AMERICA'S FIRST FAMILIES are largely unknowable. Their privacy is guarded by West Wing aides and by a team of roughly one hundred people who stay deliberately out of sight: the White House residence staff. These workers spend much of their time on the second and third floors of the fifty-five-thousand-square-foot building. It's here that the first family can escape the overwhelming pressures of the office, even if just for a couple of precious hours while they eat dinner or watch TV. Upstairs, as tourists shuffle below on the first floor and amateur photographers gather at the perimeter fence with cell phone cameras, they are free to conduct their personal lives in private.

Unlike the slew of political aides who have eagerly given interviews and published memoirs after leaving the White House, the maids, butlers, chefs, ushers, engineers, electricians, plumbers, carpenters, and florists who run America's most famous home have largely preferred to remain invisible. One worker told me that his colleagues share a "passion for anonymity." As a result, the unseen backstairs world of the White House staff has remained rich with intrigue.

I first became aware of that world when, as a member of the White House press corps, I was invited to a luncheon that Michelle Obama held for fewer than a dozen reporters in an intimate dining room on the State Floor of the White House. Dubbed the Old Family Dining Room after Jackie Kennedy created a separate dining room on the second floor that is used more routinely by current first families, the room is tucked away across from the formal State Dining Room, where I had covered dozens of events. I had never seen this private side of the White House; indeed, I didn't even know the room existed. Access to many areas of the residence is heavily restricted; reporters and photographers covering formal events, such as East Room receptions and state dinners (now often held in an impressive white pavilion on the South Lawn), are kept cordoned off from White House guests. And for these large gatherings, the White House staff is often augmented by the hiring of part-time butlers and waitstaff.

So I was surprised, on the day of the first lady's luncheon, when a handler ushered us into the relatively small and cozy Old Family Dining Room, and an elegantly dressed gentleman offered us champagne on a gleaming silver tray. The menu included salad with vegetables from the White House garden and fresh pan-roasted rockfish elegantly presented on Truman china. Each course was served by a butler who clearly had a rapport with the first lady. *This is all very* Downton Abbey, I thought. The experience left me wondering: Just who were these people, so intimate with the world's most powerful family?

As a White House reporter for Bloomberg News, I worked in one of the many tiny windowless cubbies located below the James S. Brady Press Briefing Room. The cramped basement space is a constant whirl of activity as reporters race back and forth covering events, talking to sources, and rushing back to their computers to file stories. During my time covering the White House, I traveled around the world on Air Force One and on Air Force Two (the vice president's plane)—filing reports from Mongolia, Japan, Poland, France, Portugal, China, and Colombia—but the most fascinating story turned out to be right in front of me every day: the men and women who take care of the first family, who share a fierce loyalty to the institution of the American presidency. Each staffer who has served at the White House has borne witness to history, and each has incredible stories to share.

The White House is the country's most potent and enduring symbol of the presidency. Its 132 rooms, 147 windows, 28 fireplaces, 8 staircases, and 3 elevators are spread across the 6 floors—plus 2 hidden mezzanine levels—all tucked within what appears to be a three-story building. The house is home to just one famous family at a time, but the members of the building's supporting cast are its permanent tenants.

The residence workers bring a sense of humanity and Old World values to the world's most famous eighteen acres. Rising at dawn, they sacrifice their personal lives to serve the first family with quiet, awe-inspiring dignity. For them, working in the White House, regardless of position, is a great honor. Elections may bring new faces, but they stay on from administration to administration and are careful to keep their political beliefs to themselves. They have one job: to make America's first families comfortable in the country's most public private home.

In the course of their work, many of these men and women have witnessed presidents and their families during incredibly vulnerable moments, but only a handful of residence workers have published memoirs of their time at the White House. This book marks the first time that so many have shared what it's like to devote their lives to caring for the first family. Their memories range from small acts of kindness to episodes of anger and private despair, from stories of personal quirks and foibles to moments when their everyday work was transcended by instances of national triumph or tragedy.

From playing with the Kennedy children in the Oval Office to witnessing the first African American president arrive at the White House; from being asked by Nancy Reagan to return each of her twenty-five Limoges boxes to the same exact spot after cleaning, to giving Hillary Clinton a moment of privacy during her husband's sex scandal and impeachment, the residence staff see sides of the first family no one else ever glimpses.

Though they gave me unprecedented access to their stories, recent and current residence workers follow a long-established code of ethics that values discretion and the protection of the first family's privacy above all else. Unlike most people in power-obsessed Washington, D.C., who tell each other where they work almost before offering their names, staffers avoid mentioning their extraordinary jobs. They inherited that code of honor from the previous generations who kept FDR's paralysis private by ushering guests into the room for state dinners only after the president was seated and his wheelchair rolled out of view—and who made sure that stories of JFK's philandering never left the White House gates.

Residence workers have such privileged access, in fact, that current White House aides did not want them speaking with me. One former staffer told me in an e-mail, "I think you will find that anyone who is still employed will not want to speak to you because they do not want to lose their job—yes, this is a reality. We were trained to keep what goes on inside the WH, inside the WH."

But while at first some of them were reluctant to share their experiences working in "the house," as they call it, all were incredibly gracious. Black and white, men and women, chefs, electricians, and maids, dozens of retired staffers invited me to sit across from them at their kitchen tables or to talk with them on their living room sofas. (I was pregnant with our second child at the time, which prompted lots of kind inquiries into how I was feeling and whether I wanted something to eat.) Before long, they were happily recounting decades of memories working for several presidents and their families. Many seemed oblivious to the fact that they had led remarkable lives with front-row seats to history. Their recollections were not always consistent; where many staffers had fond memories of the families they served, others told less flattering stories.

Getting them to talk wasn't always easy. Some opened up to me only after I mentioned the names of their colleagues whom I'd already interviewed. Others were guarded until we met in person, like Chief Electrician William "Bill" Cliber, who told me fascinating stories about Richard Nixon in his final days in office, and Executive Housekeeper Christine Limerick, who talked about her painful decision to temporarily leave her post because she was sick of taking abuse from a certain first lady.

Some people, like George W. Bush's favorite butler, James Ramsey, wanted to talk only about their positive experiences. Ramsey even said he was worried that the government would take away the pension he worked his entire life to earn if he shared anything negative (though there is no evidence that that would have happened). He was full of genuine love for the families he served. He passed away in 2014, but I feel fortunate to have gotten to know him and other staffers who died before they could see their stories told.

I've talked to people who worked at the White House during the time known as Camelot—including the first residence staffer to be informed of President Kennedy's assassination—and to butlers, doormen, and florists who served the Obamas. I've listened to the sons and daughters of presidents describe what it's like to grow up in the White House. And I have had candid conversations with former first ladies Rosalynn Carter, Barbara Bush, and Laura Bush, as well as many high-level White House aides. Most were genuinely eager to help bring attention to the people who work quietly and diligently behind the scenes.

Despite their sacrifice and hard work, the residence staff assiduously avoids the spotlight—and not just in a metaphorical sense. "There's an unwritten rule that we stayed in the background. If there was a camera we always ducked under it, over it, or around it," insisted Usher James W. F. "Skip" Allen. Yet the workers I interviewed had a blend of intelligence and character that made me want to learn more about their lives. Many of them also had a wry, even wicked, sense of humor. After our interview, retired butler James Hall made sure to walk me out—very slowly—through the crowded lobby of his retirement home. He wasn't just being polite, he admitted; he wanted to make sure everyone saw him with a younger woman. "It's like *Peyton Place* around here!" he said, laughing.

My research took me beyond Washington and its suburbs. Allen had retired to a sprawling six-thousand-square-foot nineteenth-century farmhouse in Bedford, Pennsylvania. We ate chicken salad sandwiches by his pool during a light drizzle as he described the close relationship between the president and the staff ("It would be nothing out of the ordinary for a president to acknowledge somebody's birthday") and the weight of the job ("Name a president. Nobody leaves the White House looking younger than they came in").

While they are overlooked in the pomp and circumstance of presidential events and state visits, White House workers are vital to the public and private lives of the American presidency. "In a way, my family and I always thought of them as cohosts with the president and the first lady," Tricia Nixon Cox, the older of President Nixon's two daughters, told me. "They made everything very beautiful and warm."

Sometimes they even help the world's most famous couple weather storms and feel normal again—if only for a few hours. At the height of the Monica Lewinsky scandal, several staffers told me, Hillary Clinton appeared tired and depressed. They said they felt sorry for her, knowing she craved the one thing she couldn't have: privacy. One staffer, Usher Worthington White, recalled clearing tourists out of the White House and keeping her Secret Service agents at bay so that the first lady could enjoy a few short hours of solitude by the pool. Having the chance to help Mrs. Clinton "meant the world to me," White said.

Residence workers sometimes get to witness the sheer joy a newly inaugurated president feels upon reaching the highest peak in American politics. In 2009, after the inaugural balls were finally over, the Obamas were settling in for their first night in the White House. But they still weren't quite ready for bed when White was dropping off some late-night papers. When he got upstairs to the second floor he heard something unusual.

"All of a sudden I heard President Obama say, 'I got this, I got this. I got the inside on this now,' and suddenly the music picked up and it was Mary J. Blige." The new residents had shed their formal wear; the president was in shirtsleeves and the first lady was wearing a T-shirt and sweatpants. The president grabbed the first lady, White recalls, and suddenly "they were dancing together" to Blige's hit "Real Love." The usher paused a moment as he told the story. "It was the most beautiful, lovely thing you could imagine."

"I bet you haven't seen anything like this in this house, have you?" Obama asked as the first couple danced.

"I can honestly say I've never heard *any* Mary J. Blige being played on this floor," White replied.

He isn't sure how long the Obamas stayed there dancing, but it was clear that they intended to savor the moment.

————

Many first families say they think of the residence staff as the true tenants of the White House. President Carter has called them "the glue that holds the house together." One staffer called his colleagues "a group of people who eat, sleep, and drink the White House."

The White House employs approximately 96 full-time and 250 part-time residence staff: ushers, chefs, florists, maids, butlers, doormen, painters, carpenters, electricians, plumbers, engineers, and calligraphers. In addition, about two dozen National Park Service staff take care of the White House grounds. The residence workers are federal employees who serve at the pleasure of the president.

The center of activity for the White House staff is the Usher's Office, located on the State Floor next to the North Portico entrance. The chief usher is in charge of the funds allocated by Congress to run the house, including the cost of heating, lighting, air-conditioning, and the staff's salaries. In 1941, when there were sixty-two people on the residence staff, the annual budget was just $152,000. Fast-forward through almost seventy-five years of added staff, operational costs, inflation, and more, and the annual budget now hovers around $13 million. (This cost is separate from the $750,000 required to repair and restore the White House every year.)

The job of the chief usher is akin to the general manager of a major hotel, but with only one tenant to serve. He or she manages the entire residence staff, working closely with the first lady. Reporting to the chief usher is a deputy and a team of ushers responsible for overseeing the various departments or "shops," such as the Housekeeping Shop or the Flower Shop. The ushers serve as contacts for visitors, including the first family's house guests, and they keep records of the president's movements within the house, which eventually get transferred to the presidential libraries for posterity.

The job of chief usher in today's White House is so complex that it demands the kind of rigor and discipline generally associated with the military. Before U.S. Coast Guard Rear Admiral Stephen Rochon was appointed chief usher by George W. Bush in 2007—becoming the eighth person, and the first African American, to serve in the role officially—he sat for eight interviews for the job, driving back and forth to the White House from his Coast Guard station at Norfolk, Virginia. His final interview was with the president in the Oval Office. Bush wondered whether Rochon would be happy with the new, misleadingly modest title.

"What do you think about this chief usher business?" Bush asked him.

Rochon replied: "Well, Mr. President, what's in a title?"

Apparently, a lot: When Rochon was hired, the post was renamed White House Chief Usher and Director of the Executive Residence, a decidedly more impressive job description. Since October 2011, the job has been held by Angella Reid, the former general manager of the Ritz-Carlton in Arlington, Virginia—the first woman and the second African American to hold the position.

No matter how august the title, the goal is simple: to provide whatever the first family needs. For Chief Usher J. B. West, that included feverishly searching the house for Caroline Kennedy's lost hamsters and calling in dozens of experts in an unending quest to satisfy President Johnson's demand for better water pressure in his shower. Jacqueline Kennedy called West "the most powerful man in Washington, next to the president."

From the highest staff position to the most entry-level one, getting hired to work at the White House is not as simple as answering an ad or applying online. "The jobs in the White House are not advertised," said Tony Savoy, head of the Operations Department until 2013. "Nearly everyone I interviewed had a family member or a friend who recommended them for the job. You're vouching for the person you're bringing in." Most workers stay on for decades, some even for generations: one family, the Ficklins, has seen nine members work in the White House.

Every administration names a social secretary. The post has traditionally gone to a woman—until 2011, when Jeremy Bernard was named to the position by the Obamas, becoming both the first male and the first openly gay social secretary. The social secretary acts as a conduit between the first family and the residence staff, and between the West Wing and the East Wing. The position involves supervision of seating for state dinners and formal events at the White House, with the secretary distributing worksheets to the residence staff showing how many people are expected and what rooms will be used for the event.

The social secretary often gets pulled between competing worlds. Letitia Baldrige, who served in the post during the Kennedy administration, showed the president letters disapproving of John-John's long hair—which the first lady loved. When the president insisted he get a haircut, Jackie Kennedy didn't speak to Baldrige for three days.

Residence workers can make the social secretary's job of navigating endless parties and following time-honored traditions much easier. Julianna Smoot, who served as the Obamas' social secretary from 2010 to 2011, credits the team of White House calligraphers, who sit in a small office down the hall from the Social Office in the East Wing, with saving her from one embarrassing oversight during her time there. One day in the late summer of 2010, one of the three calligraphers—who are responsible for creating a massive number of invitations to White House events—approached Smoot and asked, "Have you thought about Christmas?"

"It's in December. Can't we talk about it when we get closer?" Smoot said. Christmas seemed far away, and there were so many events to work on before then.

"We're actually behind on planning by now," the calligrapher told her worriedly.

Smoot was shocked. "Of course I wouldn't know that!" she recalled later. "It was this panic moment! We had to come up with a theme *and* the Christmas card. I think the reason we had Christmas in 2010 was because of the calligraphers."

The social secretary sometimes delivers bad news to the residence staff on behalf of the first lady, who usually wants to stay above the fray. When Laura Bush hired Lea Berman as her new social secretary, it fell to Berman to take Executive Chef Walter Scheib aside and tell him to stop serving "this country club food" to the family. Scheib said he'd just been following orders and besides, much of what he prepared could hardly be called "country club food." In fact, it was far from highbrow. "If the president wanted a peanut butter and honey sandwich then by god we made the best damn peanut butter and honey sandwich we could," Scheib says, adding, "This is what the president wants, be careful what you call it." When Berman started showing him dog-eared pages of Martha Stewart cookbooks, the chef was enraged.

Christine Limerick oversaw about twenty staffers in the Housekeeping Shop, which she managed from 1979 to 2008 (she took a hiatus between 1986 and 1991). Six worked on the second and third floors in the family's private living quarters, including several maids and a houseman who vacuumed and moved heavy furniture. Two staffers handled the laundry exclusively and the rest took care of the tour areas and the Oval Office, and they were supplemented by additional workers when there were house guests and big events, such as state dinners.

The White House also employs a team of florists, led by a chief florist, who prepare arrangements daily in the Flower Shop, located in a small space on the Ground Floor, nestled under the driveway of the White House's North Portico. The florists are responsible for coming up with unique arrangements that suit the first family's taste. During the holidays and around state dinners the florists call in volunteers to help; the Obamas often use outside event companies from Chicago to help stage elaborate state dinners and decorate for Christmas. The chief florist focuses on the public spaces and helps oversee all of the arrangements; the members of the Flower Shop share responsibility for decorating the entire complex, from the private quarters on the second and third floors to the West Wing, the East Wing, and the public rooms. No corner of the White House is overlooked.

Reid Cherlin, who was a spokesman for President Obama, remembers being awed by their work. "What always struck me was the flowers. Coming in in the morning in the West Wing, if you came in at the right time, the florists would be putting new bowls of peonies out," he said. "There's something about putting fresh flowers in a place where no one is necessarily going to be. It's one thing for them to be on the coffee table in the Oval Office, it's another thing to be sprucing things up in areas where people aren't even going to congregate."

Everyone works together to make the residence look as perfect as possible, said Bob Scanlan, who worked in the Flower Shop from 1998 to 2010. "If a flower was down in an arrangement, it wasn't unusual for the housekeeper to come in and say, 'You guys might want to take a look at the Red Room, there are petals on the table. I picked them up but it looks like they're dropping still.' We kept an eye out for each other because everything reflects on everybody."

The residence is served by around six permanent butlers, and dozens of part-time butlers who come in on a regular basis to help with state dinners and receptions. Of the six full-time butlers, one is designated as the head butler, or the maître d'. The task of tending to the president's more personal needs is handled by valets, who are always close at hand. There are typically two valets who work in shifts. They are military personnel who take care of the president's clothes, run errands, shine shoes, and work with the housekeepers. For example, if the president's shoes need to be resoled, a valet alerts a member of the Housekeeping Shop. When the president goes to the Oval Office in the morning, a valet stands close by in case he needs anything, including a cup of coffee, breakfast, or just a cough drop. When the president travels, a valet packs for him and often rides in a backup vehicle in the motorcade, carrying a spare shirt or tie in case the commander in chief spills something and needs a quick change of clothes.

On the very first day after his inauguration, George W. Bush was shocked when he met his valets. Laura Bush says, "These two men come and introduce themselves to George and say, 'We're your valets.' So George went in and talked to his dad and said, 'These two men just introduced themselves and said they were my valets, and I don't *need* a valet. I don't *want* a valet.' And President Bush (George H. W. Bush) said, 'You'll get used to it.'" And he did. Sooner or later, any president must have an occasion to be grateful for the luxury of not having to worry about packing a spare shirt.

———

RESIDENCE WORKERS ARE there to alleviate the burdens of daily life for the first family, who generally have no time to cook, shop, or clean. They also serve under the highest possible security—what other household has a team of snipers keeping constant watch on the roof?—and must accustom themselves to a job with little privacy. Many observers have noted that living in the White House can be like spending time in a prison—though, as Michelle Obama notes, "It's a really nice prison."

Longtime White House maid Betty Finney (nicknamed "Little Betty" because of her tiny frame) says that the high level of security helps make the people who work there, and the family, feel safe. "You know the snipers are up there to protect you. Why not feel at home?" she said. "You'd wonder where they were if you didn't see them!"

Recent security lapses, however, expose the vulnerability of this potent symbol of America's democracy and the family who call it home. They also show how multifaceted and critical the job of a residence worker can be. As the nation's first black president, President Obama reportedly faces three times as many threats as his predecessors. In 2014, former residence workers were horrified when a man armed with a knife was able to scale the White House fence, sprint across the North Lawn, and actually make his way deep into the mansion's main floor, bypassing several Secret Service officers, before he was eventually tackled by an off-duty agent. In another terrifying incident in 2011, a maid inadvertently became a sort of private investigator when she was the first person to notice a broken window and a chunk of white concrete on the floor of the Truman Balcony. Her discovery led to the realization that a man had actually fired at least seven bullets into the residence several days before. (The Secret Service knew a shooting had occurred but wrongly concluded that the shots were fired by rival gangs in a gunfight and that they were not aimed at the executive mansion.) White House maids are trained to be "very observant," and they know to report anything out of the ordinary, Limerick says, especially if it could endanger the first family.

Certainly there's nothing ordinary about life in the residence, no matter how hard the staff work to make the president and his family feel at home. Beyond the very real security concerns, the

White House bears precious little resemblance to a normal American household. The Reagans' son, Ron, told me about a visit he and his wife made to see his parents. When they arrived too late for dinner, they decided to rummage through the kitchen in the private quarters, looking for eggs and a frying pan. When a butler heard them rattling around late at night, he rushed in, looking concerned.

"Can I help you? Don't you want somebody to do that for you?" he asked earnestly.

"No, thank you," Reagan replied. "But can you tell me, where are the eggs? Where do you keep the frying pan?"

The butler didn't look pleased. The last thing the staff ever wants is to feel useless. In the end, Reagan had to ask the butler to bring up eggs from the Ground Floor kitchen; there were none in the Reagans' family kitchen.

"They really, *really* do want to do what they do. They don't want to just stand there."

Hillary Clinton was another first family member who sometimes wanted to be able to fend for herself. She designed an eat-in area in the second-floor kitchen so that her family could have their meals together informally.

"I knew I'd done the right thing when Chelsea was sick one night," she said. That night, she recalled, the staff "went crazy" when she went to make her daughter scrambled eggs.

"Oh, we'll bring an omelet from downstairs," the butler told her.

"No, I just want to make some scrambled eggs and applesauce and feed her what I would feed her if we were living anywhere else in America."

Though the first family may sometimes wish they could forget about the majesty of the residence, many of the workers said they took solace in it. "If you're having a little bit of a bad day with a member of the first family or their staff, you step away from it and you look at the house," said Limerick. "If I would see the White

House lit up at night I'd think, *I actually work inside that building, and I've had the wonderful privilege to do that.* It could set my mind straight and I could deal with the next day."

————

THE WHITE HOUSE is the physical embodiment of American democracy. It sits on eighteen acres in downtown Washington, grounds that are cared for year-round by the National Park Service. The main building, known formally as the executive mansion, is divided into public and private rooms. The mansion may look like it only has three floors, but its design is deceptive: the building actually contains six floors, plus two small mezzanine levels. In addition to two belowground floors, there is the Ground Floor, where the main kitchen, the Flower Shop, and the Carpenter's Shop are located; the State Floor, also called the first floor; the two mezzanines, which house the chief usher's office and the Pastry Kitchen; and the second and third floors, which are the first family's private quarters. The staff kitchen and storage areas are located in the basement levels. The East Wing and the West Wing have their own hidden floors, the most famous of which is the Situation Room, located underneath the West Wing. It has become a symbol of the gravity of the presidency, where the commander in chief gathers with advisers to handle major crises and conduct secure calls with foreign leaders.

The residence staff has its own cafeteria, dining room, lounge, and storage areas in the basement mezzanine (actually a full floor), located under the North Portico. Their cafeteria is separate from the main kitchen on the Ground Floor where meals are prepared for the first family and for formal occasions, including state dinners. (In addition, there is the small kitchen on the second floor of the residence that is exclusively used to prepare intimate family meals.) White House workers have traditionally gathered in the basement cafeteria to eat, talk, and unwind. For years, this was where the staff came to enjoy traditional Southern home cooking, including fried chicken, corn bread, and black-eyed peas, lovingly prepared by a team of African American cooks, including a woman named Miss Sally, who always wore elaborate hats when she wasn't working and loved to tease her colleagues—sometimes swearing like a sailor—when she served them. While the basement cafeteria was discontinued recently in an apparent cost-saving measure—much to the chagrin of the workers—it's still a gathering place, where workers bring their own food and sit down to eat and catch up.

Occasionally even top political aides come downstairs to dine with residence workers. Reggie Love, Obama's former personal assistant—known as his "body man"—grew so close to some of the butlers that he would eat with them on weekends in the kitchen when the cafeteria for West Wing staffers, known as the Navy Mess, was closed. Love left the White House in 2011, but he still plays cards with the White House butlers when he's in town.

———

THE WEST WING is home to the Oval Office and to the president's political staff. The East Wing houses the offices of the first lady and her staff. Walking between the two wings is roughly the equivalent of walking across a football field.

Every morning members of the staff have to roll out the carpets and put out ropes and stanchions in the tour areas on the Ground Floor and the State Floor. Every afternoon, after thousands of people have walked through, they have to clean, remove the stanchions, and roll down the carpets, so that if the first family wants to spend time on the State Floor it won't look so glaringly like a tourist destination.

"I didn't appreciate until I worked there that the president and the first lady aren't that far removed from all the public tours.

They're just a floor above," said Katie Johnson, President Obama's personal secretary from 2009 to 2011. Her responsibilities included keeping the president on schedule and coordinating with the first lady and the residence staff. Johnson was the person assigned with the unenviable task of telling the East Wing staff if the president was going to be running late for dinner with his family.

The residence feels "like a very, very fancy New York apartment," she said candidly. "There's all this stuff going on outside and around but once you're inside, it's your home."

Katie McCormick Lelyveld, Michelle Obama's first press secretary, would sometimes sit in an office adjacent to the beauty parlor on the second floor. She remembers how quiet those floors were compared to the hubbub below. "There aren't dozens of people flitting about in the personal home space. They very much try to treat it as a personal home. Agents aren't standing inside there, they're standing outside."

"The White House is built on a human scale," says Tricia Nixon Cox. One day, after a welcoming ceremony on the South Lawn, a visiting European prince turned to her and said, "It really is a house." He was astonished by the scale of the executive mansion, compared with the palaces he knew. "To him, it looked small!"

It may be less imposing than some royal palaces, but it is far from modest. The large Entrance Hall on the north side opens to the eighty-foot-long East Room at one end and the State Dining Room, often used for state dinners in honor of foreign heads of state, at the other. There are three rooms in between: the Green Room, the Blue Room, and the Red Room.

The first family's private rooms on the second and third floors are linked by one main corridor on each floor: sixteen rooms and six bathrooms on the second floor, another twenty rooms and nine bathrooms on the third. Maids and valets have sometimes been housed on these floors, as well as presidential children. The guest rooms do not have numbers on their doors, but they are known among the residence staff by their room numbers, just like at a hotel. Each week, each of the White House maids is assigned a roster of rooms to clean. And they all hate Room Number 328.

"It's the hardest room to clean!" says Maid Betty Finney. Room 328 has a sleigh bed, "and they're incredibly hard to make! When you make a bed you want it to look neat, and that was a hard, hard job trying to get that thing neat. We all knew it had to be done, we just dreaded it."

Each main floor boasts an oval-shaped room: the Diplomatic Reception Room on the Ground Floor, where President Roosevelt delivered his fireside chats and from where the first family usually enters the residence; the Blue Room on the State Floor, which overlooks the South Lawn and features a cut-glass French chandelier and vivid blue satin draperies; and the Yellow Oval Room on the second floor, leading to the Truman Balcony. This last was once a library with a private passage to President Lincoln's office, now the Lincoln Bedroom, created so that Lincoln could avoid the hordes of people waiting to see him in the Treaty Room; it's now a presidential study. The West Wing, where the Oval Office is located, would not be built until decades later. Until then, the residence served as the president's home and his office.

There are four staircases in the executive residence: the Grand Staircase, which goes from the State Floor to the second floor; a staircase by the president's elevator, which goes from the basement to the third floor; a spiral staircase by the staff elevator that goes from the first-floor mezzanine, where the Pastry Shop is located, to the basement; and the fourth staircase, the true "backstairs," which runs from the second floor by the Queens' Bedroom (an elegant rose-colored room named for royalty who have stayed there) to the east end of the third floor. Maids sometimes use this staircase if they need to clean rooms on the second floor and want to avoid interrupting the first family. It allows them to walk all the way up to the third floor and circle back down.

The White House was designed by the Irish-born architect James Hoban, after winning a competition devised by President George Washington and Secretary of State Thomas Jefferson. The house's design was inspired by Leinster House, an eighteenth-century Georgian mansion in Dublin that is home to Ireland's Parliament. Early residents complained that it was too big, a critique rarely heard now that state dinners sometimes have to be prepared for hundreds of guests in the cramped kitchen and almost every guest room is crammed with friends and family around the inauguration.

George Washington had predicted that Washington, D.C., would rival the beauty and grandeur of Paris and London, but at first the city lagged far behind such picturesque European capitals. In 1800, when President John Adams and his wife, Abigail, became the first residents of the White House, there were only six habitable rooms, and the Adamses brought just four servants with them. Their new home was far from complete, and Washington was such a swampy, isolated outpost that the first family got lost for hours between Baltimore and the capital. Once they finally arrived they had to enter on wooden planks; the front steps had not yet been installed. A laundry and stables dotted the area now occupied by the West Wing, and city officials even closed down a brothel operating out of the shacks of the construction workers building the White House. (Carpenters and stone carvers were so upset by the move that the brothel was relocated to a more inconspicuous part of town.)

"We have not the least fence, yard, or other convenience," Abigail wrote to her daughter. "The principal stairs are not up, and will not be this winter."

When Abigail Adams moved into the White House, she estimated that at least thirty servants would be needed to run it properly. (Nearly one hundred people work there today.) In early administrations the first families often brought their own maids, cooks, and valets, paying their personal staffs themselves. In recent decades some first families have brought a loyal employee or two from their prepresidential lives, but they mostly rely on the expertise of the residence staff.

In 1814, toward the tail end of the War of 1812, the British burned the White House to the ground. President James Madison asked Hoban to help rebuild the mansion, already a national icon. Since then, each president has sought to leave his mark on the physical building. The mansion was subjected to various Victorian embellishments during the nineteenth century, but in 1902 Theodore Roosevelt hired famed New York architects McKim, Mead & White to renovate it in keeping with its original neoclassical style. Roosevelt had the third story outfitted with guest rooms and tore down a series of giant glass conservatories—used to grow fruits and flowers for the first family—to clear a path for the expansion known as the West Wing. Later that year, Roosevelt moved his office from the second floor of the residence into the West Wing; his successor, William Howard Taft, added the Oval Office, completed in 1909.

The last major renovation came during the Truman administration, when the roof was literally caving in and the house was found to be in serious danger of collapsing. Things had gotten so dangerous that once, when the first lady was hosting a tea for the Daughters of the American Revolution in the Blue Room, the chandelier—which was as big as a refrigerator—swayed wildly above the unsuspecting guests, in part because the president was taking a bath above them on the second floor. In addition, the leg of one of Margaret Truman's pianos actually plunged through the rotted flooring of her sitting room during a particularly spirited practice session. Truman replaced the mansion's original wood framing with a new steel structure and added a second-floor outdoor space overlooking the

South Lawn that became known as the Truman Balcony, still a favorite spot for first families to relax.

No modern White House resident has transformed the White House more surely than Jacqueline Kennedy, who launched a very public effort to restore the interior (she hated the term *redecorate*), aimed at making it the "most perfect house" in the country. She asked her friend the philanthropist Rachel "Bunny" Mellon to redesign the Rose Garden and the East Garden, replacing Mamie Eisenhower's pink with soft white and pale blue. She augmented the work of the White House staff by bringing in top interior decorator Sister Parish to help in the restoration, combing the house for "treasures" and jettisoning "horrors." "If there's anything I can't stand, it's Victorian mirrors—they're hideous. Off to the dungeons with them," Jackie joked, insisting that "everything in the White House must have a reason for being there." She enlisted Henry Francis du Pont, a collector of early American furniture and an heir to the family fortune, to chair the White House Fine Arts Committee, which she created within a month of moving into the residence. Members of the committee were responsible for searching for museum-quality pieces around the country and for persuading their owners to donate them to the White House. She also established the Curator's Office, ensuring that the house's furnishings and artwork would be properly inventoried and cared for. When she gave the first-ever televised tour of the mansion, in 1962, it was watched by eighty million people and helped to make her one of the country's most popular first ladies. She was only thirty-two years old at the time.

The White House of today still bears Jackie Kennedy's stamp. She took a building that had long seemed drab and made it fashionable, bringing to the job a blend of historical sensitivity and contemporary elegance. She breathed a new Continental style into the

White House staff, hiring French chef René Verdon and appointing Oleg Cassini as official couturier. And her attentions extended to the private quarters: when the Old Family Dining Room downstairs felt too formal to serve as a gathering place for her young family, she took a second-floor space that had been Margaret Truman's bedroom and remade it as a kitchen and dining room for them.

Today the staff talks about the house with a reverence they usually reserve for their favorite first families. One residence worker said that every time he gave friends a tour of the White House he would end it by telling them to look around and soak it all in: "You have walked through exactly the same space as every president since John Adams was president."

Each time, he said, "It was thrilling."

———

THE WHITE HOUSE staff delights in knowing every inch of the mansion, its little-known corners and historical secrets. The underground locker rooms where butlers keep their crisp tuxedos and maids house their uniforms (pastel shirts and white pants) are just a short distance from a bomb shelter under the East Wing that was built for President Franklin Roosevelt during World War II; this room is now the President's Emergency Operations Center, built to withstand a nuclear detonation. The tube-shaped bunker is where the president may be taken in case of an attack. The Ground Floor Map Room was once a billiards room before it was transformed into the president's top secret planning center during World War II; it was there, surrounded by maps tracking the movements of American and enemy forces, that FDR contemplated the invasion of Normandy. Few people were ever granted the authority to glimpse inside. "When the room was to be cleaned," wrote Chief Usher J. B. West, "the security guard covered the maps with cloth, standing duty while the cleaner mopped the floor." Decades later, Bill Clinton used this room to give his televised grand jury testimony during the Lewinsky affair; and today it is used as a holding area for holiday party guests waiting to be photographed with the president and first lady in the adjoining Diplomatic Reception Room.

Other rooms tell different stories spanning centuries of American history. Abigail Adams used the grand but drafty East Room— the largest room in the White House, with ceilings more than twenty feet high—to hang laundry. The room, which later served as a temporary home for soldiers during the Civil War, now serves as the setting for most presidential press conferences. The State Dining Room, often used for highly choreographed state dinners in connection with the signing of significant military and trade agreements, was once Thomas Jefferson's office. The Green Room, now a formal sitting room on the State Floor, began as Jefferson's bedroom and breakfast room; James Monroe used it as a card parlor, and Abraham Lincoln's beloved eleven-year-old son, Willie, was embalmed there, candles illuminating his face as camellias were placed in his hands. The small Victorian-style Lincoln Sitting Room on the second floor was used as a telegraph room in the late nineteenth century; during the darkest days of Watergate, Richard Nixon sought refuge amid its heavy drapes and dark furnishings, spending hours there with music blasting, a fire blazing in the fireplace, air-conditioning cranked up as high as it would go.

On the third floor there's a sanctuary hidden from view on the roof of the South Portico with 180-degree views of the Mall and the Washington Monument. It was designed by First Lady Grace Coolidge as her "Sky Parlor." Now known as the Solarium, the airy hideaway serves as the first family's family room. It's here where young Caroline Kennedy attended kindergarten, where President

Reagan went to recuperate after being shot in an assassination attempt, and where Sasha and Malia Obama giggle with friends during sleepovers.

———

NONE OF THE residence workers I interviewed minded being called a "domestic." There's nothing demeaning about working in the White House, in *any* capacity. "When you can't afford it yourself and you're surrounded by the finest pieces of furniture and Americana in the entire country every single day, that's kind of cool," says Florist Ronn Payne.

To Executive Pastry Chef Roland Mesnier, preparing elaborate desserts for five presidents was the pinnacle of his career. "The White House is the top of the top. If it's not the top at the White House, when is it going to be the top?"

It is this distinct commitment to service, and pride in their role, that allow America's first families to work and live in the White House complex with confidence and security, and to enjoy precious moments of peace. The stories of these residence workers offer a glimpse at our presidents and their families as they live within the confines of the office, literally and symbolically. Their incredible stories—some heartwarming, some hilarious, some tragic—deserve a place in American history.

CHAPTER I

Controlled Chaos

*The transformation in the household from one Administration
to another is as sudden as death. By that I mean it leaves you with a
mysterious emptiness. In the morning you serve breakfast to a family with
whom you have spent years. At noon that family is gone out of your life
and here are new faces, new dispositions, and new likes and dislikes.*

—Alonzo Fields, butler and maître d', 1931–1953,
My 21 Years in the White House

It's the only time I ever had a job quit me.

—Walter Scheib, executive chef, 1994–2005

Once or twice a decade, on an often bone-chillingly cold day in January, Americans are riveted by the public transfer of power from one president to the next. Hundreds of thousands of people flood the National Mall to watch the president-elect take the oath of office, in a serene and carefully choreographed ceremony that Lady Bird Johnson called "the great quadrennial American pageant."

Behind the scenes, however, this peaceful ceremony is accompanied by an astounding number of complex logistics. Laura Bush calls the "transfer of families" a "choreographic masterpiece, done with exceptional speed," and its successful execution depends on the institutional knowledge and the flexibility of the residence staff. The hum of White House activity starts even earlier than usual on Inauguration Day, with workers coming in before the break of dawn. By the time their day has come to an end, a new era in American history has begun.

The White House belongs to the outgoing family until noon, when the new president's term begins. On the morning of the inauguration, the president hosts a small coffee reception for the new first family. Just before the first family departs, the staff crams into the opulent State Dining Room, where they have served so many state dinners, to say good-bye to the family. They are often overcome by the range of emotions they feel—trading one boss, and in some cases a friend, for another in the span of just six hours. In many cases they have had eight years to grow close to the departing family; they have seldom had any time to get to know the mansion's new residents. There is rarely a dry eye in the room—even though many may be excited about the future.

"When the Clintons came down and Chelsea came with them, they didn't say a word," Head Housekeeper Christine Limerick recalled about Inauguration Day 2001. "I'll get emotional about this now—[President Clinton] looked at every person dead on in the face and said, 'Thank you.' The whole room just broke up."

During the farewell, residence workers present the family with a gift—sometimes the flag that flew over the White House on the day that the president was inaugurated—placed in a beautiful hand-carved box designed by White House carpenters. In 2001, Limerick, Chief Florist Nancy Clarke, and Chief Curator Betty Monkman gave Hillary Clinton a large pillow made from swatches of fabrics that she had selected to decorate different rooms in the house.

There is very little time for reflection. At around eleven o'clock in the morning, the two first families leave the White House for the Capitol. Between then and approximately five o'clock in the afternoon—when the new president and his family return to rest and prepare for the inaugural balls—the staff must complete the job of moving one family out and another family in. In that rare moment, when the eyes of Washington and the world are trained away from the White House toward the Capitol, the staff is grateful that the public's attention is temporarily diverted from the turbulent activity within the residence walls.

Since employing professional movers for one day would require an impractical array of security checks, the residence staff is solely responsible for moving the newly elected president in and the departing president and his family out. No outside help is allowed. Throughout the day, even as they continue to perform their traditional roles, the residence workers also serve as professional movers, with just six hours to complete the move. The job is so large, and so physically demanding, that everyone is called in to help: pot washers in the kitchen help arrange furniture, and carpenters can be found placing framed photographs on side tables. The move is so labor intensive that on the day of the Clintons' arrival one staffer sustained a serious back injury from lifting a sofa and was unable to return to work for several months.

For Operations Supervisor Tony Savoy, Inauguration Day is the most important day of his career. The Operations Department usually handles receptions, dinners, rearranging furniture for the tapings of TV interviews, and outdoor events, but during the inauguration they are the team that "moves 'em in and moves 'em out," Savoy says. The trucks carrying the new family's belongings are allowed in through one set of gates, and dozens of residence workers from the Operations, Engineering, Carpenters, and Electricians shops race to remove furniture from the trucks and place them precisely where the first family's interior decorator wants them. "The best transition is when they don't lose" and get to stay another four years, Savoy joked, masking the very serious anxiety that comes with this astounding task.

In the six hours between the departure of the first family and the arrival of the newly elected president and his family, the staff has to put in fresh rugs and brand-new mattresses and headboards, remove paintings, and essentially redecorate in the incoming family's preferred style. They unpack the family's boxes, fold their clothes perfectly, and place them in their drawers. They even put toothpaste and toothbrushes on bathroom counters. No detail is overlooked.

Florist Bob Scanlan helped with the transition from Clinton to George W. Bush in 2001. As transitions go, the Bushes' was relatively easy, since they knew the territory better than most. George W. Bush was a frequent visitor to the residence when his father was president. The Bushes were used to being surrounded by a large staff, and Laura Bush recognizes that they "had a huge advantage" over other first families because they had spent so much time at the White House when the first President Bush ("old man Bush" as the staffers affectionately call him) was in office. "The only other family that had that were John Quincy and Louisa Adams."

Bill Clinton was well aware of the Bush's familiarity with the house and its staff and joked that Bush even knew where to find the light switches. Clinton, on the other hand, had been to the White House only a handful of times before his inauguration: once, as a teenage member of the American Legion Boys Nation, when he was photographed shaking President Kennedy's hand; once as a guest of the Carters in 1977 (which also marked Hillary Clinton's first visit); and several times for the National Governors Association dinners during his terms as governor of Arkansas. Before they moved in, Hillary said she had only been to the second floor once, when Barbara Bush gave her a tour after her husband won the election. She had never even seen the third floor. When they moved in, Hillary delved into the history of the house, asking curators to compile a book showing how every room looked through history back to the earliest photographs and drawings.

In the modern era, however, Barack Obama is the president who found the transition the most challenging. He moved with his family from their home in Chicago's Hyde Park neighborhood directly into the White House. The Obamas were even less accustomed to a household staff than the Clintons: they had one housekeeper in Chicago, but not a nanny, leaving their daughters, Sasha and Malia, with Michelle's mother, Marian, during the campaign. Without the benefit of growing up the son of a president—or living in the relative luxury of a governor's mansion—it took time for Obama and his family to grow comfortable with their new lives.

On January 20, 2009, 1.8 million people huddled together in twenty-eight-degree weather to watch Barack Obama become the first African American to take the oath of office. It was not only the largest crowd that had ever attended a presidential inauguration, it was also the largest attendance for any event in the history of Washington, D.C.

Most Americans had never heard of Barack Obama until 2004, when, as an Illinois state senator, he delivered an electrifying keynote address at the Democratic National Convention. His meteoric rise left the Obamas with very little time to prepare for life in the White House. Knowing this, the residence staff wanted to help ease their transition. It must have felt surreal to Obama when the chief usher turned to him and said, "Hello, Mr. President, welcome to your new home," as he walked through the imposing North Portico doors for the first time as president. During brief moments of quiet time that afternoon and evening, between parade watching on Pennsylvania Avenue and their first inaugural ball, the Obamas grazed on a buffet in the Old Family Dining Room where no detail was overlooked.

That day was the result of months of careful advance planning. For residence workers, the transition to the next administration begins about eighteen months before the inauguration, when the chief usher prepares books for the incoming president and first lady (with the added challenge of not knowing who they will be) that include a detailed White House layout, a list of staff, and an overview of allowable changes to the Oval Office.

Gary Walters, who served as chief usher from 1986 until 2007, started gathering information on the candidates during the primaries, well before a general election candidate is selected. It was particularly difficult when President Ford, President Carter, and President George H. W. Bush lost their bids for a second term. "The ownership is of the family that's there but you have to be watching out for what's going to occur," Walters said.

In December, after the election and before the inauguration, Walters would arrange for the incoming family to get a guided tour of the White House from the current first lady. It's then that the incoming first lady would be presented with a book containing the names and photographs of the people who work in the residence. The book helps the first family learn the names of everyone who works in the house and is partly a security measure, so that if they see anyone unfamiliar they can alert the Secret Service.

The departing first family pays for their personal things to be moved out of the White House. The incoming president also pays for bringing belongings into the mansion either out of the new first family's own coffers or from funds raised for the campaign or transition. It is the job of the incoming family to coordinate with the Secret Service to get their personal effects to the White House the morning of the inauguration.

One logistical challenge that comes with every inauguration is the transfer of the incoming first family's furniture and larger belongings to the White House. After the election of 1960, the

Kennedys' social secretary, Letitia Baldrige, told Jackie in a memo that she had asked the Eisenhowers' social secretary, Mary Jane McCaffree, "if we couldn't smuggle a lot of stuff over without the [Eisenhowers] knowing and she said yes, the head Usher could store cartons, suitcases, etc., out of sight and then whisk them into sight on the stroke of 12 noon. Isn't that marvelous??? Right out of Alfred Hitchcock." Baldrige recalled pulling up to the White House with Jackie's maid, Providencia Paredes, and Jack Kennedy's valet, George Thomas, in a car with the inaugural gown and all of the Kennedys' luggage. They arrived as everyone else was gathered at the Capitol for the inauguration ceremony. The snow-covered South Grounds were bathed in bright sunshine. "We had timed the pilgrimage from Georgetown to the White House so that we would not arrive before twelve noon, because at noon, officially, the new president takes possession of the White House."

Nearly a half-century later, the same conditions applied. The Obama family's advisers started meeting with residence staff soon after the election, and by the week before the inauguration, much of the Obamas' furniture had already been shipped to the White House, where it was stored in the China Room on the Ground Floor so that it could be moved quickly upstairs. The Bushes had told Chief Usher Stephen Rochon that they wanted to make the move as easy as possible for everyone, but Rochon was eager to make sure the Bushes never felt as if they were being pushed out. "We want to keep it out of the sight of the existing family. Not that they didn't know it was there, but we didn't want them to feel that we were trying to move them out."

Other Obama advisers made similar connections with the residence staff. More than two months before the inauguration, Chief Florist Nancy Clarke met with the Obamas' decorator, Michael Smith, to discuss floral arrangements for the private rooms where friends and family would be staying on the night of the inauguration.

"There's very limited time to prepare the house, so there's a whole team working on making certain that everything was as perfect as it could be in the time that we had allotted," said Social Secretary Desirée Rogers, a close confidante of the Obamas since their Chicago days and their first social secretary. On Inauguration Day "we were in the house as soon as we could be," she recalls, "laying out things, getting things ready, putting the clothing in each room."

Weeks before the inauguration, Rogers met with the florists and discussed what kind of flowers would sit on the cabaret tables and which kind of candelabras and candlelight they would use for those precious moments the first family has to enjoy their new, heady surroundings before they change for the balls.

"All those little things can make everybody feel comfortable and welcome," Florist Bob Scanlan said.

The new president filled most of the West Wing with loyal aides from his presidential campaign and from his early political career, including longtime spokesman Robert Gibbs, whom he named as his first White House press secretary, and close friend Valerie Jarrett, whom he brought on board as a senior adviser. Michelle Obama brought her own team of aides, many of whom she had known for years. A couple of days after moving in, Michelle asked her East Wing staff and the entire residence staff to gather in the East Room. Katie McCormick Lelyveld, the first lady's then press secretary, remembers her boss making it clear who was in charge.

"This is the team I walked in the door with," the first lady told the longtime residence staffers as she gestured toward her small cadre of political aides. "You guys are part of our new team," she told them before turning to address her own staffers, including Lelyveld: "It's on *you* to make sure that you know everybody here. They were here before you and they're the ones that make this place tick. We are on *their* ground now." The first lady's staff then circulated around the room, introducing themselves.

"At the time it was a matter of us investing in them to make sure that we knew what their role was, and how they fit into the bigger picture," Lelyveld said. "*We* were the new kids."

From those first days onward, Lelyveld looked to residence workers for advice. When she wanted to think of a clever way to preview the Obamas' first state dinner menu, she went down to the kitchen and asked Executive Chef Cristeta "Cris" Comerford how she thought they should lay out the room so that members of the media could see what she was preparing without distracting her from her work. When she asked workers from the Engineering and Operations departments about rearranging furniture for a TV interview on the State Floor, she was reminded that the White House is not the average household. "You're working in a museum," she says. "It's not just two chairs for an interview," but "two chairs in the Blue Room that are older than you are—by centuries—that need to be moved out of the way. So you defer to the staff whose job it is to take care of that space." (The furnishings are so precious that one housekeeper was told by his boss that if he broke a certain French gilded bronze clock that had been on display at the White House since 1817 he should not bother ever coming back. He wouldn't make enough money in his lifetime to replace it.)

On the Friday after President Obama's inauguration, the president casually made the rounds to introduce himself. When he came to the second-floor kitchen, he found several butlers gathered around the TV. He playfully punched James Jeffries on the shoulder.

"What are you looking at?" he asked them.

"We were looking at what was going on at the Lincoln Memorial before the inauguration," Jeffries replied. "Congratulations on becoming president."

"Thank you," Obama said with his trademark ear-to-ear grin and walked out of the room.

A few minutes later, when he came back into the kitchen, Jeffries got up the nerve to add: "I just congratulated you. Tomorrow, if I happen to be called to come to work, you can congratulate me for having been working here for fifty years."

"I ain't got to wait until tomorrow," Obama replied, without missing a beat. "I can do that right now. Congratulations."

Though Desirée Rogers describes their relationship with the staff as simply "very, very cordial," the new president was considerably more reserved and less chatty than his immediate predecessors. Some staffers said they missed the easy camaraderie they had established with presidents Bush, Clinton, and Bush. "With the Bushes, they wanted you to feel close to them," Chief Usher Rochon said. With the Obamas, "you had to keep it completely professional." Yet the Obamas have formed friendships with some of the men and women who work behind the scenes, and Butler James Jeffries said there's an unspoken understanding and respect between the Obamas and the largely African American butler staff about the realities of being black in America. President Obama acknowledged this when he said that part of the butlers' warmth to his family is because "they look at Malia and Sasha and they say, 'Well, this looks like my grandbaby, or this looks like my daughter.'"

Doorman Vincent Contee, eighty-four, worked every Monday and Tuesday from 1988 to 2009, escorting the president to and from the Oval Office on the elevator. "We got along swell," he recalls. "I would see him in the mornings and he would talk and ask me how my day was going." During his twenty-one years at the White House, Contee couldn't afford to get too starstruck; in addition to talking to presidents on a regular basis, he also escorted icons like Nelson Mandela and Elizabeth Taylor on the elevator to meet the president in the family's private quarters. He says even presidents can't hide their exhaustion sometimes. There would come a point when every president he served would turn to him during that short elevator ride and sigh, "I just wish I could go back to bed and sleep all day."

On the way to the Oval Office, Obama would talk sports with

Contee. "He knew I was a football fan. I'm a Redskins fan. He would tell me when they got beat, you know, what they didn't do or what they should do." Sometimes Obama would ask him to take their Portuguese water dog, Bo, out for a walk on the grounds. When they were done, Contee would bring Bo back up to his room on the third floor.

Still, the Obamas proved an especially private family, and Chief Usher Rochon sensed a certain distance between the staff and the new president. The Obamas seemed "uncomfortable," he said, having "so many butlers and housekeepers waiting on them hand and foot." For a couple who'd only recently finished paying off their own student loans, the level of personal service afforded by the White House staff must have been unnerving. "You have to give them their privacy," Contee told me. "You'd talk to them momentarily and then they would be on their way and you would be on your way."

The Obamas were especially anxious to raise their daughters in as normal an environment as possible, even while living in a household staffed with dozens of cooks, butlers, and maids. In 2011, Michelle Obama told an interviewer that her older daughter, Malia, who was thirteen at the time, was going to start doing her own laundry—and that her own mother, Marian Robinson, who lives in a suite on the third floor, would teach her. "My mother still does her own laundry. She doesn't want strangers touching her intimate wears." The first lady's former stylist, Michael "Rahni" Flowers, confirms that "Michelle is a no-nonsense kind of mother—and so is her mother. All they have to do is give you that eye, it will turn you into stone, it will stop you in your tracks."

Katie McCormick Lelyveld remembers how the first lady made the ground rules clear to her daughters. "While she appreciated that there are staff there to pay attention to those details, those staff are not there for the girls." Michelle reminded her daughters: "Don't get used to someone else making your bed, that's on your chores list."

Still, after two grueling years on the campaign trail and a frenetic schedule, the Obamas appreciated the help. "There are certain conveniences that just make what are otherwise very long days a lot easier, like someone who's in charge of figuring out your dinner plans," Lelyveld explained.

Traditions die hard at the executive mansion. When the Obamas told the butlers they could trade in their starched tuxes for button-down shirts and slacks on the weekends, not everyone took them up on the offer. "For some of the older gentlemen, who are in their seventies and eighties, they might have several tuxes that they're just used to and anything else would mean getting new clothes. They might just be more comfortable in those tuxes," Lelyveld said. When many butlers insisted on sticking with their formal wear, she said she felt awkward wearing khakis or jeans around them, even though she was used to the more comfortable dress code on the campaign trail. "I respected how much respect they had for what they did."

The Obamas clearly miss their lives in Chicago. Obama has said that "every president is acutely aware that we are just temporary residents" of the White House, adding, "we're renters here." After two grueling campaigns, the president refuses to miss family dinners more than twice a week. Those nightly meals were prepared by Sam Kass, the personal chef they had brought from Chicago, up until December 2014 when Kass left his post to move to New York.

As the president's former personal assistant Reggie Love recalls, on his walk from the living quarters to the West Wing every morning, Obama would ask Chief Usher Stephen Rochon for updates on the kinds of simple household matters that everyone deals with, whether they live in the executive mansion or a suburban cul-de-sac. "You live in a building and someone's responsible for the maintenance of the building. So if the water pressure wasn't right, or the Wi-Fi's not working, you've got to talk to somebody about it, right?"

One of the president's preoccupations, in the early days, was the White House basketball court. During the 2008 campaign, Obama had enjoyed the ritual of playing a pickup game on the days of nominating primaries and caucuses. The two times he didn't play, in New Hampshire and Nevada, he lost the contests. Not long after taking office, he told Rochon that he wanted the South Lawn tennis court, shrouded in pine trees, to be converted into a full basketball court. Removable basketball hoops were installed, new lines were painted on the court, and basketballs with White House seals were ordered. The effort cost $4,995.

The project took several months to complete. Eventually Obama grew impatient, telling Rochon on their morning walks: "You know, Admiral, this is not rocket science."

One morning, Rochon didn't mention the court's progress. When the president asked him how his "hoops were coming," he replied: "Well, Mr. President, I'm pleased to report that it will be done by eleven-thirty today."

Obama's eyes lit up. By ten-thirty, an hour before it was scheduled to be ready, he was out on the court playing with Love, a onetime forward for the Duke Blue Devils.

———

MICHELLE OBAMA'S STYLIST, Michael "Rahni" Flowers, had done her hair since she was a teenager, and he was the incoming first lady's choice for the inauguration. Though hairstylists are not officially on the residence staff, they offer a unique behind-the-scenes perspective on the events of that memorable day.

Flowers's day started at 4:00 A.M. at Blair House, the elegant town house across the street from the White House, where the president-elect and his family traditionally stay before they officially move into the executive mansion. That morning he styled Michelle, her daughters, and her mother, and he traveled with the

Obamas throughout the day, to Capitol Hill and all ten official inaugural balls that night.

Flowers noticed immediately how excited the mostly African American butlers were about the incoming president. "There was a pride that goes beyond pride—this is something that happened that they never would have dreamed in their lifetime," said Flowers, who is black himself. "I saw it in the way they talked, the way they walked. You could tell by their smiling faces—it was beyond their wildest dreams."

Everyone seemed calm that morning, he said, except for Marian Robinson, the first lady's mother. Robinson was on the verge of a dramatic change: she had just started a track club for seniors in Chicago, and had recently won a track meet, but Michelle had asked her to live with them at the White House, to help with the girls, and now she was leaving her hometown for a new—and very tightly regimented—life.

"She's a very independent woman," Flowers says. She might not have chosen the change for herself, he believes, but "she let me know that Michelle wants her to do this, and she's got the kids to think about." When she left her beloved Chicago, Robinson said, "They're dragging me with them, and I'm not that comfortable, but I'm doing exactly what you do. You do what has to be done."

Yet the incoming president seemed unfazed by the dramatic change. After delivering an ambitious inaugural address—citing policy objectives like health care reform while renewing his broader promise to change the divisive rhetoric in Washington—he asked casually, "How did I do?"

"Barack's always very calm, his mood is always controlled," Flowers said. "Michelle's a more in-the-moment type of person."

Because of a glitch in the schedule (someone forgot to account for the traditional Capitol luncheon after the oath of office) the Obamas had only forty-five minutes to prepare for the balls that evening. As they rushed to get ready, the president stopped by the small beauty parlor on the second floor of the White House and asked his wife which bow tie she thought he should wear.

"I want to look my best for you," he told her.

As he was walking out, Flowers noticed that one of the president's French cuffs didn't go through all the way.

"Barack, check your cuffs," Flowers pointed.

"Oh that's nice, people care," Obama said affably.

When the first lady's wardrobe stylist, Ikram Goldman, whose high-end Chicago boutique Michelle Obama frequented before moving into the White House, heard Flowers call the president "Barack," she snapped at him. "She suggested that I should call him 'Mr. President,'" Flowers recalled. "When I called him 'Barack' he smiled. I went to their wedding, I've met [Michelle's] dad, he hasn't changed with me," Flowers said, still obviously smarting from the rebuke. "That would have been unnatural for me." That transition—from personal names to formal titles—is a rite of passage for many friends of future presidents. The Kennedys' social secretary, Letitia Baldrige—who later became an arbiter of etiquette—had known the couple as "Jack and Jackie," but they became "Mr. President and Mrs. Kennedy" immediately after the presidential election in November 1960. "President and Mrs. Kennedy may have been young, and personal friends from earlier times, but a new aura of great dignity surrounded them now." Few people call President Obama by his first name anymore.

———

INAUGURATION DAY—AN OVERWHELMING event for any new president—begins hours before the oath of office is administered at noon at the Capitol. In the early morning he gets a national security briefing from the outgoing president's national security adviser and his own incoming national security adviser. At the end of the briefing, a senior officer from the White House military office explains the top secret codes used to launch a nuclear strike. Once he is sworn in, an aide with the "football"—a briefcase carrying the codes—will always be close by. (After he is sworn in, the president will be given the card allowing him to actually launch the strikes.) This all happens before a morning church service.

While adjusting to the weight of his new job, the new president must also get used to life in the residence. The day after his inauguration, President Obama came into the East Room to introduce himself to the staff. The president had "a look of surprise," Florist Bob Scanlan recalled. "It's like, 'Wow.' He didn't realize that there were that many people just to take care of the house." The staff Obama greeted that day was responsible not only for servicing the private quarters, but also for maintaining the State Floor, including the constant traffic from public tours.

West Wing staffers, many of whom grew used to a more ad hoc way of life during the campaign, are suddenly thrust into their new roles with little understanding of how things work. For Obama's personal secretary, Katie Johnson, Inauguration Day itself was "complete chaos." When she arrived at the White House that morning, she was told she wasn't cleared for entry. "I was on my own personal crash course," she says. (Top Obama aide Denis McDonough eventually cleared her through security.) And her problems didn't stop there. "Looking back on it, the West Wing is tiny," she says, "but at the time it felt like a maze." Once she was settled in the "Outer Oval," her small office located just outside the Oval Office, she spent much of the day getting a hurried tutorial about how to use the "shockingly complicated" phone system. During the first few weeks of the administration, she remembers being unable to transfer a call from a high-level official to the president, who was on board Air Force One. The call never went through and eventually

Obama himself had to call the person directly from the plane. "I was so panicked," Johnson recalls.

For the residence staff, of course, this was not their first rodeo, and they were able to calm Johnson's frazzled nerves. The West Wing staff relies on the Usher's Office to help them settle in, and Johnson kept the ushers busy with one question or another, including where to find the Flower Shop so that she could ask them to refill the gala apples the president keeps in the Oval Office. "I called the Usher's Office if I had questions about *anything*," she recalls. "If someone wanted some particular wine in the Oval, I'd call the Usher's Office and they would find it."

Sometimes she needed help from the valets and ushers locating important presidential memos, especially when there was a piece of paper the West Wing staff was looking for that nobody could find. "Whenever I was panicked, desperately looking for something—and the president's traveling so I can't ask him where it is—and people are telling me there's a piece of paper that has some important decision on it, and the president says he brought it down to me and I swear I don't have it, I'd ask them to check," she says breathlessly. "They'd go look for it, and ninety percent of the time they could find it."

Reggie Love remembers how patient the ushers were in helping him "navigate the back of the house of the White House." He says, "There's a nickname for every hall, there's a nickname for every room."

After a few days the Obamas started "moving about the house little by little," Scanlan recalled, usually after the tourists and most of the residence staff had left for the day. "It's a process for them too. It's a process to know almost a hundred people, because they don't see them all at once. Maybe one housekeeper, one florist at a time. You may only have one chef up there doing the cooking. They don't know all the other people who are down in those workshops and eventually they do meet them but it's over a period of time."

And eventually they get used to the help, or at least learn to live with it. "I think the White House staff has really figured out how to accommodate families and make them feel as normal as possible, even though there are dozens of people around, dropping off flowers, vacuuming, fixing things up all the time," Michelle Obama said. "You begin to see them as family in so many ways and that's the beauty of this place."

———————

EACH FIRST FAMILY behaves differently around the staff. In the late 1920s and early 1930s the family of Herbert Hoover often preferred to have the workers out of sight; the sounding of three bells would send maids, butlers, and housemen scurrying into closets. FDR and Truman were much more relaxed, telling the staff that it was all right to keep working when they walked into a room.

In modern times, relations between the first family and the staff have grown much more comfortable. Maid Ivaniz Silva said the first lady usually knows everyone's names within a week—at least those of the dozen or so maids and butlers who regularly work on the second and third floors.

One day, Silva said, she was cleaning when Barbara Bush walked in and stopped her.

"Oh, I haven't seen you yet," Mrs. Bush told her.

"But I'm in the book," she insisted.

"Are you sure?" The First Lady went to go get the book listing the residence staffers prepared by the chief usher. She returned a few minutes later.

"Oh, this is not a good enough picture. That's why I don't recognize you!" Bush teased her.

Along with new furniture and paint, each first family brings a different spirit to the White House. The sea change from the Eisenhowers to the Kennedys was both superficial—from grandparents who personified the 1950s to a beautiful young couple with two small children—and tangible. The staff had to get used to the Kennedys' more relaxed style of entertaining: black tie instead of white tie, cocktails served before dinner, and smoking allowed everywhere. At formal dinners, the Eisenhowers served six courses and sat their guests at a giant E-shaped banquet table. The Kennedys quickly decided to change the seating to fifteen round tables seating eight or ten apiece, and pared down dinners to four courses.

Jackie Kennedy, who was used to being surrounded by servants and wealth, was eager to delve right into running the 132-room mansion. The morning after her husband's inauguration, she approached Chief Usher J. B. West. "I'd like to meet all the staff today," she told him. "Could you please take me around the White House to meet them at their work?"

Reluctant to present the first lady to the staff workshops without advance warning, West suggested bringing the staff to her in groups of three instead. Each group, from the ushers and butlers to the maids and cooks, were incredibly nervous about the formal inspection. When they got off the elevator, they were startled to see the first lady wearing pants (a particularly shocking sight at the time) and brown boots, standing there with disheveled hair. As the staffers introduced themselves one by one, West recalled, Jackie tried to think of ways to memorize their names. She repeated each of them slowly and though she didn't take notes she remembered all of them. One of the maids who met her that day, Lucinda Morman, was a skilled seamstress; the first lady would later ask her to tailor her one-of-a-kind Oleg Cassini gowns.

Jackie Kennedy was a perfectionist and was deeply involved in the day-to-day operations of the residence. At night she scribbled notes to herself, checking off each item as it was completed throughout the day. She also wrote West daily notes on a yellow pad she carried everywhere.

"She always had a list for me," recalled West. "Each person that had any authority over anything, she had their name, and under it there would be all the things that she wanted to discuss with each person."

Mrs. Kennedy also noticed that some of the residence workers were nervous around the first family. She wrote a note about the maids: "They are so terrified of being in W.H.—of First Family, etc., that they are rigid with fear and get panicky—even Lucinda who knows me well still apologizes 10 minutes if she drops a pin." To help them overcome their fears, she suggested that they come to the second and third floors more often so that they get used to being around her family. "I can't teach them anything—nor have time—when they are that scared."

———

DOORMAN PRESTON BRUCE was used to the predictability of the Eisenhowers, who typically went to bed at ten o'clock. When the Kennedys returned from the inaugural balls at two o'clock in the morning, Bruce was sure they would be exhausted. Instead, they brought friends back to the White House to continue the party on the second floor—unaware that the residence workers had to stay until the first couple were safely in bed. At 3:15 A.M. Bruce escorted the last guest out and turned off the lights in the West Sitting Hall. When he got to the president's bedroom, no one was there.

"Is that you, Bruce? I'm here in the Lincoln Bedroom," the president called out. Bruce couldn't believe it. Workers thought the Lincoln Bedroom was cursed. Kennedy ordered a Coke and asked Bruce to open a window to let the cold night air in. Jackie called out from the Queens' Bedroom across the hall and asked the ever-obliging Bruce for an aperitif. He did not get home until after four o'clock in the morning.

Despite that long first night, Bruce learned to love the Kennedys, and because he worked nights he got a glimpse of the more intimate side of the family. He'd laugh when he witnessed the beautiful young couple scamper between each other's bedrooms late at night when he brought up their after-dinner drinks. ("Don't worry, Bruce. We know you're married too," Jackie Kennedy would say, her eyes twinkling.)

From 1953 to 1977 Bruce arrived at the White House at three o'clock in the afternoon, greeting dignitaries at the door, calming nervous visitors before they met the president, escorting the president from the Oval Office to his residence at night, and waiting until he was in bed to go home. He was a star at the White House. Other staffers praised his elegance and his ability to remain calm under the enormous pressure of his job. Butler Lynwood Westray calls him a "diplomat."

"That's why he was so well liked, some people have it and some don't. He had it."

The day after the Kennedy inauguration, Bruce escorted the president and the first lady upstairs after dinner. He breathed a sigh of relief at the thought of getting home at a decent hour. "Bang! The elevator door opened in the hallway across from the Usher's Office. Out popped the president. He charged down the hall, the Secret Service in hot pursuit," Bruce wrote. Kennedy wanted to take a late-night walk and marched out the Northwest Gate into the freezing cold air without a coat. "Only twenty-four hours in the White House, and he had to escape."

The Secret Service had to rein Kennedy in and told him he would have to limit walks to the eighteen acres surrounding the White House. From then on, Bruce was always prepared with two overcoats: one if the president decided to leave for his walk through the first-floor doors, and another if he chose the Ground Floor. Whenever he offered the president a coat and rain boots, the commander in chief protested. "He was like a little schoolboy, bound to run off unprotected into the cold."

———

NOT EVERY FIRST family has enjoyed such a joyous arrival as the Kennedys. On the Monday after the 1992 election, the Clintons called interior decorator Kaki Hockersmith and asked her to perform the monumental task of redecorating the White House. Even though she had decorated the Arkansas governor's mansion for them, she wasn't expecting the call—she recalls being "very, very surprised"—but she accepted the invitation. Between the election and the inauguration, she visited the governor's mansion several times to show the Clintons the different fabrics and furnishings she had selected for the residence.

"On the first of those occasions President Clinton was in a meeting with his transition staff and Hillary called him out of the meeting," she said. She splayed out drapery swatches and rug designs on the kitchen counter to show him. (Clinton is the rare modern president who has shown such an interest in décor.) In the ensuing weeks, Hockersmith made several trips to the White House to work with the curators. They brought her to the huge climate-controlled storage facility about eleven miles outside of Washington in Riverdale, Maryland, where every piece of furniture that was once in the White House is stored in a warehouse. Incoming families can pick pieces they want to take out of storage and bring back to the residence.

The furniture in Riverdale is methodically organized into categories with rows of desks and writing tables situated alongside chests and rugs that sat in the Oval Office during different administrations. Pieces from different eras, each with an extensive provenance, are described and catalogued. The curators know where every candlestick and side table can be found in the massive space. There's even a conservation studio with X-ray equipment where photography can be done for guidebooks. It is a far cry from the ramshackle storage facility a stunned Jackie Kennedy visited at Fort Washington along the Potomac River in Maryland, where she was appalled to find precious antiques lying on the dirt floor.

Hockersmith carried with her a detailed floor plan, keeping track of the desired locations for pieces already in the house and new pieces from the warehouse. "We had this very ambitious plan," Hockersmith said, sounding exhausted by the memory.

The Clintons began Inauguration Day with an interfaith church service. Afterward they stopped at Blair House before arriving at the White House at 10:27 A.M.—twenty-seven minutes late. The Bushes stood at the North Portico waiting to greet them.

"Welcome to your new house," President George H. W. Bush told twelve-year-old Chelsea, who petted the Bush's springer spaniel, Millie. The outgoing president wished his successor good luck— and, following tradition, left a note in the desk in the Oval Office offering advice to his successor. (When Clinton left office eight years later, he wrote a note to President George W. Bush and left behind the note that Bush's father had left for him.) Details of the notes have not been made public.

On the big day, Hillary Clinton told Hockersmith that she didn't want her to miss the inaugural ceremony, held at the West Front of the U.S. Capitol. But she needed her to get back to the White House as soon as it was over.

"We have to figure out a way to get you out of that mess and quickly back to the White House," Hillary told her.

After the hour-long inaugural ceremony, Hillary told Hockersmith to look for a colonel on a corner in a van who would whisk her back to the White House to help oversee the move.

"I thought, how in the world are they going to work this out?" Hockersmith says.

Amid the cheering throng of people gathered at the Capitol on

January 20, 1993, Hockersmith was astonished to see the van waiting for her. Every time they hit a security barrier, the police moved
it. The crowd lining Pennsylvania Avenue awaiting the new president waved excitedly at her van. "They thought we might be someone really famous."

"We just drove up to the South Lawn with a view of two large
moving vans that said 'Little Rock, Arkansas' on them," she says.
"Quite an exciting drive."

The Clintons spent roughly $400,000 redecorating the White
House, all financed by private donations. But the effort raised some
eyebrows, both within and outside the mansion. Even the normally
discreet residence workers have called Hockersmith's efforts disor-
ganized, her expectations too high.

Chief Electrician Bill Cliber, who worked on nine transitions,
said that the Clintons' arrival was by far the most difficult. Shortly
before the inauguration, Hockersmith told him that he and the
other electricians needed to rehang seven chandeliers—*now.*

"Why does it have to be done now? Let them move in and we'll
do it one a day," said Cliber.

"No, they want them all changed before they come in the door,"
she replied.

Cliber had no choice. He went to the second-floor Treaty Room,
which Clinton would use as a private study, to start work on one of
the chandeliers.

Almost as soon as the Clintons returned from the inaugural
parade, Hillary appeared in the Treaty Room. "How long are you
going to be in this room?" she asked Cliber.

"Truthfully, I'm looking at maybe four hours," he told her as he
handled the elaborate crystal chandelier that was dismantled on the
floor.

"Hmm, we'll see about that," she said, and stormed out.

Hockersmith poked her head in and told him to leave the room within twenty minutes. Cliber said he'd need more time just to collect the hundreds and hundreds of priceless crystals strewn about the floor. She replied: "Don't worry about it. They can be replaced."

"No, ma'am. This is crystal that can't be replaced," he told her indignantly.

Cliber did as he was told, leaving the Treaty Room a mess with crystals everywhere. But he wasn't about to let the first lady, or her decorator, have the final word. Chief Curator Rex Scouten (who was well respected on the staff and had been an usher and then chief usher from 1969 to 1986 before he took the job as curator) locked the door to protect the chandelier until Cliber could get back to work. The electrician wasn't allowed back in the room for three weeks.

Gary Walters is always careful not to single out any one administration for criticism. But when I asked him how the Clinton move-in went there was a long pause: "That's when you get the most difficulty, when you're going from one administration to another of different parties." The Clintons, he said, "had no concept of what the White House was like." He had to go up to the residence multiple times a day to answer questions.

Usher Nancy Mitchell was on duty early in the morning when the first couple came home from the inaugural balls. "President Clinton wanted to make a phone call, so I had gone upstairs with him and I hear this roar from him, 'Nancy!' and I say, 'Yes, sir.' He says, 'How do I make a phone call?'" When the president picked up the phone, he was greeted not by a dial tone but by a White House operator; he was shocked that he couldn't just dial a number himself. The entire phone system was changed shortly thereafter.

It did not help that the Clintons invited friends from Little Rock ("friends of Bill's," or "FOBs") to help them unpack, which only served to complicate matters.

"We've been doing this for two hundred years," said Usher Chris

Emery. "They made all these promises to various people to come in and help. Of course we were upset, it was such a mess." Emery, who had a difficult relationship with the Clintons and would eventually be fired during their administration, said that many FOBs actually had criminal records. According to Emery, the Secret Service called the Usher's Office several times to report that some of the Arkansas guests had not passed their background checks and were deemed "do not admits." Emery told agents, "The president's expecting them. Make it happen." They ended up having to assign Secret Service officers on every floor: "Typically if you bring a worker that has a 'hit' [on his background check] they have to be escorted." Before long, much to Emery's chagrin, there were several people with "hits" at the house.

Hockersmith took a hands-on approach to some elements of the redecoration, including the placement of the Clintons' personal photographs and the knickknacks they brought with them from Little Rock, including a memorable collection of frogs. When Hillary and Bill were dating, it seemed, he had charmed her with a story from his childhood. The punch line was: "You can't tell how far a frog will jump until you punch him." Translation: You never know how far you can go until you try—an apt anecdote for the ambitious young couple. When her husband first ran for office, Hillary gave Bill a drawing of a frog being punched and jumping with the saying underneath. In 1993, for her birthday, Bill gave her a glass frog wearing a crown and a note that read: "This could have been me if you hadn't come along."

To Hockersmith, initially unaware of their sentimental significance, the frogs looked like a mishmash of misguided gifts. "Somebody goes to your house and they think, 'Oh they must like frogs.' Then you're given a frog for your birthday." She did her best to make them work.

When the first family returns to the White House from the

parade viewing stands, Hockersmith recalls, "That's when everyone else disappears." The residence workers, who have been working to make the house perfect all day long, rush back to their respective shops to give the family some much-needed privacy.

Hockersmith would become a White House fixture, staying in the Queens' Bedroom off and on throughout Bill Clinton's eight years in the White House as redecoration efforts continued. Her guest room on the second floor was separated from their living quarters by pocket doors that close off the west end from the east end of the residence. She tried to make the house brighter, especially focusing on turning a drab second-floor Butler's Pantry into an eat-in kitchen where Chelsea could do her homework. But the redecoration was met with mixed reviews, with Hockersmith's elaborate Victorian furnishings in the Lincoln Sitting Room coming in for particular criticism.

———

THERE HAS BEEN no transition in modern memory as shocking as the sudden and violent upheaval that brought the arrival of Lyndon B. Johnson and his family to the White House. The residence staff had to help a devastated first lady and her two children move out, even as they were grieving themselves, and at the same time they had to help the Johnsons move in. And it all had to be done without making Mrs. Kennedy feel rushed, or the Johnsons feel as though they were being ignored. "I've been on panels with other social secretaries and they make it all sound so exciting when they got there," says Lady Bird's social secretary, Bess Abell, a Katharine Hepburn–esque presence who speaks with great affection about the Johnsons. "I moved into the White House on an entirely different occasion. Instead of coming in with the excitement and the thrill of an inauguration, we moved into a house that was covered with black crepe on all the chandeliers and the columns."

The new first lady, Lady Bird Johnson, often lamented the difficult position her family were suddenly thrust into. "People see the living and wish for the dead," she'd say.

Out of respect for the president's widow, Lyndon B. Johnson—who was largely disliked by Kennedy's staff—did not move into the White House until December 7, 1963. He started working out of the Oval Office on November 26; before then he worked out of Room 274 in the Old Executive Office Building next door to the White House. Some of Johnson's advisers argued that moving in to the residence on December 7, the twenty-second anniversary of the horrific attack on Pearl Harbor, would be disrespectful. Others simply wanted to give Mrs. Kennedy more time before leaving the White House. Every move the Johnsons made must have been excruciating since nothing they did could help endear them to President Kennedy's heartbroken aides.

Luci Baines Johnson, just sixteen years old at the time, remembers eavesdropping as her parents had what she called the "only argument" she can remember them ever having. "We have to move December seventh, Bird," Johnson told his wife. "Lyndon, any day but that. Any day but that," her mother pleaded, but in vain.

When the Johnson family finally arrived, their daughter Luci brought their beagles, "Him" and "Her," in her convertible. Lady Bird and Bess and her press secretary, Liz Carpenter, brought breakable items, along with a portrait of House Speaker Sam Rayburn, a fellow Texan who was Johnson's mentor.

At first the Johnsons seemed to treat the White House gingerly, as though they were impinging on sacred ground. But the residence staff, unlike Kennedy's political aides, never made them feel like interlopers. "I never felt a sense of, 'How could you be here?'" Luci told me. "It was, 'Oh, how tough to have you come here this way. How can we help? How can we teach?'"

Not everyone was welcoming. After Kennedy's assassination,

Traphes Bryant, an electrician who started caring for the first family's dogs with the Kennedys (they had nine dogs at one point) and didn't stop until the Nixons, was wary of President Johnson. "I was losing a dog and gaining a president I didn't know. Not only didn't I know him, I didn't think I wanted to know him. He wasn't boyish or good-natured or quick-witted like Kennedy, and I heard him cussing out the help when things weren't done fast enough." Bryant describes the abrupt shift at the White House to accommodate the new president: "Terriers were out and beagles were in. Jackie pink was out, Lady Bird yellow was in. Chowder was out and chili was in." He hoped that one thing would remain the same, that Johnson would appreciate the way that he trained presidential dogs to greet their owners on the South Lawn when they returned from a trip on the marine helicopter. President Kennedy thoroughly enjoyed the tradition. He always gave a broad smile and greeted the waiting dogs "as if they were his distinguished hosts."

After the Kennedys' abrupt departure he writes touchingly, "Toddlers were out and teenagers were in," referring to Caroline and John-John's successors at the White House, the Johnsons' teenage daughters, Luci and Lynda. Ultimately, though, Bryant would grow to love the Johnsons.

In her memoir, Lady Bird Johnson described the impossible task of trying to replace Jackie, marveling at the "element of steel and stamina" that must have flowed through her predecessor's veins. She said she felt as though she were "suddenly onstage for a part I never rehearsed."

While the new president was working in his temporary quarters, the White House staff had quietly made arrangements for the transition. Just four days after the assassination, Chief Usher J. B. West visited Lady Bird at the Johnsons' Washington mansion, known as the Elms, where they discussed what furniture the Johnsons would bring with them to the White House.

Later that afternoon, Mrs. Johnson had tea with JFK's widow at the White House. The outgoing first lady graciously showed her successor the second floor, allowing her to consider how her furniture would fit into the bedroom and sitting room Mrs. Kennedy had occupied for almost three years. "Don't be frightened of this house—some of the happiest years of my marriage have been spent here—you will be happy here," Jackie said. Lady Bird said she told her this so often during her tour that it felt "as though she were trying to reassure me."

Jackie told her that J. B. West and Curator Jim Ketchum were the most dependable members of the residence staff. Ketchum, who served as the White House chief curator from 1963 to 1970, fondly recalls his first meeting with Lady Bird shortly after the family moved in. As one of four people on the curatorial staff, Ketchum was in charge of cataloguing and protecting every piece of furniture and artwork in the White House's private collection, ranging from masterpieces by John Singer Sargent to porcelain dating back to George Washington.

Lady Bird asked Ketchum to set up time after she moved in for "walk and learns," so she could go through each room with him and learn more about its history and its furnishings. She said she needed to have a working knowledge of the residence so that she could take friends and guests on tours, one of her duties as first lady. She took her new role very seriously—not surprising, as she had earned a reputation as a pinch hitter for Jackie Kennedy during the previous administration. When Jackie didn't feel like doing something, Lady Bird dutifully stepped in.

Ketchum's first meeting with the new first lady was not at all glamorous. When Lady Bird called down to the Curator's Office and asked him to come upstairs, he recalls, "I found her in a closet, between her bedroom and sitting room, on her hands and knees with a cardboard box open in front of her," he said. She was surrounded by about twenty porcelain birds all carefully wrapped and

brought from the Elms. He got down on the floor and began to help
her unwrap each bird.

"What neither one of us realized is that the light for the closet
was in the door jamb. And as we started, and we had the birds kind
of lined up on the floor, Bonner Arrington [the carpenter foreman]
and one of his colleagues from the Carpenter's Shop were moving a
sofa and went right down this narrow corridor and of course closed
the door. So there we were, playing touchy-feely, trying to protect
the birds and figure out how one could get up without stepping on
something," he laughed. They managed to find the light switch and
remarkably they left the birds unharmed.

Soon after they moved in, the president and the first lady were
invited to adviser Walter Jenkins's house for dinner. Their absence
gave "a breathing spell to the staff here at the White House who
must have been carrying on with heavy hearts," Lady Bird said.

The Jenkins's daughter, Beth, was a close friend of Luci's, and she
came to the White House that night for a sleepover. "All I had felt was
the challenge and the burden of this transition," Luci told me.

Her room in the White House had a fireplace—"I'd never had
something so delicious as a fireplace in my bedroom"—so she lit a
fire. Neither girl knew anything about fireplaces, though, and the
room soon filled up with smoke. Luci frantically tried using a juice
glass filled with water, and then a trash can, to douse the flames.
Finally she climbed up on her desk and opened a window to let
the smoke out—and was horrified when she saw a White House
policeman looking in at her in her nightgown. Once they realized
what was happening, staff ran in to help.

"My mother felt it was very appropriate that I help clean the
smoke stains off the walls of my bedroom that first week," she said,
still embarrassed decades later. "It was literally a baptism by fire." She
scrubbed alongside the maids, none of whom made her feel guilty.

A LITTLE MORE than a decade later, the residence staff found themselves once again confronted with a sudden and unceremonious transition, when President Richard Nixon announced his resignation on August 8, 1974.

"The transfer of power was shockingly abrupt, yet orderly as it had been after the assassination of President Kennedy," wrote Doorman Preston Bruce. Yet despite the fact that the Watergate scandal had been raging for two years, and calls for Nixon's resignation had mounted through the summer, no one inside the White House was expecting it. After all, no president had ever resigned before. The staff had no clue until Pat Nixon called down, asking for some packing boxes.

At seven-thirty on the morning after he announced his resignation, Nixon was in bare feet and pajamas when Executive Chef Henry Haller found him sitting alone in the Family Kitchen. He usually ate a light breakfast of cereal, juice, and fresh fruit, but that morning he ordered corned beef hash with a poached egg.

Nixon walked up to Haller and grabbed his hand: "Chef, I have been eating all over the world, your food is the best."

Later that morning, just before walking to the helicopter on the South Lawn and giving his famous V-for-victory salute, Nixon made an emotional farewell speech to his staff in the East Room. As the staff gathered for the event, Painter Cletus Clark unexpectedly found himself in the middle of the drama. "I was in the East Room painting the stage. I was the only one in there on the residence staff," he said. "The next thing you know I looked up and all these people started coming into the East Room—I couldn't get out! And the paint wasn't even dry!"

He told the Secret Service agents who were in place before the president's arrival to make sure the president was careful not to touch the wet paint.

"The room was filling up. I grabbed my little bucket and went over there on the south side and mixed in with the crowd. I put my bucket down between my feet and stayed in there."

Standing in his all-white uniform, Clark listened as the thirty-seventh president began good-byes by praising the residence staff, who, as usual, stayed in the shadows. "This house has a great heart and that heart comes from those who serve. I was rather sorry they didn't come down; we said good-bye to them upstairs," Nixon said, already wistful. "But they're really great. I recall after so many times I've made speeches, some of them pretty tough, you'd always come back, or after a hard day, and my days usually run rather long, I'd always get a lift from them. Because I might be a little down, but they always smiled."

The residence staff took on the familiar role of movers that day, packing up the first family's things and managing as seamless a transition as they could under the circumstances.

Barbara Bush, whose husband was then the chairman of the Republican National Committee, described in amazement witnessing just how quickly the White House was handed over to the Fords. "The day President Nixon resigned we went down to the White House, we met there for his resignation and Jerry Ford's swearing in hours later. After we waved good-bye to the Nixons, the pictures on the wall were all of Jerry Ford's family. We were standing at the helicopter waving good-bye while they changed the pictures."

———

THE NIXONS' FORMAL style was replaced by the more relaxed attitude of Gerald and Betty Ford, who allowed their four children to wear jeans anywhere in the White House. Susan Ford even roller-skated on the State Floor's pristine floors while her parents were traveling, which she says she's embarrassed to admit now.

Betty Ford was fiercely independent, and when she got the tour of the second-floor family quarters she immediately rejected the idea of sleeping in a separate bedroom from her husband. "Well, there'll be no need for that," she told the head usher.

She could not understand why the maids and butlers were so quiet around her. She worried that they didn't like her. She soon found out that Pat Nixon had preferred it that way.

Carpenter Milton Frame was impressed by Betty Ford's approachable manner. "I do recall that Mrs. Ford, she would invite you to sit down and have a cup of tea," he said fondly. She asked him where he was from and made small talk, an act of kindness that her predecessor would never have initiated.

She also enjoyed teasing the staff. During a tour of the private quarters, her press secretary, Sheila Rabb Weidenfeld, noticed a flower vase featuring the figures of two angels, with their hands almost touching. A cigarette was perched in one of the angel's hands. "Oh, that," the first lady said, laughing. "I put it there. That's just my way of testing whether the maids have cleaned the room!"

––––––

NEW FAMILIES MUST get used to a big staff—and to paying shockingly high monthly bills. Contrary to popular belief, the first family pays for all of their own personal expenses. And almost every first lady ends up pleading with the chief usher to keep costs down.

The family pays for their own dry cleaning, which is farmed out to a local dry cleaner chosen by the head housekeeper or the family themselves. During the first Bush and the Clinton administrations, Executive Housekeeper Christine Limerick said, they often used the nearby Willard Hotel. Even that basic service has to be conducted in secrecy: the family's clothing is dropped off and picked up discreetly by members of the Operations Department.

The first family is also required to cover their personal food and drink expenses—including not just their own meals but also those of their personal guests, which can include dozens of friends and family over the inauguration or the holidays. Walters told me that "each and every" first lady, except for Barbara Bush, has seemed surprised and not very pleased to discover this. Many have asked for menus featuring cheaper cuts of meat to cut down on the enormous monthly costs; the Carters even asked to be served leftovers for their own personal meals.

Even Jackie Kennedy instructed the chief usher to "run this place just like you'd run it for the *chinchiest* president who ever got elected!" She dropped her voice comically, adding: "We don't have nearly as much money as you read in the papers!"

Her husband was obsessed with the food bill, talking in great detail with the ushers about how to keep the milk bill down at their Hyannis home. The Kennedys' social secretary, Nancy Tuckerman, said she never saw him sit still for that long or be that interested in anything for more than five minutes. The liquor bill multiplied during the Kennedy years and that's because, before Kennedy took office, the White House amazingly and very discreetly accepted bootleg whiskey from the General Services Administration. A new regulation would have made it impossible for the White House to continue doing so without making it public, so the president quickly ordered an end to the practice and sent Housekeeper Anne Lincoln to shop for inexpensive booze. Kennedy had his own private liquor cabinet tucked away in a closet on the third floor and the only people with the key were Lincoln and his valet. He was always mindful of the cost of living in the White House, even though he wouldn't be asked to pay for the bulk of the alcohol himself because it was mostly used for official entertaining.

Obama aide Reggie Love was twenty-seven years old when he arrived at the White House and remembers the first time Admiral

Rochon walked him through the Obamas' monthly bill. "I saw the number and I was like, 'I see the numbers, I see all the things itemized, but for me, a person who's only lived in a household of one with no children, I have no real way to look at that and say, 'You know what, this seems about right.'"

The executive chef sends the first lady a weekly menu every Sunday. If she finds something there that she doesn't like, or feels is too extravagant for a family meal, she may ask the chef to look for an alternative.

Luci Baines Johnson said her mother talked "constantly" about the exorbitant costs of living at the White House. After she got married, Luci went with her family to Camp David for the weekend—and received a bill for the food she ate while she was there. She was astonished.

"Oh yes, we've always been billed, but when you were a minor living in our home we paid it for you," Lady Bird Johnson told her irate daughter.

"My mother was quite stunned that *I* was stunned!" she said, laughing.

Somehow, seeing a line-item breakdown at the end of the month makes the prices seem higher than if the family were going to the grocery store, or out to eat. President Ford's daughter, Susan, said that her father would wave the bill at her and warn her, "You need to be aware that when you have a bunch of friends over I do see this."

Rosalynn Carter vividly remembers her family's first monthly bill: $600. "It doesn't sound like very much, but that was enormous to me back in '76!" She thought the prices were higher than they would be outside the White House because the food has to be examined to make sure it hasn't been poisoned.

The food bills weren't the only costs that worried the Carters, according to Florist Ronn Payne. Jimmy Carter wanted his flowers on the cheap too. Even though the first family doesn't usually pay for flowers, Carter didn't believe the government needed to foot the bill for elaborate arrangements either. "We had to go out and pick flowers to do dinners," Payne remembers. "We would go to the city parks to cut flowers." He and other staffers took field trips to Rock Creek Park to pick daffodils and the National Zoo to collect wild-flowers. "Police would actually stop us. One guy was arrested and they had to go and get him out of jail for picking daffodils on that big hillside in Rock Creek Park to do a dinner." The White House intervened to get him released, Payne said.

"We'd buy dried flowers from the market, or we'd have our garden club ladies dry their own garden flowers, and that's what we had to use." In other administrations it was not uncommon to spend $50,000 on flowers for a state dinner, with single arrangements cost-ing several thousand dollars.

Barbara Bush, every bit the patrician matriarch, has no sympa-thy for any first lady who is surprised when she receives her family's monthly food bill. Or any bill, for that matter. "If they were shocked, there's something wrong with them," she says sternly. "We had lots of guests, as did George W., and we paid for those private guests. But the bill would come and it would say, 'One egg: eighteen cents.' Mrs. So and So had an egg and a piece of toast. It's cheaper to eat at the White House." She points out that, while the first family has to pay for food and dry cleaning, they don't have to pay for electricity, air-conditioning, flowers, butlers, plumbers, or "yard people," making their cost of living a relative bargain—especially for a family like the Bushes, who were accustomed to having hired help. "I thought it was very cheap to live at the White House!" she said. "I'd like to go back and live there and not have the responsibility."

Laura Bush's mother-in-law may have prepared her for the cost of living in the White House, but she was still surprised when she got her first bill. She noted how expensive it was to throw her husband a birthday party because they had to pay time and a half for staff who worked after five o'clock in the evening.

Executive Chef Walter Scheib also reported that he sometimes got calls from the chief usher, saying that the first lady's office had asked him to keep the cost of ingredients down, or requesting that fewer cooks be used in the kitchen.

"Chef, did you really need that many people to produce that event?" Chief Usher Gary Walters would ask him.

"Well, Gary, maybe not. Maybe we could have done it with a couple less people," the uncompromising Scheib would reply. "Let's play this scenario out: we made a mistake at the White House, and we're sitting across the table from Mrs. Bush or Mrs. Clinton, and we're trying to explain why her name is being bandied around by all the late-night comedians. 'But the good news, Mrs. Bush, the good news, Mrs. Clinton, is, we saved five hundred dollars.' How do you think that discussion's going to go?"

Above all else, he said, "Our goal was to make sure that the first family was never embarrassed." No matter the cost.

———

WHEN A NEW family moves in, routines change abruptly. The Obamas have pushed their wake-up time back slightly later than their recent predecessors; they prefer to turn off their own lights at night; and they want gala apples in addition to the usual flowers in the Oval Office. The apples added a fresh task for the florists: they have to be checked every day, because the president encourages people to eat them and the supply dwindles fast. Florists are out of the Oval Office no later than 7:30 A.M., when President Obama is usually making his way to work.

While the Obama family's requests don't veer too far from those of previous first families, when their first social secretary, Desirée Rogers, arrived with them in 2009, she was committed to shaking up tradition by bringing a new energy and new ideas to the staid executive mansion. A Harvard MBA and descendant of a Creole voodoo priestess, Rogers was the first African American social secretary, so her very presence defied tradition. In her first sixty days in the post, she coordinated more than fifty events. That's twice as many as President George W. Bush held during the same period of his first term, and surpassed even the pace of the party-loving Clintons. She sought to change the way the White House worked, mixing and matching china from different eras at formal dinners and including Republicans in every congressional event. She also involved herself in details traditionally handled by the residence staff, deeply irritating some of them.

"She really was in her own little world when she came in the door," Florist Bob Scanlan said. "She made it quite clear that they didn't want what we had been doing and they were looking for a new look. I can't tell you how many times we heard [Rogers ask for] 'the Four Seasons look.'" He interpreted Rogers's edict as a request for more contemporary floral arrangements, with flowers placed at an angle, as opposed to the more traditional oasis arrangement, an array of lush fresh-cut flowers stuck in foam. Scanlan said that he and his colleagues bristled when a woman was brought in for several weeks to "revamp the Flower Shop" because, he said, they were told they were stuck in the past.

Scanlan said that from the beginning many of the florists viewed Rogers as disrespectful of the mansion's long-standing traditions and were happy to see her go fifteen months later (after a scandal involving gate-crashers who managed to infiltrate the Obamas' first state dinner without an invitation). "When you become part of that house and you are a florist, there's a certain element and a certain look that belongs strictly for that house. It's not just the first family's, it's the public's too. We're doing flowers for the country." Rogers remembers the controversy over the flowers a little differently. She says she didn't ask for changes immediately and stuck to tradition, at least on Inauguration Day. "There was a certain way that flowers were done in the house," she said, adding that there was nothing new done on Inauguration Day to incorporate the first family's style. "Remember, this is before they ever got into the house. They're not able to say 'we like this' or 'we like that,' 'more of this' or 'less of that.' So it was pretty much set up the way it had historically been set up over the years by that florist."

When I asked Chief Usher Admiral Rochon what it was like working with Rogers, he joked that he might need to take an Excedrin. Rogers had been a successful businesswoman, but when it came to the White House transition, she had unrealistic expectations.

"It wasn't exacting, it was just impossible," he said, exasperated by the memory. She wanted the walls to be painted and dry by the time the Obamas came back from the inaugural parade, Rochon recalls. "We would have to convince them that, no, you can't have a mural on this wall, because it has to be done after President Bush leaves."

The new family is not allowed to change the historic State and Ground floors, but they are free to make a variety of changes on the second and third floors once they actually move in. The staff even closed a wall up in Malia's room because it led to an open walkway and the teenager wanted more privacy. Such changes, however, must wait until the limousine carries away the outgoing first family.

Executive Pastry Chef Roland Mesnier had extensive experience in the hotel industry, having worked at London's Savoy Hotel and at the Homestead in Virginia's Allegheny Mountains, and he earned a reputation for quickly figuring out what the president wanted. Instead of listening to Obama's political advisers, who all claimed they knew what kind of food the president and first lady preferred, he discreetly approached family members when they visited the White House.

One aide to George W. Bush told Mesnier not to worry about making elaborate birthday cakes. Instead, he suggested, just make an angel food cake with strawberries. "I never made an angel food cake with strawberry in the hole!" said Mesnier, a boisterous, plump Frenchman with rosy cheeks. "After they see what you can do, forget about what they used to have."

———————

AFTER AMERICAN VOTERS elect a new president, all eyes turn to the future. For the residence workers, though, life goes on. David Hume Kennerly, President Ford's White House photographer and a close Ford family friend, said that working at the White House is like being on a movie set: "When the movie's over you go on to the next gig."

For the residence staff, it's not always easy to deal with the revolving door of families. Inauguration Day feels like starting a new job, working for the most powerful family in the world with no certainty about what they expect. Will the first lady, who has much more direct contact with the staff than the president, find fault with the food, or the flower arrangements, or the way the beds are made? "There are thousands of things like that running through your mind," Scanlan confessed. "Is she going to call up and say, 'I hate this'? They can do whatever they want."

Executive Chef Walter Scheib was hired by Hillary Clinton and fired by Laura Bush. For him, the transition to Bush was painful. After serving the Clintons haute American cuisine for almost the entirety of their two terms, he didn't know what the Bushes expected. Almost overnight, he had to go from preparing layered late-summer vegetables with lemongrass and red curry to serving up Tex-Mex Chex and BLTs. (President Clinton satisfied most of his unhealthy food cravings when he was on the road and away from the watchful eye of the first lady who even requested that calorie counts be included on family dinner menus.)

"It's the only time I ever had a job quit me: the physical plan was the same, all the pots and pans were the same, the refrigerator was the same, all the ovens were the same, but you didn't know your job anymore. You had to relearn your job literally in an afternoon."

Mesnier describes saying good-bye to the departing family as "little short of funereal."

Leaving the happy environment of the White House often isn't any easier for the first family. President George H. W. Bush broke down crying when he saw the staff gathered before him. He was rendered speechless. "We were too choked up with emotion to say what we felt, but I think they knew the affection we had for them all," recalled Barbara Bush. Before leaving for the Capitol, she raced through the Red and Blue Rooms to hug all the butlers privately. "From then on it was all downhill. The hard part for me was over."

The transition back to civilian life is difficult, no matter how much presidents and first ladies say they crave a return to privacy. When the Reagans said their good-byes to the residence staff in the State Dining Room, the president joked: "You know the only problem about leaving the White House: When I will wake up tomorrow morning, how am I going to turn the electricity on? I haven't done it in eight years. You have done it for me all these years. How will I turn the switch on? I don't know." (Nancy Reagan said her husband loved the luxury of the residence, referring to it as an eight-star hotel. She agreed. "Every evening, while I took a bath, one of the maids would come by and remove my clothes for laundering or dry cleaning. The bed would always be turned down. Five minutes after Ronnie came home and hung up his suit, it would disappear from the closet to be pressed, cleaned, or brushed.")

In her memoir, Barbara Bush offers a rare glimpse of how sheltered the first family becomes after years of having cooks, maids, and butlers. The Bushes had spent decades in public service and were famously not accustomed to buying groceries. (During his 1992 reelection campaign, Bush was ridiculed after he marveled at a supermarket scanner.) Not long after leaving office, Barbara Bush says, her husband took his first trip to Sam's Club and "bought the world's biggest jar of spaghetti sauce and some spaghetti" for dinner.

While he sat down to watch the evening news, the former first lady started to cook. She accidentally knocked the enormous jar of sauce off the counter, sending it crashing onto the kitchen floor. Their dinner plans ruined, they scrambled for an alternative. "That was the night George and I made an amazing discovery: You can call out for pizza!"

Sometimes the good-byes are funny. Lyndon Johnson's youngest daughter, Luci, now sixty-seven, entered nursing school while she was living at the White House, and for months she kept the cat fetus she used for dissection in class in the third-floor Solarium's refrigerator. She fondly referred to the fetus as "Crunchy" because it was housed in a crunchy peanut butter jar. On the day she left, one staffer, a maid named Clara to whom she had grown particularly close, thrust the jar into her hands and said, "This is the only good thing I can think about you leaving." The two hugged and "cried our eyes out."

"I knew it would never be the same," Luci said. "I knew that she would be turning those energies and that deference and that grace just as quickly as I walked out the door to trying to help the Nixon girls feel just as much at home as she had made me. The allegiance that the White House domestic staff feels toward the White House and toward the president and his family who occupy it is something that makes you feel very proud to be an American."

White House Electrician and Dog Keeper Traphes Bryant, who was skeptical of LBJ when he first moved into the residence so full of bluster, was devastated when the Johnsons moved back to Texas in 1969. "It was over. It was really over. It was a relief. It was not a relief. It was as if someone told me I would never see a member of my family again," he wrote in his memoir. "I had known LBJ and felt closer than a brother. And now if we met again, we would be almost like strangers. I felt lost. Then free, as I realized I wouldn't have to take his guff anymore."

———

SOME TRANSITIONS ARE easier than others. President George W. Bush and his family brought only one chest of drawers and some family photos, because, Laura Bush said, "part of the fun" of living at the White House is going to the warehouse in Maryland and picking out pieces from the White House collection to furnish the house. It helped that the Bushes already knew the layout of the house. "You could hardly take a breath and it was done," Bob Scanlan said of their move-in.

Before the Bushes could start choosing furniture, however, they had to deal with a most unexpected complication: the 2000 recount, which kept the outcome of the election a mystery until December 12, more than a month after the votes were cast. Perhaps no one, aside from the candidates themselves, was watching the unfolding drama of the election quite as closely as the residence workers. Between Election Day and the day the Supreme Court upheld Bush's victory, Walters scoured the news constantly, anxious to learn whom they would be catering to: George W. Bush or Al Gore. After the decision was handed down, Laura Bush had less than half the normal amount of time to prepare for their move.

The recount was highly contentious, with the entire national election hinging on the results in Florida, and when the verdict came down against Gore, Bill Clinton's staff was furious. The younger Clinton aides, in particular, were vocal about their disdain for the incoming president. One staffer shouted at Chef Mesnier, in no uncertain terms, that Bush would be a one-term president: "We'll kick his ass out of here!" he yelled at the chef. In keeping with the residence staff's credo to be apolitical Mesnier says, "I let him have his say and said nothing myself." (He says that the Clintons themselves weren't happy about their staff's behavior, loyalty notwithstanding.)

Regardless of who won the election, the Clintons hated to leave. Hillary Clinton said that even after eight years of living in the residence, and enduring incredibly painful times there, she still views the White House "with the same awe I felt as a little girl pressing my face up to the gate to get a better look." The whole family, including Chelsea, took advantage of their private theater one last time to watch the movie *State and Main* well after midnight the night before President George W. Bush's inauguration. They didn't want to miss a minute that the house was still under their temporary ownership. "The fun of that night left them so tired that when Barbara, Jenna, and I glanced over at Bill during George's inaugural address, he was dozing," Laura Bush recalled.

President Clinton confessed to the Bushes on the morning of the inauguration that he had put off packing for so long that, right at the end, "he was packing simply by pulling out drawers and dumping their contents into boxes."

While Hillary Clinton always appreciated the majesty of the White House, she had her regrets. She told Laura Bush that she wished that she hadn't insisted on having an office in the West Wing and that she had not decided to turn down invitations just because her schedule was too packed. She always felt particularly guilty about declining an invitation from Jackie Kennedy to attend the ballet. Jackie died a few months later. Her advice to Bush: Don't lose sight of what's important.

WORKERS OFTEN FOUND themselves at the center of world events. Betty Monkman, who served in the curator's office from 1967 to 2002, eventually becoming chief curator, was responsible for supervising the workers who hung and removed artwork for each new incoming first family. During the transition from Carter to Reagan, she remembers, the staff turned on televisions throughout the residence as they worked so that they could watch the final throes of the tense Iran hostage crisis. "President Carter had been up in the Oval Office all night long with his staff and barely got over to the house to dress for his ten A.M. event with President Reagan," Monkman said. "Nobody knew what was going to happen. The whole country was waiting." The Iranians released the remaining fifty-two hostages minutes after Reagan was sworn in as the nation's fortieth president—one last dig at Carter, who had worked day and night to bring about their release before the end of his administration.

No matter what occurs outside the White House, the staff is always singularly focused on the move. "We were constantly on our feet," Monkman said. "Once, in the Ford administration, we were doing something in Susan Ford's bedroom and President Ford just happened to come around when people were starting to disassemble things to say good-bye to the household staff. Right before he went downstairs he made it a mission to come by and thank everybody for their work and that was something the staff appreciated." As soon as he left, the rush was on.

Though they try not to get too attached to the mansion's current residents, the staff often seems to be pulling for the incumbent to be reelected, whether Democrat or Republican. When Bill Clinton defeated the first President Bush, Chef Mesnier felt the outcome was a "veritable disaster." He had grown so close to the Bushes that he was truly unsure whether he would be able to serve another president.

He wasn't alone: when other residence staffers called out sick after President Clinton's election, the joke was that they had caught the "Republican flu."

In part, this is because the arrival of a new family means casting aside everything they've learned about each member of the outgoing first family and starting fresh. But most accounts agree that the residence workers' devotion to President George H. W. Bush was more than customary—it was genuine, almost profound. The Bushes were generally easy to please, and the residence workers found themselves quickly at ease with them. Even before she moved into the White House, Chief Usher Gary Walters reported, Barbara Bush assured him that she wouldn't be making any changes in the kitchen. "I've never had a bad meal [at the White House], so you just have the chefs put whatever they want to on the menu every evening and we'll be surprised at what we eat each night."

"What if you don't like something?" he asked her, unaccustomed to such an easygoing first lady after working for Nancy Reagan.

"Then we'll tell the chef not to have it again," she told him.

———

ON NOVEMBER 11, 1968, days after Richard M. Nixon won the presidential election, he and his wife, Pat, were guests of the Johnsons at the White House. Johnson and Nixon were bitter political enemies, but they made nice during a four-hour lunch. Johnson surprised even his wife with his civility. "Lyndon, I thought, was generous and rather fatherly," Lady Bird said. "I thought, it was not so much Nixon the man he was talking to, but the next President of this country."

Lady Bird showed the incoming first lady the second and third floors, reassuring her of "the efficiency, devotion, and impersonal professionalism" of the residence staff.

During the stress and strain of the move, first ladies have been seen on the morning of the inauguration stealing a quiet moment to themselves. "You wonder what must be going through their minds," mused Head Housekeeper Christine Limerick. The Johnsons had a particular affinity for life in the residence. Lady Bird recalled wandering through the second and third floors in her robe with a cup of coffee early on the morning of Inauguration Day, her final day in the White House. A little more than five years earlier, she and her family moved into a White House consumed by grief. On the evening of December 7, 1963, just as Jackie Kennedy was moving out, Lady Bird must have been moved to tears by a note the first lady left behind. "I wish you a happy arrival in your new house, Lady Bird," Jackie wrote. "Remember—you will be happy here." All those years later, the grief of those first few months must have come rushing back.

She stood in the Yellow Oval Room and the Lincoln Sitting Room, wanting to soak in their rich history one last time. She said a final, private good-bye to the place she and her family had called home for so many years. "This was partly the housewifely need to see whether any personal object had been left anywhere," she said, "but mostly just to stand still and absorb."

Lady Bird peeked into her daughter Luci's room, which was strewn with half-filled bags and boxes, and leafed through a guest book showing all the guests who had stayed with them over the years. When she walked up to the Solarium she was struck by how different it looked without their furniture. "Its personality all stripped away and looking cold and clinical now, and what a gay, happy room it had been—the citadel of the young." On the State Floor she could smell the ammonia as maids, butlers, and almost everyone else on the residence staff pitched in to ready the house for the Nixons.

As the inaugural parade was going on, the staff fulfilled an unusual request. The outgoing president had been a devoted consumer of television news, and had filled the White House with sets. "Lyndon Johnson would sit like a king with four sets on in a row, watching himself," according to Bryant. "There he'd be, throwing out comments and switching the sound from one to another, or keeping several sets on together, with the sound turned up loud." Richard Nixon, in contrast, was famously uncomfortable with the medium, and after his election the residence staff were instructed to remove most of the sets from the house. Some were still being yanked out even as staffers tried to catch a glimpse of the inaugural parade on TV.

Late that morning, as President Johnson and President-elect Nixon headed off to the Capitol together, Lady Bird shared a car with Pat Nixon. As she drove away, the last thing Lady Bird saw through her rearview window was Maître d' John Ficklin and Butler Wilson Jerman watching the Johnsons depart. She blew them a kiss good-bye. It must have been bittersweet to know that the next time she returned to her beloved White House, she would be just another guest.

CHAPTER II

Discretion

*Secrecy, loyalty, discretion applies to the humblest, not so
much personal loyalty to the incumbent as loyalty to the office.
The atmosphere of the house would be intolerable if the President had to
look on all hands as eaves-droppers; he must take their loyalty for granted.
State and personal secrets aren't shouted, but in a house so uttered daily
with confidences, some must reach the ears of the least employee.*

—IRWIN "IKE" HOOVER, CHIEF USHER, 1913–1933, "WHO'S WHO, AND WHY,
IN THE WHITE HOUSE," *SATURDAY EVENING POST*, FEBRUARY 10, 1934

*Q: "Why don't you have a lot of photos?"
A: "Because I knew where the cameras were."*

—NELSON PIERCE, USHER, 1961–1987

"Sce no evil, hear no evil, speak no evil," residence workers
often respond when they are asked to share details about
the private moments of the first families. If they share one
unifying quality, it is the ability to keep secrets, especially when
they are still on the job. James Jeffries was the only current residence worker who was willing to discuss his experiences; retired

staffers often rebuffed several approaches before they agreed to share their memories, and even then some of them tried to mask painful or negative stories by painting them in a good light, no matter how strained they seemed. The stories shared here represent only what they felt they could divulge, and in almost every case, reflect their efforts to present their experiences in a thoughtful and deliberate manner. Still, their recollections pull back the curtain and provide fascinating and sometimes shocking insights into the personalities of the occupants of the executive mansion.

Butlers, maids, and valets have the most intimate exposure to the first family. They are also the hardest workers to get to open up, because they guard so passionately the trust the first family places in them. They are the first people to see the first family in the morning and the last people to see them at night. These residence workers—along with a few others, such as the family chefs—watch the presidents and first ladies as they conduct themselves as husband and wife: fighting, laughing, crying, and being each other's most trusted advisers. All of these residence workers will doubtless take plenty of secrets to their graves.

One telling example of the importance of the staff's discretion comes not from a staffer but from a first family member. Ron Reagan remembers visiting his parents at the White House during the Iran-Contra affair, before his father's administration admitted to helping sell arms to Iran in exchange for the release of hostages and funding for the Contra rebels in Nicaragua. During the visit, the president's son, then in his midtwenties, was amazed at how candid his family was in front of the help. They shared dinner that night in the Family Dining Room on the second floor, and then repaired to the West Sitting Hall on the second floor—a more informal room with a stunning floor-to-ceiling half-moon window looking out over the West Colonnade and the West Wing—where the younger Reagan found himself pushing his father about the Iran-Contra situation.

"I was getting a little heated about this at a certain point," he says, "and realized suddenly as I was berating my father that somebody was standing there with a plate of cookies. I felt immediately like, 'Oh, God, this is not good'—doing this in public, as it were." But he was amazed to realize that the presence of the servants "seemed to be of no concern" to his parents. "The staff there is so discreet that there really wasn't any concern that somebody was going to run and tell stories to the papers." Such discretion is mandatory, Reagan reflects now. If the president had to worry about the staff talking to the press, "life there would be almost unbearable. You need a retreat you can go to and not be constantly scrutinized."

Building up to this level of trust can take time, and each administration is different. Everyone on staff knows when the first family finally trusts them, said Chief Usher Gary Walters. For Walters, his favorite moment of a new administration comes when the president calls him by his first name.

"The residence staff knows when the comfortableness gets to the point where we can all collectively say, 'Ahhhhhh.' It happens usually with the butlers or with the ushers when a conversation is going on and you walk into the room and the conversation doesn't stop. It continues. That's a collective sigh, we know we have proven that we can be trusted."

There are times, however, when the president needs total privacy. As Butler Herman Thompson recalls, even the approachable George H. W. Bush would sometimes say "Thank you very much," to one of the residence workers. "That meant for you to turn around and go back out."

JAMES RAMSEY

Each president has a favorite butler, and for President George W. Bush it was James Ramsey, or just plain "Ramsey," as he was affectionately called around the residence. He was a consummate professional, but he liked trading zingers with President George W. Bush, and their rapport led to a real bond between the men; Ramsey was one of the few residence staffers invited by the Bushes to fly with them on Air Force One to work at their ranch in Crawford, Texas. He zealously guarded the family's privacy, never talking to the press or causing the president to doubt his loyalty. He also turned down invitations to go out drinking with his colleagues because, he said, other people "get you in trouble."

Ramsey had a joyful and ready smile, and he seemed genuinely in awe of the families he served during three decades as a White House butler. Reggie Love, President Obama's young, handsome, and gregarious personal assistant, remembers Ramsey's contagious sense of humor. "He'd joke, 'I'm seventy years old. When you're my age, hopefully you'll look half as good as I do.'"

Ramsey sported a bright silver mustache, shaving it off only after he retired in 2010. He dry-cleaned all his clothes, even his undershirts, and always made sure his nails were manicured because people would see his hands when he was serving them. He was not at all ashamed of his love of self-pampering: "I want to look nice all the way: nails done, hair groomed," he said. "I was a butler at the White House!"

A self-described ladies' man, Ramsey dated quite a bit after getting divorced and even introduced some of his girlfriends to President George W. Bush at staff holiday parties. He sometimes told the Bush daughters about his dates. "Jenna, Barbara—I loved them to death. They were my friends. . . . If they ask, I tell them, 'I got a lady friend. I ain't that old, am I?'"

George W. Bush, whom Ramsey affectionately called the "young Bush," would tease him mercilessly—and Ramsey gave as good as he got. He fondly recalled one day when he was serving refreshments at a T-ball game on the South Lawn and the president came out from the Diplomatic Reception Room. "Do some work, Ramsey!" the president joked. That's just the way their relationship was, he said: they were casual with each other, even though it was clear who was in charge.

President George W. Bush loved having a little fun with the residence workers. He would turn framed photos on their sides when the butlers and maids weren't looking and chase imaginary flies with flyswatters as they walked by. "There were great practical jokes that the president would play on the butlers," recalled Andy Card, Bush's chief of staff.

"Bush," Ramsey said, pausing. "I'll never forget his family. If I live to be one hundred, I'll never forget his family."

Ramsey's small apartment, which he called his "bachelor pad," was plastered with astounding photos of himself with presidents and other historic figures, including Nelson Mandela ("Oh, I got a lot of them baby"), and personal notes from President Reagan and Hillary Clinton thanking him for his help with state dinners. One photo is autographed by President Obama: "You are a great friend and will be missed," the president wrote.

He was so proud of his job at the White House that his friend, fellow butler Buddy Carter, teased him: "Ramsey—he sleeps in his damn White House pass."

While the first family is in their private quarters on the second and third floors of the White House, a butler is almost always available—in the second-floor pantry or nearby—waiting to serve. The rooms are equipped with buzzers that go off in the pantry when their service is requested, but Ramsey rarely needed them: "I could sense it if they wanted something."

It's easy to see why Ramsey was so beloved. He kept his sweet Southern accent from his years growing up in Yanceyville, North Carolina. His stepfather was a tobacco farmer (he never met his father), and he spent much of his childhood using the family's mule to plow the tobacco field.

"It was rough. I told my dad, I said, 'When I graduate from high school, I got to go. I can't stay here.' He said, 'How are you going to live?' And I said, 'That's a chance I got to take.' So when I came to Washington I didn't know nobody."

He finally got to Washington when he was twenty years old. He had nowhere to stay until he found a sympathetic owner of a gas station who let him sleep at the station and wash up in the bathroom. Eventually he found a room on Rhode Island Avenue Northwest for ten dollars a week, and while he was there he befriended someone who worked at the glamorous art deco Kennedy Warren apartment building in northwest Washington. He told his friend that he was a good worker and his friend got him an interview. He was hired on the spot.

Not long after that, at a party, he met someone who worked at the White House. Ramsey asked him if he could get him a job there. The first thing this White House staffer asked Ramsey was, "Do you have a record?"

"No, man, I ain't got no record," Ramsey replied.

"If you do, don't bother filling the papers out," he said skeptically. "They're not going to hire you with *any* kind of record." (Operations Supervisor Tony Savoy remembers being shocked to learn how many job applicants had serious criminal records. "Everybody comes there and they have a clean record. Until you do the background check. With the background check all these little skeletons start coming out of the closet. One boy came in during the Clinton administration and he told us, at the very last minute, that he was arrested and convicted of rape. We have thirteen-year-old Chelsea upstairs! That application went in the trash can.")

Ramsey's record was unblemished, so he filled out the application and waited. "I passed the White House going to the Kennedy Warren, oh my god for two or three years, and I said, 'I wonder how in the world it would be working in that place?'" he said, smiling. But it took a few years until the White House finally called him. When they met him, Maître d' Eugene Allen and then–Chief Usher Rex Scouten hired him the same day.

Starting as a butler during Carter's presidency, Ramsey worked at the White House for thirty years, serving six presidents: Jimmy Carter, Ronald Reagan, George H. W. Bush, Bill Clinton, George W. Bush, and Barack Obama. He credits Eugene Allen—"He talked to me like I was his son"—with advising him to keep his nose clean and keep anything he heard in the residence to himself. (The 2013 film *Lee Daniels' The Butler* was loosely based on Allen's life.)

Even decades later, Ramsey would not betray Allen's instruction— he would never reveal anything private about those he served to the outside world. "You're not working at no McDonald's or Gino's, you're working down here at the house," Allen told Ramsey. "If you get in trouble or say the wrong thing, you might be history."

That code of silence didn't extend to his colleagues. Chief Usher Stephen Rochon remembered that Ramsey was the first residence worker to welcome him and that he went out of his way to tell Rochon what was happening on the second and third floors.

————

THE RESPONSIBILITY OF being privy to the family's inner sanctum was never lost on loyal staff like Wilson Jerman, a soft-spoken eighty-five-year-old when I interviewed him recently. Starting as a houseman in 1957, he retired as a butler in 1993, then came out of retirement in 2003 (he missed "the house") and worked as a part-time doorman until 2010. Like a doorman in any building, he saw everyone coming and going and held their secrets.

Jerman views his loyalty to the first family and his guarding of their privacy as a natural response to the trust they place in him. "It makes you feel good that you could just go up there and walk in the first lady's bedroom and pick up whatever she asked you to go get."

Katie Johnson, President Obama's former personal secretary, said she used to love quizzing the butlers. When she asked one butler what had changed the most in the White House over his several decades of service, he mentioned two things: more women and no more drinking at lunch.

"People used to drink really heavily in the middle of the day," he told her. "One reason they had so many staff was, they were making martinis for these meetings in the middle of the day, which would never happen now," she said. "Can you imagine if someone went to a Cabinet meeting and asked for a dry martini?"

Nelson Pierce, a White House usher for twenty-six years who passed away in 2014 at eighty-nine years old, was often required to bring the president documents classified as "eyes only," papers so sensitive that only the president is authorized to see them. I was lucky enough to have interviewed Pierce before his passing. He told me that one day he had to bring something to President Lyndon Johnson to sign during a luncheon with Secretary of State Dean Rusk, Secretary of Defense Robert McNamara, and at least a half dozen other advisers. They were almost certainly talking about Vietnam at the time.

Pierce stood anxiously next to the president, waiting for him to sign the document when he heard something unusual: "Secretary McNamara was raising his voice and yelling at the president. He was mad about something. I could not repeat a single word he said or the president said to him. I have no idea and I would swear on a stack of Bibles I don't remember a single word that was said because you blank it out. Even under hypnosis I don't think they'd be able to get anything."

Decades later, White House Chief of Staff Andrew Card said that during Oval Office meetings with George W. Bush he noticed that some of his fellow advisers got nervous when butlers and residence staff came in.

"They were trying to be as nonintrusive as possible at the same time they were trying to serve. I think other people were more uncomfortable with the presence of a butler than the president or the first lady ever were. They didn't know if they should stop talking!"

Yet the very thing that the staff most pride themselves on—their ability to fade into the background—can also be dehumanizing. Having the president count on their ability to tune out conversations has sometimes made residence workers feel as though they don't exist at all.

"People would say anything around you. It was surprising to me," said Butler Herman Thompson, who worked part-time from the Kennedy era until the end of the first Bush administration. "Sometimes the conversation in the State Dining Room, when you were working in there, you would think that they'd be whispering certain things. It was almost like you weren't there."

In some cases, the president or the first lady have proved uncomfortably oblivious to the workers nearby. Nelson Pierce remembered his embarrassment one night, when he was bringing some bags up to the Reagans' room, and Nancy Reagan yelled at her husband, the most powerful man in the world, right in front of him. "She cussed him out for having the TV on. He said, 'Honey, I'm just watching the news.' As soon as she opened the door, she was into him like you wouldn't believe. Right in front of me. I thought she would fuss at him in private. He was watching the eleven o'clock news. She thought he should be asleep. I was a little surprised, so I dropped the luggage and got out as soon as I could."

President Johnson often undressed in front of staffers and was famous for rattling off orders while he was sitting on the toilet. Once, reporter Frank Cormier was shocked to see Air Force One Steward Sergeant and Valet Paul Glynn kneel before the president while they were in midair and wash his feet—all the more so because Johnson never once acknowledged Glynn.

"Talking all the while, Johnson paid no heed except to cross his legs in the opposite direction when it was time for Glynn to attend to the other foot," Cormier observed. After witnessing this, Cormier said, he was unfazed when he learned that Glynn also cut Johnson's toenails.

Most of the time, however, working on such an intimate basis for the most powerful family in the world makes the staff feel respected. And it's in their interests to keep quiet about whatever they hear. Susan Ford, who was just seventeen when her father took over the presidency, said, "These people wouldn't be there for so many years if they talked."

White House painter Cletus Clark, who served presidents from Nixon to George W. Bush, never spilled secrets. "I'm just like a ghost. I've always stayed to myself. And I know right from wrong."

"They serve from president to president, they know all of the families, and they are always discreet," Laura Bush told me—in a much more measured voice than her mother-in-law. They maintain their discretion even when chatting with the first families themselves. "They don't tell about the presidents that lived there before you or anything about their family, which we admired and respected because, of course, we wanted them to treat us the same when we left."

The kinds of memories of everyday life that are treasured by most families are especially dear to the first families, who have often invited residence workers to join them on their downtime. Laura Bush says that her husband and Butler Ron Guy shared a love for fishing. "Any time the butlers came to our ranch, which they did when we hosted heads of state at our ranch, George and Ron Guy would bass fish at every free moment they had. I have a great big blowup of a photograph of George and Vice President Cheney and Ron Guy out on the little electric bass boat that we have at our ranch, fishing."

"There are just a lot of ways that we knew each person who worked there. We knew them so well," Mrs. Bush said. "Harold Hancock, I remember, was one of the doormen who we loved. He was such a gentle and lovely man and he died while we lived there. I have a wonderful photograph of him standing at the door waiting for the president to come back with Spot, our dog. . . . They were always great to all the animals. They acted like they were really wild about all the animals, whether they were or not!"

Luci Baines Johnson says she loved Wilson Jerman and remembers him vividly even now, nearly fifty years after leaving the White House. "He had a smile that could soothe a savage breast," she said in her slow Southern drawl.

In an ultimate example of discretion, Jerman found a way to dodge people's questions by never really admitting where he worked. "I'd say, 'I work at 1600 Pennsylvania Avenue,' and 99 percent of the people don't know where that is. They'd ask you, 'What warehouse is that? What building is that?' I'd say 'It's downtown.'" He didn't want to answer the barrage of questions that would follow if he told them the truth.

Like Ramsey, Jerman was so worried about saying something that would get him fired that he did not talk about his job at all when he worked there. "There would be too many questions asked," he said. "You see, you never see. You hear, you never hear. And you don't know nothing."

Even in the face of unfolding history, Jerman maintained focus on his job and seemed completely uninterested in breaking any news. In the early evening on April 15, 1986, Jerman and Chef Frank Ruta were preparing dinner for the Reagans when the president walked in. He often came into the kitchen, but this time he wasn't just checking in to see how they were doing.

"I just want you boys to know that in five minutes we're going to begin bombing Libya, and I want you to be the first to know," Reagan announced.

"That's nice, Mr. President," Jerman replied, "but what time would you like to have dinner?"

Reagan stopped, thought for a second, and said, "You better ask my wife that."

Ruta laughed, recalling the stunned look on Reagan's face. A moment later, Mrs. Reagan whisked her husband out of the kitchen; she was always wary of having him talk too much to the staff, especially when it came to divulging national security secrets.

Ruta was just twenty-two when he started in the White House kitchen, where he prepared most of the Reagans' family meals. He told me that Nancy Reagan protected her husband fiercely—her devotion to him was complete and genuine—but that Mrs. Reagan never had anything to worry about from the residence workers. Ruta never gossiped, and he never asked the maids and butlers to share any gossip either. "Their privacy has to be respected. You're not there to be the public's eye."

Sometimes staffers cannot help but witness private moments. Every evening, the usher on night duty brings up the president's briefing book, which contains sensitive material put together by the West Wing staff to prepare him for the next day, and turns off the lights. Usher Chris Emery remembers often finding the Reagans in the sitting room together after dinner when he was dropping off the briefing book. "Sometimes they'd be watching *Who's the Boss*—the TV was very loud because he was a little hard of hearing. It'd be eight or nine o'clock and he'd be there with these big black government-issue glasses in his red robe, in a flowered chair with a dinner tray next to him stacked with papers, working. Mrs. Reagan would be right next to him, and a lot of times I'd go up and they'd be holding hands. There was nobody around to see it."

Painter Cletus Clark said he took pains to avoid disturbing the family, even though it meant complicating his job. "They really didn't want us around there that much. You had to work around the first family as much as possible. When they're in the West Sitting Hall and we had to go down to the Queens' Bedroom, which is on the East Side, we used to have to go up to the third floor and walk down the hall and come down the back stairway. You've got to keep working."

Clark's loyalty to the job was clear when he was instructed to do some painting work at the home of Charles "Bebe" Rebozo, President Nixon's best friend. The press soon got hold of the story and questioned the use of White House staff for a personal job.

"I did what they told me to do," Clark said. "I don't ask no questions."

Barbara Bush says that the residence staff "probably gossip less than one gossips normally." Of course, she added mischievously, "I've got to say that we do have the perfect family."

Rosalynn Carter appreciated the staff's discretion. "I just trusted them completely. They were all so good. I don't remember ever covering up anything, but I don't ever remember them trying to listen in. I guess they were doing things around while we were talking but I don't remember that at all."

These workers hate the spotlight. Usher Nelson Pierce, who was a thin man with a gentle smile, didn't have many photos of his time at the White House, largely because he dodged photographers so conscientiously during his twenty-six years there (1961 to 1987). "I wasn't there to be photographed," said Pierce. "I got caught three times on television: once was when I was plugging in the Christmas lights on the North Portico and the cameras weren't supposed to be taking pictures, but they were. And then twice when holding an umbrella: once for the president and once for the first lady when they got off the chopper."

————

DISCRETION IS ESPECIALLY important when it comes to protecting the way food is secured for the first family. For large orders, the White House uses prescreened food supply companies whose workers are fully vetted by the FBI and the Secret Service. The items are picked up by Secret Service officers and brought to the White House. If the president takes a liking to a certain snack he encounters during his travels and wants it sent back to the White House, arrangements are sometimes made to have it sent to residence staff at their home addresses so that no one knows it's going to the president.

When it comes to the first family's regular meals, though, the raw materials are bought anonymously by residence workers to ensure safety. Storeroom Manager William "Bill" Hamilton, the longest-serving residence worker in recent history (he started when President Eisenhower was in office and retired in 2013), was responsible for buying food for family meals and occasionally for larger dinners. A slim, bald seventy-seven-year-old who looks remarkably young, Hamilton often ran to a local grocery store to pick up whatever the family needed, from toilet paper to apples. He still will not reveal which store he went to. ("The Secret Service won't let me say!") The anonymity was crucial: no one knew he was shopping for the first family, and no one was interested in poisoning his food.

Hamilton's office was located underneath the North Portico, across from the White House Ground Floor Kitchen, making it convenient for him to stay in touch with the executive chef about which ingredients were needed for the family's meals. When shopping time came, Hamilton generally traveled to the market in a Secret Service van made to look like a normal SUV, rather than one of the imposing black vans in the White House motorcade. "Just like any van, except that we take all the seats and stuff out of it, but on the outside it looks like any other van."

Because no packages are accepted through the mail at the White House compound, everything has to be cleared through the Secret Service in a building in remote Maryland. Whenever someone asked Executive Pastry Chef Roland Mesnier how they could send the president something special, he would tell them not to bother. "You can send it but they're not going to see it. It's going to be destroyed."

When the president eats meals outside the White House, a member of the military is generally assigned to monitor the kitchen, watch the food being prepared, and taste it to make sure it's safe. Jane Erkenbeck, an assistant to Nancy Reagan, said that her hotel room was always next to the first lady's, in part to make it easier for Mrs. Reagan to get room service meals delivered safely and expeditiously. Erkenbeck herself would order the food, she recalls, and "it was always delivered to me, it was never delivered to her. Then I would take it into her room."

———

WORKING AT THE White House also requires a degree of composure under unusual circumstances, even from workers who don't necessarily have daily exposure to the first family. Plumbing Foreman Reds Arrington and his brother, Bonner, who was the carpenter foreman, were warned by their uncle—who got them their jobs—about the importance of keeping their own counsel.

"They all kept their mouths shut," said Margaret Arrington, Reds Arrington's widow. Now that so much time has passed, she feels free to share some of what her husband saw behind closed doors.

"When the family was around," she recalled, her husband and his brother usually "disappeared," staying out of the way. But "they did any job they were asked to do. One job was to move some chairs for Jackie Kennedy. When they got off of the elevator, she was sitting at the end of the hall on the phone and had her leg propped up, crossed at the ankle, fiddling with her toes." The first lady was wearing pants, and her casual demeanor caught them off-guard. "They were so shocked, seeing her sitting there in a very unladylike position, that they both ran straight into a wall with the chairs!" They hit the wall so hard, they were worried they'd damaged the priceless antiques.

If the first lady or the president decides to come down for an impromptu visit, workers try to look out for one another, sending along advance notice so their colleagues won't be caught by surprise. According to Reggie Love, the Secret Service or the president's secretary would call the Usher's Office to let them know when the president was heading to the residence or to visit any of the shops downstairs.

As Cletus Clark remembers, when Betty Ford came downstairs to the basement to thank him before her husband left office, he got a call a few minutes before from the Usher's Office: "The first lady's coming down, so carry yourself accordingly."

CHRISTINE LIMERICK

Executive Housekeeper Christine Limerick worked at the
White House for thirty-four years, retiring in 2008. Unlike some
of her colleagues' homes, her yellow ranch house in Delaware is not
a shrine to her White House years. (Instead a whole room of her
house is devoted to her teddy bear collection.) The only hint of her
fascinating career is a Christmas card from the Clintons hanging
in the dining room. A friendly woman with close-cropped white
hair, Limerick started dating her husband, Robert, when he was
an engineer at the White House. She is completely unaffected by
her close relationship with the most famous families in the world.
And she is absolutely beloved by the staff she worked with for so
many years.

Limerick "was my boss and she was a friend," said Betty Finney,
a White House maid from 1993 until 2007. "She would do anything
in the world to help you if you needed help."

She took an unlikely path to 1600 Pennsylvania Avenue. In 1972, she dropped out of a graduate program in Chinese history at the prestigious George Washington University in Washington, D.C., to become a cocktail waitress at the elegant Mayflower Hotel off of Connecticut Avenue. Her father was upset and was no happier when she joined the hotel's housekeeping training program. "I didn't raise my daughter to be a toilet bowl cleaner," he told her.

That would all change.

"When I got the job at the White House I called him up and I said, 'Your daughter is now the toilet bowl cleaner for the White House. How do you feel about that?'"

In her role as executive housekeeper, Limerick was in charge of hiring and firing maids (in consultation with the chief usher). During her time in the job, she recalls, a couple of maids left after a few weeks—either because they were too starstruck to do their job in proximity to the most powerful couple in the world, or because they lacked the necessary discretion.

"You have a balance between serving the family and knowing when you need to get out of their way," she said. "Some of these people might not be the best bed maker in the world, they might not win an award for that, but they knew when the family needed them and when it was time to vacate the premises."

The Clintons were her favorite family to serve. She said they were the most passionate first couple, their infamous ups and downs playing out in the private quarters. During the Clinton era, Limerick recalls, working at the White House was a roller-coaster ride. The couple sometimes got into pitched battles, shocking the staff with their vicious cursing, and sometimes they went through periods of stony silence. During happier times, though, they were liable to wander around the residence late at night when they couldn't sleep, chatting giddily and marveling at the house.

Ivaniz Silva, who worked with Limerick at the Mayflower, was hired by her as a White House housekeeper in 1985. Retired since 2008, she lives near Howard University with her younger sister, Sylvia, who still works as a maid at the residence. During her time at the White House, Ivaniz had to get up at 5:30 A.M. and take two buses to get to the residence in time for her shift at seven-thirty. "If we got any snow," she recalls, "I had to walk." The rotation was three weeks on the morning shift, from seven-thirty to four in the afternoon, and one week on the evening shift, which ran from noon to around 8:00 P.M.

She always did what was asked of her. If a guest needed something beyond her normal duties, like hemming a dress, she would do it. She sewed the most for the Clintons and for Laura Bush.

Limerick describes a delicate dance the maids must do as they try not to disturb the first family. "We worked two steps behind them," she recalled. "If they walk in the room, they look at you and say, 'You can finish, you don't have to leave.' If they tell you to stay, you do what you need to do, but you have an ability to let what's going on around you just go over your head. If they're having a meeting or a conversation between the president and the first lady—maybe it's heated, maybe it's not, maybe it's passionate, maybe it's not—you just ask, 'Can I stay, can I finish?' You just do what you do, either you forget it or you file it away." Even if the family wanted time alone, the residence workers would often leave one room and go to work in an adjoining chamber. "If they want privacy, they close the doors that are connected to the bathroom and we don't leave."

Limerick said maids follow the same code as butlers: they see but they don't see, they hear but they don't hear. They don't speak to members of the first family or their guests unless spoken to, and they never approach them with personal requests.

At times, the maids have had to turn a blind eye to the youthful misbehavior of the first family's children—including underage drinking among some of the teenagers. The residence workers generally sympathize with kids who grow up in the White House, with so little privacy. "I was no angel when I was twenty, twenty-one," Limerick recalled, identifying with some of the kids. "They party, and they like to have friends over, and so you see all that," she says. And most of the workers believe it's better for them to drink inside the gates than outside, where it could jeopardize both their physical safety and their parents' reputations.

Susan Ford, who moved into the residence as a teenager, re-members the staff "gently nudging" her when she was behaving inappropriately. But, she says, their admonishments didn't carry the same weight as her parents'. Some things she and her friends did, like shooting off fireworks from the White House grounds on the Fourth of July (which is illegal in Washington, D.C.), they did be-cause they knew they could get away with it. "Who's going to come behind the White House gate and arrest you?" Ford says that un-derage drinking was easy to do in the residence: the refrigerator in the Solarium was stocked with soda and beer to offer guests. "What teenager's not going to drink beer if it's put there in front of them?"

President Carter's three adult sons spent plenty of time at the White House during his presidency. Florist Ronn Payne, who started at the White House during the Nixon administration and left under Clinton, said he had to do more than freshen the floral arrangements in the Carters' sons' rooms on the third floor. "I would regularly have to move bongs," he said. (The unabashed pot-smoking in the president's house was confirmed by another member of the household staff on the condition of anonymity.) If any of the Carter sons were found with the illegal drug on the street they would have been arrested, but they smoked inside the White House without fear of any repercussions.

President Carter's mother, Lillian, and younger brother, Billy, were also fixtures at the White House. They were colorful char-acters: Lillian, in her eighties at the time, was known to enjoy her bourbon (the president told the staff to keep her away from alcohol, so she would send a butler out to pick up a bottle of Jack Daniel's from a liquor store on Connecticut Avenue and deliver it to her room), and Billy was involved in several scandals while his brother was president. The household staff called Carter's brother "Billy Beer" after the beer he so enthusiastically promoted, and whenever he was drunk they made sure he "wouldn't hit the streets," Butler Herman Thompson said. "If they knew that you were really intoxicated and you were close to the president, like a brother or cousin, you weren't going *anywhere*."

One Fourth of July during President George W. Bush's administration, after his daughters Jenna and Barbara were old enough to drink legally, their parents left them at the White House alone while they went off to Camp David.

"They allowed Jenna and Barbara to have a party on the second floor and we cleared all the furniture out of the Yellow Oval Room and they danced. They were up all night long," Limerick said, smiling at the memory. "We shut off the Lincoln and Queens' bedrooms—they couldn't go there—but they could go every place else that they wanted to go. And they partied, and then the next morning we had a brunch for them. Some of them stayed up all night and some of them were a little bit hungover, but it's better than them being on the street."

The residence staff often come to the rescue of the first family, seeking to shelter them from public scrutiny and embarrassment. Usher Skip Allen remembers being called by the Secret Service duty desk when a sniper stationed on the roof of the White House saw something unusual. The Bush daughters were having another party in the Solarium, and it spilled outside to the walkway and onto the roof, as they often did when the weather was nice. Apparently, one of the guests had dared another to touch the flagpole. "It's not the safest place to be even in the daylight. You can trip over numerous hazards," Allen said. "There is only a narrow walkway to transit the roof safely, and all the bright lights shine directly on the flag, blinding anyone who's not used to going up there."

The snipers decided that the embarrassing and potentially dangerous situation would best be handled by someone on the residence staff. By the time Allen got to the roof, the inebriated partygoer was already on his way down.

Allen never said a word.

———

IN A HOUSE where even a minor bit of gossip could make national headlines, Bill and Hillary Clinton had a difficult time learning to trust the staff. The reason they changed the White House phone system was to ensure that no one could listen in on their private conversations—a move that frustrated the ushers, who had a trusted system in place for the purpose of directing calls.

When a call came in for a member of the first family, an operator would call the call box in the Usher's Office. "If it was a call for the first lady, we'd put a little key in the first lady's slot and it would ring a bell with her code so she could pick up any phone that was up there close by and the operator would connect her," Skip Allen explained. "That went in during the Carter administration because there were so many people living at the White House at the time that everybody had their own specific ring. The president would have just the one ring, the first lady would have two rings, and Chelsea would have three short rings."

Each morning, the president is awakened by a phone call from the White House operators. Most presidents get up by 5:30 or 6:00 A.M., and an usher is on duty as early as 5:30 in case the president needs anything.

The day after President Clinton's inauguration, whoever woke him up got a surprise. The Clintons didn't get back from the inaugural balls until two o'clock in the morning. When an usher placed his wake-up call for 5:00 A.M., as they had done every day for his predecessor, the president thundered: "Can't a person get some sleep around here?" (President Clinton was a famous night owl, like President Johnson before him, and his habits drove the staff crazy: some nights, the ushers weren't dismissed to go home until two o'clock in the morning.)

The Clintons, Allen said, decided that "too many people could listen in on them" under the old phone system, so they had all the White House phones changed over to interior circuitry so that if the first lady was in the bedroom and the president was in the study she could ring him from room to room without going through the operator. "That kind of negated the security of the phone system. Then anybody could pick up upstairs in any room," Allen said, still exasperated by the change.

The Clintons' preoccupation with secrecy made relations with the staff "chaotic" for their entire eight years in office, Allen said. At least one residence worker, Florist Wendy Elsasser, attributes their anxiety to parental concerns: "I think protecting Chelsea may have had a lot to do with, for lack of a better term, their standoffishness with the staff."

But it seems clear that the Clintons had little reason to worry about the residence staff leaking any secrets. Even now, years later, most staffers keep quiet when asked about what went on behind closed doors. Discretion is built into the DNA of most of them; they know that their restraint is fundamental to the protection of the presidency—and that, without it, life in the executive mansion would be impossible to endure.

CHAPTER III

Devotion

> CARSON: *Downton is a great house, Mr. Bates, and the*
> *Crawleys are a great family. We live by certain standards and*
> *those standards can at first seem daunting.*
> BATES: *Of course—*
> CARSON: *If you find yourself tongue-tied in the presence of his*
> *lordship, I can only assure you that his manners and grace will soon*
> *help you to perform your duties to the best of your ability.*
>
> —DOWNTON ABBEY, EPISODE 1, SEASON 1

Sundays and holidays are only words" to a White House usher, observed Irwin "Ike" Hoover, who served as chief usher from 1913 until his death in 1933.

Residence staffers have such devotion to their jobs that they sometimes refuse to go home, even when they're told to. Lady Bird Johnson was so disturbed by her husband's nocturnal habits that she called Chief Usher J. B. West to her dressing room one morning after the butlers had been sent home at midnight the night before.

"I am so distressed about the servants having to stay so late," she said. "I've long since given up on my husband eating dinner at a decent hour. Can't we just have Zephyr [the Johnsons' family cook] fix something that can be kept warm—or I'll go in and warm it up for him—or if I'm asleep he can easily serve himself? Then we can just send the butlers home at eight o'clock every night, the way they're supposed to."

When West passed her question to Maître d' Charles Ficklin, he was incensed. It was their pleasure to stay as long as the president wanted them to stay. "The president of the United States having to serve himself dinner? Never!" Ficklin said.

Charles's brother John, also a butler, concurred. "We've served the presidents and first ladies every meal in formal service as long as I can remember. Even if it's a cheese sandwich or a bowl of chili or a boiled egg. That's a tradition."

When West told Lady Bird that there would be a full-fledged revolt if they were sent home early, she replied: "I've never seen such a house. First it takes two engineers to light the fireplaces—they won't let me do it. And now the servants don't want to go home at night."

Gary Walters, who was chief usher from Reagan to George W. Bush, was in charge of hiring and firing staff. He always warned them during the job interview: "This is certainly not a nine-to-five job." He felt the toll himself; one of the reasons he retired was so that he could set his own schedule and actually go on vacation with his family.

"I had given assigned times that people were scheduled to work, but they all knew that any particular day the world situation drives what the presidency does, and that at any given time they may be called upon to stay over and work or come in early, or come in at the last minute or stay there for multiple days. It all revolved around the schedule of the presidency."

For Walters, interruptions from his family life were routine. In 1991, he was just pulling out of the White House driveway, heading out to a University of Maryland basketball game, when he got word that the United States, along with an international coalition, had begun bombing Iraqi forces in Kuwait. "So I drove out one gate, and before I got down Pennsylvania Avenue very far I came in the other gate."

Painter Cletus Clark, who worked at the White House from 1969 to 2008, said that during those years he gave up his life for the job. He always had his walkie-talkie on and was regularly called in from home to work on the weekends because of the whims of the first family. "If the first lady wanted to move a picture and make a hole in the wall, they'd hunt me down to get me to come down there and fix it."

Clark's friend, Operations Supervisor Tony Savoy, worked closely with him. If the first lady decided she wanted to change a paint color, the two of them made the gargantuan assignment look effortless. "We had to strip all the rooms, move all the furniture. They'd paint the room on Friday and Saturday and we'd come in Sunday and put all the furniture back," said Savoy. "When [the first family] came home on Sunday night or Monday, it would look like they never left."

No one ever wanted to say no to the president or to the first lady. And every first lady is impatient. "Everybody's scared of them. They won't tell the first lady the truth," Clark says. "She might say, 'Can you paint the whole White House in one day?' They'd say, 'Yes, ma'am.' They're not going to say no. Nobody wants to jeopardize their job by telling the truth."

Clark said he could never take his time, even when he was working on difficult projects like finding the exact shade of yellow to freshen up the Yellow Oval Room. No record remained of what color had been used the last time it was painted, years before. Because his office was in the basement and had no natural light, he had to go back and forth outside with sample colors to see how they actually looked in the sunlight. His dedication did not go unnoticed.

Laura Bush told him he was "born to be a painter," he recalled, his chin raised proudly.

Often world events made the president's job all-consuming, and the residence staff needed all hands on deck. Jimmy Carter lived in an almost constant state of agitation, brought on by a nation facing double-digit inflation, endless lines at gas stations, and an energy crisis. (Rosalynn said her husband kept the residence so cold—he asked that the White House be kept at sixty-five degrees—that one of the maids took pity on her and bought her long underwear!)

But most of all it was the Iran hostage crisis that left Carter, and those who served him, exhausted. For 444 excruciating days, the residence staff had to adapt to the president's new schedule, turned on its head because of the more than eight-hour time difference with Iran. Every day, the kitchen staff set out sandwiches and cookies late at night in the Oval Office for the president and his exhausted foreign policy staff. In the mornings Carter marched into the Oval Office by five o'clock, so staff had to have it clean with fresh floral arrangements no later than 4:45.

Mrs. Carter remembers the staff being especially attentive during the crisis. "They were concerned about us," Rosalynn recalled gratefully. The staff also gave them the private time they desperately needed. In quiet moments, the president would sit with his wife and relax on the Truman Balcony in the afternoons. "That was good, quiet time for us."

Thirty-five years later, Carter's loss to Ronald Reagan still feels personal, Mrs. Carter recalled. Staying in the White House for more than two months after being voted out of office was excruciating. "You lose the election on November fourth and then you're just ready to go home." Florist Ronn Payne remembers the toll it took on the family. "They sobbed for two weeks. I mean uncontrollably. You couldn't go to the second floor without hearing it."

———————

Working in the residence becomes a way of life. Storeroom Manager Bill Hamilton retired after fifty-five years on the residence staff. Not long after he left, he finally took his wife, Theresa, to London and Paris for their fifty-eighth wedding anniversary. They have seven children, thirteen grandchildren, and four great-grandchildren. Neither had ever been to Europe before; they could never find the time to get away.

"My wife is the only girl I ever dated in my life. We met in the fifth grade," he said, just loudly enough so that his wife could hear him in the next room. "When I told my mother that this was the lady I was going to marry, my mother turned around and slapped me out of the chair. . . . She said I didn't know nothing about it."

Hamilton was hired as a houseman at the age of twenty. Like almost everyone on staff, he got the job because he knew someone who worked there. His good friend Wilson Jerman, whom he met while he was working at the Wardman Park Hotel in Washington, brought him in for an interview. The two still call each other every couple of weeks to catch up, arguing playfully about who actually served longer.

Another residence worker who was all too familiar with the unusual demands of the job is the appropriately named carpenter Milton Frame, now seventy-two. Frame started his White House career in 1961 helping Traphes Bryant take care of the Kennedy family's dogs, and spent the next thirty-six years commuting an hour and a half each way from his home in rural Virginia to the Carpenter's Shop. When he retired in 1997 as the carpenter foreman, he was happy to stop waking up at four o'clock in the morning to get to work by six-thirty.

Milton's father, Wilford Frame, was also a White House

carpenter. That connection helped to make the interview process more casual for Milton than for those without a family connection. He met with Chief Usher J. B. West on a Sunday morning.

"Would you like to work at the White House?" West asked him.

"Well, sir, I'm looking for a job," Frame replied. He was working odd jobs at the time.

"If I should hire you, when would you be able to start?"

"Any time that you tell me, sir."

Frame started the next day, and from the very beginning, he put in long days and nights. Anxious to make sure his staff could keep up with the Kennedys' constant entertaining, West put them through unannounced training exercises. "One night we had a dry run," Frame said, laughing improbably at the memory. "We spent all night putting up a stage in the East Room and as soon as we got it up Mr. West said, 'Take her down.'" West stood by watching the time, clocking how long it would take to set up the stage. (About four hours to put up and an hour and a half to take down, says Frame.)

Many staffers' days were made even longer by their commutes downtown. Most days, well before dawn, Operations Supervisor Tony Savoy could be found sitting in his car in the parking lot waiting for the Secret Service to let him in at five in the morning. His shift did not start until six-thirty, but he wanted to beat beltway traffic. He usually put in a thousand hours of overtime a year, sometimes working a solid month without a day off. He retired in 2013 and says he's planning on doing "anything I feel like doing"— including, he added, doing "nothing in particular."

———

WHEN ASKED TO name the sacrifices they made for the job, few people ever mention the money. The residence staff are federal employees whose pay is "administratively determined," rather than dictated by a government service pay scale. Their pay is based on experience level and the complexity of the job. Some workers make $30,000 a year; those at the top of the pay scale, like the chief usher, executive chef, pastry chef, executive housekeeper, and maître d', can pull down more than $100,000.

Executive Pastry Chef Roland Mesnier turned down jobs with salaries of several hundred thousand dollars, at restaurants in Las Vegas and the Ritz in Paris, to work at the White House. "I could have made triple—quadruple—what I made at the White House!"

Mesnier is a bit of a legend on staff. He started at the White House in 1979 and left in 2006. He took his job incredibly seriously, comparing his desserts to works of art and giving them elaborate names. Who could resist "the Australian Black Pearl," a white chocolate seashell complete with chocolate seaweed and small chocolate fish that he made for the Australian state dinner, or "Sweet Serenity-Bonsai Garden," a sour cherry sorbet with almond mousse, tiny macaroons, and bits of nougat, accented with fresh peaches and cherries filled with kumquat puree, in honor of a state dinner for Japan? He spent long days thinking up the concoctions in the third-floor office he shared with the executive chef and the assistant chef. He occasionally stayed late enough to make use of the room next door, equipped with a bed and a sofa and set aside for overnight stays. Mesnier's love for his job is contagious. Seven years after retiring, he told me that he still worries about the first family. Even today, when he hears about an upcoming state dinner, he starts planning elaborate desserts in his dreams.

Still, even the most passionate staff admit there is a price to be paid for life at the White House. Mesnier acknowledges that he missed more birthdays and family dinners than he cares to count. He often planned weekend dinners out with his wife and son, only to call and cancel on the ride home from work on Friday because the first family had decided to have a birthday party or a pool party on Sunday and he knew he'd need to be there. That's how he kept his job, he said: by knowing that the White House always came first. Residence workers who did not put their jobs above their personal lives were eventually fired, he says, as the first family could decide to fire a residence staff member at any time, without explanation.

"The family knows what's going on, trust me," he says. "They're not in the back of the house checking everything, but there are people who let them know." In particular, the social secretaries often serve as conduits between the residence staff and the first family.

Working for the Clintons took the biggest physical toll on the perfectionist chef. They hosted twenty-nine state dinners during their time in the White House, compared to six during President George W. Bush's presidency. For their millennial New Year's celebration alone, they invited fifteen hundred people. Mesnier didn't leave work until seven o'clock the next morning.

"The Clintons about killed me. My legs are shot, totally shot. I didn't sit—I could not sit. You have to move. In a sixteen-hour day I may have sat twenty minutes, that's it. I took my meals standing up."

Mesnier and his wife picked a date for his retirement four years before he actually retired.

Even when he did finally retire he couldn't completely sever ties with the White House, returning twice when asked personally by Laura Bush. "I made [George W. Bush's] birthday cake and then I retired again. And then two weeks later she called me to come back again and I went back until December 2006. I don't think that ever happened before with any staff."

The pressure to please the first family may never have been greater than when the Reagans were in office. Nancy Reagan went so far as to arrange the serving platters herself, insisting that the staff should prepare no "gray food," only vibrantly colored meals. Before each state dinner, the executive chef would plan every course in consultation with the first lady; then, several weeks beforehand, the Reagans would serve the meal to a small group of friends and ask them how they liked each dish. The first lady would examine the platter and instruct the chef, " 'No, I think the roast beef should go here'—she'd point—'and I think it would look better if the peas were on this side,' " recalls Usher Skip Allen. And if a dinner wasn't exactly the way she wanted it, then "watch out," Allen said. He said she sometimes called the Usher's Office asking to see the chef on the second floor. "If it was really bad, if she was expecting asparagus and got green beans, you had to have a good excuse." Mesnier recalls creating one dessert after another for a state dinner until Nancy Reagan was satisfied.

One incident haunts him still. With days to go before a Tuesday state dinner in honor of Queen Beatrix and Prince Claus of the Netherlands, in April 1982, Nancy Reagan was seated at a long table in her beloved Solarium, having lunch with the president, who was seated at the opposite end. After Mrs. Reagan rejected two dessert options, Roland returned to present her with a third. When she was unhappy everyone on staff knew the cue: she would cock her head to the right and give a little smile. She cocked her head.

"Roland, I'm sorry but that's not going to do again."

"Okay, madam."

President Reagan interjected from the other end of the table: "Honey, leave the chef alone. That's a beautiful dessert. Let's do that, that's beautiful."

"Ronnie, just eat your soup, this is not your concern," she said.

He looked down at his bowl and finished his soup without another word.

Mesnier was beside himself. "I went back to the kitchen—that was a Sunday, I remember—I was turning around in the kitchen and I was really contemplating suicide," Mesnier said. "What am I going to do? How many years [will] I have to do that? For eight years? I was really in despair, total despair. I said I don't know what to make, I don't know what to do. Then the phone rang and she asked me to come back upstairs to see her."

She told Mesnier that she had finally decided what she wanted him to make: elaborate sugar baskets with three sugar tulips in each basket. He would have to make fifteen baskets for the dinner, each of which would take several hours—along with the tulips, the desserts inside each basket, and cookies to accompany it all.

"This is what I would like you to do," she told him calmly, pleased by her own wonderful idea.

"Mrs. Reagan, this is very nice and very beautiful and I really think that would be great, but I only have two days left until the dinner."

She smiled and tilted her head to the right: "Roland, you have two *days* and two *nights* before the dinner."

Roland had no choice. "You say, 'Thank you, madam, for the wonderful idea.' [Then] you click your heels, turn around, and go to work."

He dug in and worked day and night. After the state dinner, when he knew the first lady was happy with the result, he drove home late that night elated. He had met the challenge.

Looking back, Mesnier appreciates the way Nancy Reagan pushed him, however harrowing it must have felt at the time. On that long drive home, he recalls, "I thought, *I can make it happen.* This is how you measure a person, when you're trapped like this: How is that person going to make it happen? You do whatever it takes."

On December 8, 1987, the Reagans hosted a widely anticipated state dinner for Mikhail Gorbachev and his wife, Raisa. It was the first time a Soviet leader had come to Washington since Nikita Khrushchev in 1959. The onus of pulling off this hugely important visit was carried, in part, by the residence staff.

"Nancy Reagan and her social secretary came into the Flower Shop and she told us she wanted to 'blow [Raisa's] socks off,'" said Florist Ronn Payne. "So we did. We changed every single flower in the house three times in one day: for the morning arrival, for the afternoon lunch, and for the state dinner. Every single flower, three times, every one."

———————

SOME RESIDENCE WORKERS try too hard to play the role of the devoted staffer, and they usually don't last. Worthington White, a six-foot-two, four-hundred-pound former tackle at Virginia Tech who worked as a White House usher from 1980 to 2012, says the reason he stayed for so long was because he knew when to keep quiet. When staffers tried "to laugh at jokes that weren't funny," or vied for "face time—anything to get their face in front of the president's face and the first lady's face," he says, it never worked.

"They hated that," White insisted. "That's what I used to tell new employees when they came in: the worst thing you can do is try to be phony. These are the most confident politicians on the face of the earth. You need to be yourself. They'll like you, or they won't, but you can't fool them."

———————

THOUGH THEIR JOBS as butlers, maids, florists, and chefs may seem familiar, residence workers are keenly aware that they must also safeguard the president and his family from an increasing number of threats in a post–9/11 world. According to reporting by the *Washington Post*, it was a maid, and not a Secret Service officer, who first discovered evidence that someone had fired shots into the first family's living quarters. At 8:50 on a sleepy Friday night on November 11, 2011, a twenty-one-year-old man named Oscar Ortega-Hernandez parked his black 1998 Honda Accord on Constitution Avenue, rolled down the passenger-side window, and shot his semiautomatic rifle nearly seven hundred yards across the South Lawn toward the White House. At least seven bullets hit the second and third floors of the first family's private residence, smashing a window outside the Yellow Oval Room, the family's formal living room. The president and the first lady were out of town, and their daughter Malia was out with friends, but their younger daughter, Sasha, and the first lady's mother, Marian Robinson, were inside the residence at the time of the shooting. Several Secret Service officers heard the shots but were told to stand down. It was wrongly concluded that the shots were fired by rival gangs and that none were aimed at the White House.

Four days later, around noon on Tuesday, November 15, a maid asked Assistant Usher Reginald Dickson to meet her at the Truman Balcony where she had noticed a broken window and a chunk of white concrete lying on the floor. When Dickson arrived he spotted a bullet hole and a dent in a windowsill and quickly reported the maid's discovery to the Secret Service. The FBI soon started an investigation. They found a bullet in a window frame and metal fragments from a window ledge. (The windows had antique glass on the outside and bulletproof glass on the inside.) The president was still traveling, but the first lady had arrived home earlier that morning and was taking a nap. Dickson went to check on her, assuming she had already been briefed about the shots fired into her home, but she had not. Top Obama aides decided they would tell the president first and let him tell his wife about the frightening incident. Keeping her in the dark turned out to be a very bad decision.

The first lady was understandably furious when she heard the news from Dickson. When former Secret Service director Mark Sullivan was summoned to the White House to discuss the shooting, Michelle Obama was so angry that her voice could reportedly be heard through a closed door. If it weren't for an observant maid and a diligent usher, the bullets may have been discovered much later, or possibly not at all.

Chief Usher Stephen Rochon, who had retired several months before the shooting, had hired Dickson for the position and says that he is particularly close with the first family. Rochon is not surprised that Dickson and an unnamed maid played such a central role in bringing the shooting to light. "The staff are trained to keep their eyes open and bring anything unusual, whether it be a broken window or a package left after a tour, to the attention of the ushers. The ushers will go to the Secret Service." He added: "We are not just there to clean the house and serve meals."

In another scary security breach, on September 19, 2014, a man armed with a knife launched over the North Lawn fence, ran past several Secret Service officers, and sprinted into the White House. Once inside, he overpowered one officer and barreled past the stairway leading to the second floor of the residence and into the East Room. (The Usher's Office had reportedly asked that an alarm near the main entrance of the mansion be muted because it was too loud. If it had been operating normally, it would have alerted every officer on the ground about the break-in.) The intruder, named Omar Gonzalez, was finally stopped by an off-duty Secret Service agent near the doorway of the Green Room.

Skip Allen, who was a member of the Secret Service uniformed division for eight years before becoming an usher in 1979, is aghast by these security breaches. "I saw one fence jumper when I was in the Usher's Office," he recalled. "He made it as far as the middle of the North Grounds and by that time he was surrounded by Secret Service officers. I just don't understand how somebody could get from the front gate into the East Room without somebody doing something."

Other threats to the president and his family have been less obvious, but no less treacherous. Executive Chef Walter Scheib says that his goal was not only to keep the first family healthy, but to keep them alive. "This is no small consideration given all the people that dislike the president for whatever reason, whether it's international or national."

Scheib, who worked for the Clintons and for George W. Bush's family, said that "there is no one more important to the physical safety of the president than the pastry chef and the chef." Mesnier agrees. Even after 9/11, he says, no food tasters stood by in the kitchen. "We were it. We were truly, truly trusted that nothing will happen."

Lyndon Johnson had ways of getting around the rules governing food deliveries to the White House (which were less stringent in the 1960s). The president happened to love the blintzes made by Secretary of Defense Robert McNamara's wife, Margaret, and from time to time she asked her husband to get a batch to Johnson by handing them off to someone at the White House. Once McNamara gave the blintzes to a police officer, who handed them to the Secret Service. The blintzes were destroyed, and when McNamara asked Johnson if he enjoyed his wife's latest batch of blintzes, the president grew furious.

"You leave my food alone!" the mercurial Johnson shouted at a Secret Service agent who was unlucky enough to be in his path that day. "Use that thing on top of your head that's supposed to have a brain. Did you think the Secretary of Defense is going to kill me?"

Mesnier took advantage of the system only once. In preparing for the Reagans' state dinner for Mikhail Gorbachev, Mesnier used raspberries in the elaborate dessert—because in Russia raspberries "are so expensive they're like gold, like caviar." A few days after the Soviet premier arrived back home, Mesnier was in the kitchen with another chef when a large brown box from Gorbachev somehow made its way there. He knew that whatever was in the box would have to be destroyed immediately—but first he decided to open it.

When he looked inside, he was thrilled to find two large tins each filled with seven pounds of the finest Russian caviar. "I don't care what you do with yours," he told his colleague, "but I'm taking mine home. I'm willing to die for that!"

The residence staffers' long hours and incredible loyalty do not go unnoticed by the first family. President Ford knew that Doorman Frederick "Freddie" Mayfield liked to swim, so one day he told him to bring his bathing suit, and the two of them swam laps together. They came back inside, laughing and wrapped up in towels.

First ladies often have an unspoken understanding with their favorite members of the household staff: they will help them out in a bind. In 1986, Nancy Reagan's maid, Anita Castelo, was accused of helping two fellow Paraguayan natives smuggle 350,000 rounds of .22 caliber ammunition to Paraguay. The first lady provided an affidavit attesting to Castelo's integrity. Charges against Castelo were dropped just as the Iran-Contra affair, which involved arms smuggling on a much larger scale, was starting to make national news. The president was being charged with sanctioning the sale of arms to Iran in exchange for the release of hostages and funding for the Contra rebels in Nicaragua; the White House doubtless hoped to keep the Castelo charges quiet as the Iran-Contra story was about to break. Yet Nancy Reagan wanted Castelo to stay so badly that she was willing to risk public embarrassment to keep her.

———

THE RESIDENCE WORKERS' exceptional devotion to President George H. W. Bush and his family seems to have stemmed from the family's accessible demeanor. The Bushes put everyone at ease around them. Barbara Bush remembered one scene during the Persian Gulf War when she was anxiously watching the news. As she was waiting for her husband to walk in, White House Maître d' George Hannie asked her, "What would you like to drink? And what do you think Pops would like?" (While some in the media have taken to calling him "Poppy" Bush since his son's presidency, "Pops" was a nickname from President Bush's youth; while he was in the White House, no one outside his family used the nickname.)

She laughed at the memory. "I said to him—and he knew *I* was joking, and I knew *he* was joking; we were that close—'George, you can't say that about the president of the United States.'"

Without missing a beat, Hannie replied, "Trust me, Mrs. Bush, at the White House presidents come and go. But George Hannie stays."

"We had that kind of a relationship, where you could tease and laugh. And yet, when sad things happened to either one of us, we were supportive," Barbara Bush said.

Houseman Linsey Little said the first President Bush was more approachable than any other president (including his own son). "Old man Bush, they were more out there. The other one, all he'd do is speak to you and keep walking. No conversation, no nothing. But old man, he was lovely—him and his wife."

Born in Robbinsville, North Carolina—a town of fewer than one thousand people—Little had to leave school in the seventh grade to help take care of his six brothers and sisters. His father was a share-cropper, but Little escaped the backbreaking work of peanut, cotton, and tobacco farming to head north to Washington in the early 1950s.

He started working at the White House in 1979, leaving his town house—which is so close to FedEx Field that he can hear the cheers from the crowd on game day—at 5:00 a.m. in order to make it to work by six o'clock. He would have the house ready for public tours by seven-thirty, setting up ropes, mopping floors, and rolling out carpets. When the tours were over he'd take it all down, only to start again the next morning. After a quick breakfast he'd get a call from Executive Housekeeper Christine Limerick, who would tell him and his colleagues when the family was up so that they could go to the second floor and vacuum while the maids dusted and made up the beds.

LINSEY LITTLE

Little's relationship with the first President Bush extended far beyond cleaning up around the house. Little was one of a handful of household staff who played horseshoes with the president several times a month, sometimes two or three times a week.

The president and his son Marvin would happily head out to the horseshoe pitch next to the swimming pool and play with Little and his supervisor when they got off work. They all got so into the game that Little even had T-shirts made that read HOUSEMEN'S PRIDE.

"We always beat him, until the end," Little said, laughing. "The last year we were there, he and Marvin won the championship." Barbara Bush said she and the president were upset when they left because they knew the Clintons weren't likely to continue the tradition.

Once, the president even asked Little to join him in the Family Dining Room on the second floor. "He told me to have a seat at the table and we sat there and talked," Little said, shaking his head.

"Sitting at the table with the president, having a conversation. None of the rest of them would have done a thing like that."

Bush quickly forgave mistakes that would have enraged other presidents. One summer weekend, he was out playing horseshoes and asked a staffer for some bug spray. The worker had sprayed the president from head to toe before he realized he'd accidentally used a container of industrial strength pesticide. Minutes later, when the mistake was discovered, the staffer "literally ran" to the doctor always stationed nearby, said Usher Worthington White.

"By the time they got there the president's face was already red," White said. Bush needed to be "decontaminated" in the shower.

"President Bush, being who President Bush was, said, 'Okay, okay, okay, we just want to get back to our horseshoe tournament!'" No one was fired.

The Bushes genuinely seemed to appreciate the workers' sacrifices, and in turn the staff went out of its way to make them happy. The kitchen staff knew that Barbara Bush hated it when people sang "Happy Birthday to You." "On the campaign trail I would have four birthday cakes in one day from people who really didn't give a darn about me," she told me with her usual candor.

"One day I came home for lunch and there was a dessert on my plate—incidentally, you do eat very well at the White House—and there was a little tiny square cake and it had the musical notes to 'Happy Birthday to You.' They didn't say it, they didn't sing it. It was just notes." Mesnier had made the cake for her to enjoy quietly while she read a book by herself at lunch.

Barbara Bush stopped by the Flower Shop almost every morning just to say hello, sometimes wearing a bathrobe over her bathing suit before her morning swim. And she would joke with Mesnier when she ran into him in the hallway, hitting him playfully with a folder and teasing, "What are you doing here? Don't you have any cookies to bake or anything?"

Operations Supervisor Tony Savoy said she treated all the staffers like she was their grandmother. "If you were in the elevator, she would get in the elevator with you. She'd say, 'Oh, no, boys, don't get off the elevator. I'm going upstairs too.'"

In 1992, when Hurricane Iniki devastated Hawaii, Florist Wendy Elsasser was desperate to reach her parents, who had retired there. She went days without hearing from them, but she refused to interrupt the Bushes with her personal concerns. Finally, one Sunday when she was changing the floral arrangements in the living quarters, Barbara Bush asked how she was doing.

"I'm okay, Mrs. Bush, thank you," she replied, trying to mask her worry. She kept on working. A few minutes later Barbara Bush was standing next to her again. "What's really going on?" she asked. "That did not sound like Wendy to me."

Her eyes filled with tears. "Mrs. Bush, my parents are in that hurricane, and I haven't heard from them for days, and I'm just so upset. I'm just so preoccupied with that."

Without hesitating, Bush told her, "Wendy, if you can think of anything I can do to help you I will." There was nothing the first lady could do, of course, but Elsasser was moved by her concern. (A few days later, she finally heard from her parents.)

Usher Chris Emery remembers "going numb" after receiving an unexpected call from the Bushes the day his father died. It was Thanksgiving, and the Bushes were at Camp David celebrating the holiday. Less than thirty minutes after he called to tell his boss, Gary Walters, about losing his father, he got a call from the military operator at Camp David who told him, "Stand by for the president."

President Bush "said he was so sorry to learn about my father," Emery recalls, "and asked me if there was anything he could do." Emery thanked him, but there was nothing to be done. The president paused.

"Stand by, Chris. Bar [Barbara Bush] is here and she wants to talk to you too."

"Can you imagine?" Emery said, still stunned.

The Bushes took special care to make sure that members of the residence staff had time with their families. When Emery was on night duty, he was expected to wait until the president and first lady told him he could go home. "The Reagans would buzz twice at nine or ten o'clock, which meant I would go up and turn off the lights and call the admin operator and tell them I'm leaving. With the Bushes, Mrs. Bush would call sometimes and say, 'What are you still doing here? Go home to your family!' It would be eight o'clock."

Barbara Bush and Emery still exchange e-mails a couple of times a year. The former first lady signs off: "Love, BPB."

★

CHAPTER IV

Extraordinary Demands

A shower that had volume and force was one of life's few comforts.

—Luci Baines Johnson

Serving the first family goes well beyond dealing with the world's most trying hotel guests: if they wanted napoleons from the bakery at the Watergate Hotel (as Tricia Nixon often did), then that's what they got. If they needed someone to listen without judgment as they talked about the excruciating decisions they had to make every day, then a sympathetic ear was provided. But some presidents have made demands that proved impossible to meet.

President Lyndon Johnson, a crass, boisterous character, was rarely satisfied with anything. ("Move it, damn it, move your ass," he was heard to cry throughout his administration. "When are you going to get the lead out of your ass?") Butler Wilson Jerman remembers serving shrimp creole and rice to the president on the Truman Balcony. The tray of rice came with two serving forks. "He looked up at me and said—I'm not gonna use [the exact words] he said, but, 'How you think I'm gonna get this rice outta here with two forks?' I said, 'I'm sorry, Mr. President. I'll get a spoon right away.'"

Johnson's intensity, and his outright bullying, caused many staffers to go out of their way to avoid him. "The clearest sign of how different he was from other presidents was that normally a half a dozen staffers and hangers-on would walk the president from the Oval Office to the residence," said former chief usher Rex Scouten. "With President Johnson, only the Secret Service agents walked home with him."

Doorman Preston Bruce first ran afoul of Johnson on the very day the Johnsons moved into the White House. That day, the president invited more than two hundred people to a reception in the family's private quarters, bringing together former Kennedy advisers and his staff. Bruce was struggling to handle the elevator alone when suddenly he saw the light blinking off and on. That could only mean the president was calling for it. And he was not happy.

By the time Bruce made it to the second floor Johnson was fuming. "Where have you been? I've been *waiting* and *waiting* for this elevator!" the president screamed, puffing out his chest and looming over Bruce—giving him what came to be known as "The Treatment," which he used to intimidate members of Congress.

"Mr. President," Bruce said, not ceding his ground. "I've been trying to get your guests out of the house. I know how to do it, but I must have time."

Johnson continued bellowing at Bruce in front of Kennedy staffers Ted Sorensen and Ken O'Donnell. Bruce was humiliated. "I will not work here any longer, being treated like this!" he told Usher Nelson Pierce later that night. "I'm never going to get over President Kennedy's death."

The next day, Johnson acted as though nothing had happened— and Bruce decided that the only way to manage this new difficult president would be to refuse to back down. "It was obvious to me that if I started scraping and bowing when he lost his temper, that would be the end of me." Bruce knew Johnson was a bully from the start, what he respected was strength. "If I was right and stood my ground I'd have a friend for life." It turns out Bruce *was* right: before he left office, Johnson credited the doorman with being one of the people who helped him survive the job. The thirty-sixth president was complicated.

Johnson loved toilet humor and aroused roars of laughter once he got going. One day he broke a toilet seat and "all hell broke loose," according to Electrician and Dog Keeper Traphes Bryant. An extra-large wooden seat was ordered as quickly as possible. Far from being embarrassed, Johnson bragged to his male friends about his new custom seat and styled himself somewhat of an expert on the subject. "He knew the good points and the bad points of all the kinds he could have had: plastic, nonplastic, bamboo, flowered, Grecian, or Early American."

Johnson would tell his friends: "Now don't anyone dare say it's to fit the Number One ass of the nation."

Johnson, who started his career as a high school teacher, roamed the halls of the White House, giving everyone—including his family—letter grades on their performance. He stuck his head into the different shops in the basement, shouting a grade at each worker.

Once he stuck his head in the Electrician's Shop and told Bill Cliber: "Today you got an F." Cliber doesn't remember why.

Then again, said Butler Herman Thompson, "Sometimes we would have a dinner and after the dinner was all over and the guests were gone he would come in and he would say, 'Hey fellas. You all did a good job tonight.'"

Plumbing Foreman Reds Arrington, who got his nickname because of his mane of bright red hair, may have found Johnson amusing at first, but he was soon made completely miserable by the president's eccentric demands. Arrington, who started in the White

House in 1946 and retired in 1979, passed away in 2007, but his wife, Margaret, wrote down many of his stories. She remembers how Johnson's erratic schedule affected their lives and the lives of their three daughters. "We were at a restaurant in Annapolis and they came through saying 'White House calling Mr. Arrington, White House calling Mr. Arrington.' I just thought that was so funny. It was President Johnson wanting something done with his commode."

Johnson tortured Reds with his obsession with the water pressure and temperature of his shower. No matter what the staff did, the water never came hard enough or hot enough for Johnson. When the president was in a mood to dole out letter grades, the shower got an F every time.

Johnson's shower fixation was made clear from the start to the still-grieving staff. On December 9, 1963, just as Chief Usher J. B. West was returning from his first day off since President Kennedy's assassination, he was summoned to meet with President Johnson at the Ground Floor elevator landing immediately. It was two days after the Johnsons had moved into the White House, and the president had a pressing matter to discuss.

"Mr. West, if you can't get that shower of mine fixed, I'm going to have to move back to the Elms," he said sternly and walked away. The Elms was the Johnsons' Washington, D.C., mansion and it was equipped with a shower like nothing the staff had ever seen: water charging out of multiple nozzles in every direction with needlelike intensity and a hugely powerful force. One nozzle was pointed directly at the president's penis, which he nicknamed "Jumbo." Another shot right up his rear. It elicits chuckles now, but Johnson's shower fixation came to define his relationship with some of the residence staff.

Johnson wanted the water pressure at the White House to be just like his shower at home—the equivalent of a fire hose—and he wanted a simple switch to change the temperature from hot to cold immediately. Never warm.

A few minutes after West got his dressing-down from the president, Lady Bird Johnson asked to speak with him in the small Queens' Sitting Room on the second floor.

"I guess you've been told about the shower," she said.

"Yes, ma'am."

"Anything that's done here, or needs to be done, remember this: my husband comes first, the girls second, and I will be satisfied with what's left." (She told Executive Chef Henry Haller the same thing: "Your main role will be to make the president happy.")

The Kennedys never complained about the shower, so the engineers were at a loss. A team was sent to the Elms to study the plumbing, and Reds was even sent to the Johnsons' ranch near Stonewall, Texas (nicknamed the "Texas White House"), to increase the water pressure and heat there to nearly scalding temperatures. When he found out that a new shower for the president would require laying new pipe and putting in a new pump, Johnson demanded that the military pay for it. The project, which cost tens of thousands of dollars, was paid for with classified funds that were supposed to be earmarked for security. "We ended up with four pumps, and then we had to increase the size of our water lines because the other parts of the house were being sucked dry," Arrington told *Life* magazine.

Margaret Arrington remembered Johnson calling Reds himself while he was sitting in the Plumber's Shop, located underground between the White House and the West Wing. "If I can move ten thousand troops in a day, you can certainly fix the bathroom any way I want it!" Johnson howled, his voice echoing down the halls of the White House.

Reds spent more than five years consumed by that shower; at one point he was even hospitalized for several days because of a nervous breakdown. Johnson was so obsessed that he brought his own special shower nozzle when he traveled, along with dozens of cases of Cutty Sark whiskey. Johnson also wanted his bathroom to be incredibly bright, and asked for mirrors to be installed on the ceiling. Reds and his team installed so many lights that they had to put in fans to keep the heat down. The shower's extreme temperatures regularly set off the fire alarm.

One day, Margaret said, when Reds looked in Johnson's shaving mirror, he screamed. "He could see all the veins on his face. He said it was scary!"

More and more people, including members of the Park Service, were summoned to 1600 Pennsylvania Avenue in an effort to fix the shower crisis. Usher Rex Scouten even jumped in the shower in his bathing suit to test it out. "It threw him up against the wall, it was so strong," Margaret said. "Reds said he came out as red as a lobster."

Five replacement showers, including one custom-built by the same manufacturer that designed the shower at the Elms, were installed, but they wouldn't do. The plumbers even had a special water tank installed with its own pump to up the pressure, and added six different nozzles located at different heights so that the spray would hit every part of the body. The pumps sprayed hundreds of gallons of water per minute—*more* than a fire hose. Still not good enough.

Cliber, who started at the White House when he was just twenty years old and stayed on for forty-one years, said Johnson once asked him to come into his bathroom and watch him test out the shower.

"Are you ready for a man's test?" the president said, standing stark naked in front of the electrician, one of the dozens of staff members brought in to address the domestic crisis.

"I'm going to throw it to you this time," Cliber said.

"Okay, give it your best shot," Johnson said as he jumped in.

When Cliber turned the shower handle on, Johnson yelped in pain, the pressure was so intense. "Whoa! What are you doing to me?" But a minute later he was screaming in ecstasy. "Wait, this feels good! Whoa!" It blasted him against the wall and he came out beet red.

And yet it still wasn't quite right.

The last day Arrington saw Johnson in the White House, the president was sitting on the toilet. Reds had to work on something in the president's bathroom and was standing outside, waiting for the president to come out.

"Come on in," Johnson bellowed.

Reds walked in sheepishly.

"I just want to tell you that the shower is my delight, and I appreciate everything you did."

For Reds, that one small sign of gratitude made those stressful years less painful to remember. Margaret said that Lady Bird invited them to their Texas ranch for "one more hoorah!" after Johnson died. "It was just wonderful. We had a picnic supper and I was with movie stars and generals and, gosh, I was just eating it up!"

Johnson's older daughter, Lynda, would later thank Reds and his wife in person: "When Daddy was happy we were all happy, and we thank Mr. Arrington for that!"

When I interviewed her younger sister, Luci, she was more reflective about her father's shower obsession. "A shower that had volume and force was one of life's few comforts," she told me. She is keenly aware of her father's legacy and how it has been marred by Vietnam. "I'm sure he probably expressed very specific guidelines and expectations and probably expressed them with a firm hand. But it's not much to ask for when you are the leader of the free world, getting that small little bit of solace and creature comfort."

And yet, as soon as Lyndon Johnson was gone from the White House, his shower was too. Richard Nixon took one look at the elaborate setup and said: "Get rid of this stuff."

———————

DESPITE HIS EXTRAORDINARY demands, LBJ had the complete loyalty of his staffers. Social Secretary Bess Abell, who affectionately called Johnson "the big boss," came in for some intense presidential pressure. After Abell gave birth to her first son, Johnson called her at the hospital and asked, "What did you name that boy?" When she told him "Daniel," he replied: "Oh too bad, if you'd named him Lyndon, I'd have given him a heifer calf."

She was sure to name her second son "Lyndon" after that. "He wanted everyone to name their baby after him," she said.

Lynda Bird Johnson Robb said that her father "considered it a supreme compliment" when people named their children after him. And he was never afraid to push. One of Lynda's friends told her about a conversation she had with her father before her son was born. "You're going to name the baby Lyndon, aren't you?" Johnson asked her, his imposing six-foot-three-inch frame looming over her.

"No, we have this name we picked out," she stammered.

When she saw the disappointment on his face she added: "But you know we love *all* of the Johnsons, and so we're going to give our boy 'Johnson' as a middle name."

Lynda laughed at the memory. "I don't know if that was really for us or just to make Daddy a little happier!"

When he first took office, Johnson ordered a budget reduction in every executive department. Convinced that an enormous amount of electricity was being wasted at the White House, he terrorized anyone who forgot to turn off the light when they left a room. The Eisenhowers had established a tradition that all the lights in the State rooms should be kept on until midnight, but Johnson demanded an end to that. He personally wandered the halls looking for any transgressions and if he saw a light on somewhere that he didn't want to investigate himself, he called the Usher's Office and asked them to find out who was there. If the room was empty, he became furious.

Carpenter Isaac Avery was working late one night in the Carpenter's Shop when all of a sudden the room went pitch-black. "Goddammit, who turned off the light?" Avery yelled. There was a pause.

"*I* did," a deep voice growled from the hallway.

Avery turned on the light switch and walked out into the hall to investigate. He saw the president standing there flanked by two Secret Service agents.

"I didn't realize you fellows worked so late," Johnson said, mellowing as he realized his mistake.

"I was finishing the frames for all those pictures you sent over," Avery told him, stunned.

Another unlucky staffer was working in the Carpenter's Shop, putting pull chains on some fluorescent lights, when Johnson caught him working with the lights on—in the daylight.

"He just went after him profusely," Bill Cliber recalled, shivering at the memory.

Everywhere the residence staff went, Cliber said, they learned to carry flashlights for fear of getting caught in utter darkness.

Finally, one of Johnson's requests seemed to go too far. The stairs were all lighted for safety, but the president was convinced this was burning too much energy.

"You have to turn off all the step lights," Johnson told Cliber.

"Mr. President, you can't turn the step lights out. This is a big building. Everybody thinks it's only three stories high—it's eight floors inside this White House [including two small mezzanine levels]. And these are all marble steps and boy, you slip on those and you hurt yourself."

"Well, are you sure?" Johnson wanted so badly to keep those lights off.

"Yes, sir, I'm sure."

"Okay, keep the lights on the steps," Johnson replied, in a rare concession. Still, every once in a while he would stop into Cliber's basement office and plead: "You still got those step lights on?"

The only person who really stood up to Johnson (even Doorman Preston Bruce had to be careful how he talked to his boss) was Zephyr Wright, the Johnsons' family cook, whom they'd brought with them from Texas. She first realized that she had to "talk up to him" well before he became president.

One night Johnson came home at about eleven-thirty, and asked for dinner. Even for Johnson this was unusually late, so late that Wright had gone downstairs to lie on her bed and rest. When he called her to serve him, she forgot to turn off the lights before she went back upstairs. When he saw that the downstairs light was still on, he threatened to take the cost of the electricity out of her pay.

She was enraged. "Well you just do that, because I have always lived at home where I had to pay my own light bill. Nobody ever told me anything about turning off the lights. But if you would come home on time, you wouldn't have to worry about me turning off the lights, because they wouldn't be on if you'd get here on time."

Her approach worked: "Of course after that he didn't say any more to me."

———

LYNDON JOHNSON WAS not the only White House occupant who tested the nerves of the staff. Ronn Payne remembers one day when Nancy Reagan called him into the West Sitting Hall on the second floor, where she was sitting under its large half-moon window.

"Ronn, the lights," she motioned theatrically above her. "They're not on."

Payne, a florist, was far from an electrician. He looked around the room and noticed a light switch on the wall.

"I thought to myself, *There's a light switch right here. Do I turn it on and make her look like an ass, or do I say, 'I'll call the electrician?'* "

He decided to hit the switch, turning on every light in the room. Like a queen, the first lady looked up at him and said, "Thank you," without a trace of embarrassment.

"She was spoiled rotten," Payne said, making a face. "When she wanted something she wanted it last month, and if you tried to persuade her [to change] from white freesia to white snaps because white freesia wasn't available anywhere in the world, she would say, 'You'll find a way.' " And they did: the florists would have flowers flown in overnight from Europe just to satisfy her.

Still, Payne, like Chef Mesnier, says he appreciated how straightforward Mrs. Reagan was about what she wanted. And if you did as she asked, she was happy.

"I remember hearing her call for her personal maid one day and it scared the dickens out of me—just her tone. I never wanted to be on the wrong side of her," said fellow florist Wendy Elsasser.

Cletus Clark, whose hours were supposed to be from seven-thirty in the morning to four o'clock in the afternoon, remembers just how punishing his schedule was when Mrs. Reagan decided to redecorate the second and third floors.

"She didn't ever want me to come home! We worked ten hours a day, seven days a week, and I'd see her around eight o'clock at night and she'd say, 'Where are you going?' I'd say, 'I've got to go home.' " It got so bad, he said, that when he saw her in the West Sitting Hall he would walk down the stairs on the east side of the mansion so that she wouldn't see him leave. "I just had to come home. After seven days a week, continuously, it wears and tears your body."

Nancy Reagan had personal quirks that almost rivaled Lyndon Johnson's. She could not abide long hair on women, and she made the housekeeping staff label her clothes with purchase dates and when the item was last worn.

She also had several collectibles she wanted proudly displayed at the White House, including a group of small hand-painted porcelain Limoges boxes, around twenty-five in all, to be arranged meticulously on a table. She also had a collection of porcelain eggs and a collection of plates. ("They had an incredible amount of stuff and that's because they don't have to clean," Executive Housekeeper Christine Limerick said, with a wry smile.) If anyone moved any of them by even an inch Nancy Reagan would take notice. Likewise, she demanded that all her silver frames and expensive perfume bottles be arranged perfectly on the bathroom countertop—and be put back exactly in their original places after cleaning, or else.

Though she conscientiously avoids badmouthing her former bosses, Limerick makes an exception for the "very tough" Nancy Reagan. She vividly recalls the transgression that eventually led her to leave the White House for five years. "At the beginning of their administration there were several items that were broken: one by Housekeeping, one by the Secret Service, and one by the Operations Department." Mrs. Reagan blamed Limerick. "She chewed me out. She really did."

She went after Limerick with such venom, and for so long, that Chief Usher Rex Scouten eventually went up to the second floor to intervene. "Chris, you can go," Scouten said, turning to speak to her and volunteering to take her place for the verbal beating. Later on he told Limerick why he'd saved her: "You'd heard enough." The first lady then turned her wrath on Scouten, whom she adored so much that she actually named her Cavalier King Charles spaniel "Rex" after him. She even called Scouten "the second most important man in my life." All that was not enough to spare him from the remnants of her tirade.

More than two decades later, Limerick is still shaken by the incident. She remembers exactly what was broken: "One was a Limoges plate; one was a candlestick; another time a Secret Service guy tripped on the table and some things fell." They were all just accidents. But that didn't matter to the first lady. "She actually was so upset that she had me pack up a lot of her personal belongings that she had out on the mantel in the private living quarters. They stayed packed up for several months. Then finally things settled down and we unpacked them again."

After the blowup, Limerick decided on a new protocol to keep track of any potential problems. The residence maids dusted and straightened throughout the house every day, but once a month they would do a more extensive cleaning of each room. Going forward, Limerick decided to have the first family's bedrooms, bathrooms, sitting rooms, and offices photographed before each monthly cleaning, so that she could have a record showing that everything was put back in its place.

The hardest part for Limerick was that she and the first lady had a close working relationship. Limerick even wrapped personal presents for the first lady to give to her friends. While she was taking heat from Mrs. Reagan, though, she could not defend herself; all she could do was continue to apologize, head bowed.

"In my whole career I never had a complaint about the linen or the beds," she said. "The ladies who worked for me, they could put me to shame. And I can make a pretty good bed."

In 1986, after working at the White House for seven years, she left to return to the Mayflower Hotel. She then spent a couple of years in Hawaii before going back to the White House in 1991. She admits that she left, in part, because the struggle to keep up with the first lady's demands was wearing on her. "It wasn't because Mrs. Reagan was who or what she was. It was because I realized that I was getting close to talking back." That would have been a cardinal sin at the White House, and she knew it.

During Limerick's five-year hiatus, her replacement would wreak havoc at the White House. The new head of housekeeping had problems coping with the stress of the job, and stories of her bizarre behavior eventually reached Limerick. According to Roland Mesnier, the chief housekeeper "went to the storeroom one day and requested to buy ten thousand teddy bears for the children of the world." She actually filled out a purchase order for the stuffed animals, he says. Another time, according to florists Ronn Payne and Wendy Elsasser, she came to work with bright turquoise triangles painted on her eyelids. She was known for walking through the basement hallways spraying air freshener outside the staff office, yelling, "This place stinks!"

The Secret Service wanted the woman fired after these troubling signs, staffers said, but Limerick's successor was allowed to stay. Limerick attributes the woman's survival there to Barbara Bush, who was very "sympathetic" to her. Elsasser agreed; she felt that Mrs. Bush gave the troubled staffer so many chances because she wanted to see her get better. "Mrs. Bush has a heart of gold," Chef Mesnier said. (In her interview for this book, Barbara Bush chose not to discuss Limerick's successor, other than to confirm that she did have trouble handling the pressures of the job.)

Finally, the head housekeeper's behavior was too much even for Mrs. Bush. One day, Skip Allen, the usher assigned to oversee the Housekeeping Department, was called upstairs urgently. Wendy Elsasser had been preparing to change the floral arrangements in the Center Hall entryway leading to Jenna and Barbara Bush's bedrooms when the head of housekeeping grabbed a pillow (hand-stitched by the first lady) and threw it at her, screaming, "This is bullshit!" Jenna and Barbara stood by as the incident played out, terrified. It is unclear what set her off.

Once her grandchildren were involved, the first lady decided that Limerick's replacement had to go. Allen helped to escort her out of the building as she screamed. "She was not going quietly," he said.

WHEN SHE RETURNED to the White House, Christine Limerick found herself working under easier regimes—first for Mrs. Bush, then for Hillary Clinton. Some residence workers found Mrs. Clinton challenging to work with, but Limerick saw her as a positive presence in the residence.

"Hillary was very, very sympathetic to working women. She got along very well with the housekeepers; she communicated with all of them. She knew everybody's strengths and weaknesses." She knows that some of the men on staff might disagree with her assessment but chalks that up to a variety of factors. "Some of it was their fault," she says of the men, but she also feels it reflected the first lady's special consideration for the female staffers. "I believe in my mind that she was tougher on men than she was on women. She'd cut us a break if we did something wrong."

Once, Limerick remembers, Hillary asked her to dye one of her turquoise suits a different color. "I'm usually pretty good with clothing," she said with a giggle. "It was a washable fabric. It was a size ten when we started, and about a size two when I finished! And she thought it was funny."

Bill Clinton wasn't always as understanding. President Clinton is allergic to pine, but for Christmas the first lady wanted a real tree for a few days in the Yellow Oval Room on the second floor. The plan was to put the tree up around December 19, and take it down by December 28.

Limerick's job was to lay out all the family's personal decorations. Then the Flower Shop and the Electrician's Shop would come up and put the lights up. Limerick knew how much the president liked putting up the decorations with Chelsea; it helped him feel like every other father celebrating Christmas with his family, if only for a few hours.

That year, though, the first lady wanted to get a head start. "The president has something this evening. Would you just put up almost everything except these two dozen here?" Hillary asked Limerick, pointing to a box of ornaments. The housekeeper did as she was asked. When the president came up to the second floor after the event and saw some of the decorations already hanging on the tree, he was furious.

"Who did this?" he yelled.

"Chris, the housekeeper," a butler told him.

As the butler told Limerick later, the president mumbled something to the effect of, "Well, she better be careful about whether she's going to have a job."

Around midnight, one of the butlers called Limerick to tell her what had happened. She was worried but she trusted that Hillary would defend her. The next morning, a Saturday, she reported to the third floor to wrap presents for the family.

Mrs. Clinton came through the door, exasperated, "No good deed goes unpunished in this house. I've had a conversation with Bill, don't worry about it."

"Thank you," Christine said, breathing a sigh of relief.

Another time, Limerick got a call at home from one of President Clinton's personal valets saying that he didn't like one of the tailors she had recommended. She had given him a list of about four. "This is at two in the morning," Limerick marveled, "and the valet's babbling about how the president's mad and I better be careful."

When she came to work the next day she called the president's office. She was sick of hearing everything secondhand, and she was suspicious that the butlers and valets were making matters seem worse than they were, overinterpreting every little thing the president said, even embellishing things for dramatic effect.

"I understand I'm in some hot water because the president didn't like the tailor," she said to Clinton's secretary, Betty Currie.

"Wait a minute, the president's right here," Currie said, handing the phone to the president.

"Sir, I'm sorry."

"It's no big deal," he told her, laughing it off.

All that panicking for nothing, she thought.

According to Skip Allen, the Clintons weren't always consistent in their requests. "When they asked for something and you gave it to them, it wasn't what they really wanted," Allen said. "They didn't know how to ask for exactly what they wanted, so they kept asking for things they thought they'd like but didn't."

Allen remembers one phone call from Hillary Clinton. The kitchen had brought out a particular chicken dish too often, she said, and she wanted the chef to stop serving it. "So I called the chef and I told him we have to take the chicken dish off the menu, that they didn't want it anymore. And a couple of months later I get a call from the first lady saying, 'Ask the chef, how come he never serves that chicken dish we like so much?' " He exhaled loudly. "That's the way it went for eight years."

The Clintons were just the opposite of the Reagans, staffers say. If they were up at one or two o'clock in the morning and couldn't sleep, they would start rearranging furniture. According to Allen, who also oversaw the Curator's Office, this furniture shuffling was a nightmare for the curators, who log every piece of furniture in the White House collection each year. "They just took it upon themselves to move a lamp from one room to the next, or a table or chair. Then, when the curators went up to take inventory, [the records] would say, so-and-so chair is in the study, and they [would] have to look all over the house for that chair because the Clintons had moved it up to the third floor in one of the guest rooms. . . . It just made everything so complicated."

The Clintons also seemed oblivious to the protocols involving mealtime—and everyone was too scared to tell them. Chef John

Moeller, who worked in the kitchen from 1992 to 2005, never knew when the first family wanted to eat, or how many people he would need to serve. "With the Bushes we consistently got a call ahead of time saying something like, 'Two for lunch at twelve-thirty.' With the Clintons, we wouldn't know what was going to happen until it actually happened!"

A week after the Clintons moved in, Butler Buddy Carter ran into the kitchen in a panic to tell Moeller that the family was seated and ready for their dinner—*now*. "I have it, but I've got to get it hot, give me a minute," Moeller told him. From then on he would always have a meal at the ready around lunch and dinnertime.

The Clintons' friends and political aides also liked to give the staff advice, sometimes steering them in the wrong direction. "They told us that Mrs. Clinton used a certain type of shampoo and deodorant, so we went out and we bought maybe twenty containers," Limerick recalls, laughing. "I learned how stupid that was because then [Hillary Clinton] said to me, 'Chris, I don't like this stuff.'"

Sometimes efforts to please the first family put White House guests in peril. Every year the holiday season brings an internal debate about how best to decorate the State Floor. Head Florist Nancy Clarke liked to place dozens of votive candles on the buffet tables, but Chef Mesnier insisted it was a fire hazard. *But Mrs. Clinton wants them*, Clarke insisted.

"One particular year, we had this lady wearing a fox around her neck. She leaned over the table to grab some cookies, and of course the votive ignited the fox because she came too close. Thank God we had a quick butler there who yanked the fox away from her and threw some water on it and extinguished the fire," Mesnier recalled. "Of course after *that*, there were no more votives on my tables!"

CHAPTER V

Dark Days

He said when he got up in the middle of the night he ran into the bathroom door. But we're pretty sure she clocked him with a book.

—Residence worker on life in the Clinton White House
during the Monica Lewinsky scandal

There was blood all over the president and first lady's bed.

A member of the residence staff got a frantic call from the maid who found the mess. Someone needed to come quickly and inspect the damage.

The blood was Bill Clinton's. The president had to get several stitches to his head. He insisted that he'd hurt himself running into the bathroom door in the middle of the night. But not everyone was convinced.

"We're pretty sure she clocked him with a book," one worker said. And who would know better than the residence staff? The incident came shortly after the president's affair with a White House intern became public knowledge—clearly a time of crisis in the Clintons' marriage. And there were at least twenty books on the bedside table for his betrayed wife to choose from, including the Bible.

In November 1995 Clinton began an affair with Monica Lew-insky, a twenty-two-year-old White House intern. He had almost a dozen sexual encounters with her over the next year and a half, most of them in the Oval Office. When the affair became public more than two years after it started, the media firestorm consumed the rest of his presidency. The revelation stemmed from more than four years of investigation by Independent Counsel Kenneth Starr that looked into other charges, including the Whitewater land deal and the firing of several longtime White House employees in the Travel Office, a scandal known as Travelgate. Although they were not part of the residence staff, Usher Skip Allen says he remembers how upset some of his colleagues became after the dismissals in the Travel Office. After all, most of the residence staff had devoted their entire careers to their jobs at the White House and some were start-ing to feel vulnerable. "The mood in the house was a little on the tense side, because everybody was career and you never can tell, if it ever got going, how many people or who they would fire." Career government employees are like professors with tenure who are very hard to fire, he says, and it was shocking to see them dismissed so summarily. The Clintons were also battling criticism that they had used the Lincoln Bedroom to woo wealthy donors.

On August 17, 1998, Clinton became the first president to testify as the subject of a grand jury investigation. Chief Electrician Bill Cliber, who helped set up the power for Clinton's marathon four-and-a-half-hour testimony—conducted via closed-circuit television—recalls that the president was "in a really bad mood" that day. Later that evening, Clinton confessed to the "inappropriate relationship" with Lewinsky in a nationwide television broadcast. Four months later, in December, the Republican-led House voted to impeach him, though he was ac-quitted after a five-week trial in the Senate.

The public did not learn about Monica Lewinsky until January 1998. But some residence workers knew about the affair when it was still occurring, between November 1995 and March 1997. The butlers saw the president and Lewinsky in the family movie theater, and the two of them were seen together so frequently that the workers started letting one another know when they'd had a Lewinsky sighting. The butlers, who are closest to the family, zealously guard such secrets, but from time to time they share fragments of stories with their colleagues—because the information could be useful, or sometimes just to prove their access.

One household staffer, who asked not to be named, remembers standing in the main hallway behind the kitchen that was used by East Wing and West Wing aides. "That's her—that's the girlfriend," a butler whispered, nudging her as Lewinsky walked by. "Yep, she's the one. She was in the theater the other night."

Nearly two decades later, many residence workers are still wary of discussing the fights they witnessed between the Clintons. But they all felt the general gloom that hung over the second and third floors as the saga dragged on throughout 1998.

The residence staff witnessed the fallout from the affair and the toll it took on Hillary Clinton, but West Wing aides had long suspected the kind of drama that was playing out on the second floor of the executive mansion. "She would have hit him with a frying pan if one had been handed to her," said the first lady's close friend and political adviser Susan Thomases in an interview with the Miller Center at the University of Virginia for their collection of oral histories documenting Bill Clinton's presidency. "I don't think she ever in her mind imagined leaving him or divorcing him."

Betty Finney, now seventy-eight, started as a White House maid in 1993. She spent most of her time in the family's private quarters and remembers well how things changed in those final years. "Things were definitely more tense. You just felt bad for the entire family and what they were going through," she says. "You could feel the sadness. There wasn't as much laughter."

Florist Bob Scanlan was less guarded about the atmosphere: "It was like a morgue when you'd go up to the second floor. Mrs. Clinton was nowhere to be found."

And when it wasn't eerily quiet, the mansion was the scene of intrigue and heated arguments. One incident occurred around Christmas 1996, while the president's affair with Lewinsky was still ongoing.

The Housekeeping Shop was going about their usual assignment of wrapping presents for the first family. Sometimes they were asked to wrap more than four hundred gifts for friends, relatives, and staffers. Gift wrapping was an elaborate process, beginning in the Reagan administration (when standards were particularly exacting), with careful logs recording details of each present that was wrapped. (These logs were shredded each time a new first family moved in.) The staffers who wrapped the presents always included a gift tag and a description of what was in the package, discreetly tucked underneath a ribbon. They then placed the wrapped gifts on a designated table in the West Sitting Hall or in the Yellow Oval Room.

That holiday season, one staffer remembers noticing an unusual gift, a copy of *Leaves of Grass* by Walt Whitman, which she was asked to wrap. She put the wrapped book on the table and thought nothing more of it. A couple of months later, in February 1997, the president gave Lewinsky a gift: a copy of *Leaves of Grass*. Only later did the staffer learn that the present she had wrapped was most likely the same one that was given to the president's mistress.

After the holidays, the staffer said, the president desperately wanted to retrieve a book from the Clintons' bedroom, but the first lady was not yet dressed, and no one wanted to disturb her. "Betty Currie [the president's secretary] called the valet, and he came to me and asked me if I'd go in and I said, '*No way,*'" the worker recalls. (When the door to the first couple's bedroom is shut, it is the equivalent of a DO NOT DISTURB sign on a hotel door.) "Finally, I think Betty Currie called Mrs. Clinton directly."

Moments later, a book came flying out of their bedroom. Hillary had hurled it into the hallway. The president's valet picked it up and brought it to Currie. It's not certain whether the book the first lady threw out of their bedroom was the same book that the president gave Lewinsky, but the staffer's memories paint a picture of the tension.

Florist Ronn Payne remembers one day when he was coming up the service elevator with a cart to pick up old floral arrangements and saw two butlers gathered outside the West Sitting Hall listening in as the Clintons argued viciously with each other. The butlers motioned him over and put their fingers to their lips, telling him to be quiet. All of a sudden he heard the first lady bellow "goddamn bastard!" at the president—and then he heard someone throw a heavy object across the room. The rumor among the staff was that she threw a lamp. The butlers, Payne said, were told to clean up the mess. In an interview with Barbara Walters, Mrs. Clinton made light of the story, which had made its way into the gossip columns. "I have a pretty good arm," she said. "If I'd thrown a lamp at somebody, I think you would have known about it."

Payne wasn't surprised at the outburst. "You heard so much foul language" in the Clinton White House, he said. "When you're somebody's domestic, you know what's going on."

Payne tested positive for HIV while working at the White House and became very ill, losing forty-three pounds at one point. He wanted to take a leave of absence, but he was told he had one of two options: quit or retire. He chose to retire early. He hoped to be able to return when he got his health back, since he said that several other retired workers had come back to work. "You can imagine what I looked like. I know they wouldn't want me upstairs," he says. "I wanted to get my strength and my weight back." Once he did feel up to working again, however, he was told he couldn't return because he had retired with disability. He was never told explicitly that he was fired because he was HIV-positive, and he doesn't know who was ultimately behind the decision—it almost certainly did not rise to the attention of the Clintons—and he did not formally challenge it. But it had been a standing rule for several years, including during previous administrations, that staff with HIV were not allowed to have any exposure to the first family. "I saw them make it very difficult for other people who became HIV-positive," Payne says. "Some were put down in the basement to work in the laundry room. Others were put out on the lawn." And florists are in every room of the executive mansion, including the family's bedrooms, so returning to his old job was impossible. He was heartbroken about the painful way his White House career came to an end, and is remembered fondly by many of the colleagues he left behind.

————

DURING THE HEIGHT of the drama, Hillary routinely missed afternoon appointments. The details of running the executive mansion, understandably, took a backseat to saving her husband's presidency and their marriage. For three or four months in 1998, the president slept on a sofa in a private study attached to their bedroom on the second floor. Most of the women on the residence staff thought he got what he deserved.

Even Butler James Ramsey, a self-proclaimed ladies' man, blushed when the subject came up. He said Clinton was his "buddy, but . . . come on now." As usual, during the Lewinsky scandal Ramsey said he kept his "mouth shut."

Some on the staff have said that Hillary knew about Lewinsky long before it came out, and that what really upset her was not the affair itself but its discovery and the media feeding frenzy that followed.

The first lady's temper was notoriously short during those difficult months. Butler James Hall remembers serving coffee and tea in the Blue Room during a reception for a foreign leader. Suddenly, the first lady approached him while he was still standing behind the bar.

"You must have been staring into space!" she upbraided him. "*I* had to take the prime minister's wife's cup. . . . She was finished and looking for some place to put it." Hall was dumbfounded—other butlers were working the reception with trays collecting drinks, and his job was to serve the drinks—but he knew that defending himself would be pointless. Clinton complained to the Usher's Office, and Hall wasn't asked back for a month.

"Working there during the impeachment wasn't bad," said former storeroom manager Bill Hamilton, but he agreed that working with Mrs. Clinton in those difficult months was a challenge. "It was just so overwhelming for her and if you said something to her she'd snap," Hamilton recalled, shaking his head. Still, he says that he loved working for the Clintons, and although he retired in 2013, he sometimes wishes he had stayed at the White House, knowing that Hillary Clinton might one day return as America's first female president. He says he would love to work for her again, even after the tumult of her eight years in the residence.

He is entirely sympathetic toward the first lady in those darkest days. "It happened and she knew it happened and everybody was looking at her," Hamilton said.

Pastry Chef Roland Mesnier said he wanted to help Hillary feel better in any way he could. Her favorite dessert was mocha cake, and at the height of the scandal, he recalls, "I made many, many mocha cakes. You better believe it," he said, chuckling. In the late afternoons, Hillary would call the Pastry Shop. In a small, unassuming voice—a far cry from her usual strong, self-confident tone—she'd ask, "Roland, can I have a mocha cake tonight?"

One sunny weekend in August 1998, just before the president made his confession to the country, the first lady called Usher Worthington White with an unusual request.

"Worthington, I want to go to the pool but I don't want to see *anybody* except *you*," she said.

"Yes, ma'am, I understand," he replied sympathetically.

White knew exactly what she meant. She did not want to see her Secret Service detail, she did not want to see anyone tending to the White House's extensive grounds, and she certainly did not want to see anyone on a tour of the West Wing. "She wasn't up for any of that," he recalled. She just wanted a few hours of peace.

White told her he would need five minutes to clear the premises. He ran to find her lead Secret Service agent and told him they would have to work together to make it happen. And fast.

"It was a twenty-second conversation but I know what she meant. 'If anybody sees her, or she sees *anybody*, I'm going to get fired, I know it,'" he told the agent. "'And you probably will too.'"

So the Secret Service agents assigned to protect the first lady agreed to trail her, even though protocol calls for one agent to walk ahead of her and one to walk behind.

"She's not going to turn around and look for you," White told them. "She just doesn't want to see your face. And she doesn't want you looking at her face."

He met Clinton at the elevator and escorted her to the pool with the agents walking behind them and no one else in sight. She was wearing red reading glasses and she was carrying a couple of books. She didn't have on any makeup and her hair wasn't done. To White, she seemed heartbroken.

They didn't exchange a single word on the walk to the pool.

"Ma'am, do you need any butler service?" White asked her after she got settled in.

"No."

"You need anything at all?"

"No, it's just a beautiful day and I want to just sit here and enjoy some sunshine. I'll call you when I'm ready to go back."

"Okay, ma'am," White replied. "It's twelve o'clock now, and I get off at one and someone else will be in."

Clinton looked intently at him. "I'll call *you* when I'm done."

"Yes, ma'am," White replied, knowing that that meant he would have to stay until whenever she chose to leave. He didn't get the call until nearly three-thirty that afternoon.

When he returned, White accompanied the first lady on another wordless walk from the pool to the second floor. Before she stepped off the elevator, the besieged first lady let him know how much his efforts meant to her.

"She grabbed me by my hands and gave them a little squeeze and looked me directly in my eyes and just said, 'Thank you.'"

"It touched my heart," White said of her gratitude. "It meant the world to me."

A few of the household workers even found themselves dragged into the unfolding drama. At one point, Houseman Linsey Little was called to the second floor to answer questions about the affair. When he got upstairs, he was met by an intimidating federal agent, who asked him if he'd ever seen Lewinsky before. No, he answered nervously.

"They want to make you feel like they think you know something," he said. He insists that he'd never seen anything untoward, but even if he had, he admits he would have been reluctant to risk his job and end up on the news himself. "They'd have your name up in bright lights," he said.

Mesnier described 1998 as a "very sad time" watching two brilliant people consumed by scandal. And like so many others, he felt terrible for the Clintons' daughter, Chelsea.

In an iconic photograph taken August 18, 1998, the day after her father's embarrassing admission, Chelsea held both of her parents' hands as they walked to the helicopter on the South Lawn. Mesnier shook his head at the thought of what the young woman went through. "Chelsea was absolutely the sweetest person you'll ever meet, and then to see them going through a stupid thing like this? *Stupid*. There was a lot of hardship."

────────

Usher Skip Allen admits that it was easier to serve the families he liked than it was to pretend.

"But we pretend very well," he said.

Allen cannot hide his reservations about the Clintons. Over lunch by the pool at his large home in rural Pennsylvania, he fondly recalled how Mrs. Clinton always asked him to help her by tying bows on her outfits, something she couldn't do herself. But he said the Clintons never fully trusted the residence staff and were particularly suspicious of the Usher's Office. "They were about the most paranoid people I'd ever seen in my life."

Allen isn't the only one with bitter memories of the Clinton White House. Usher Chris Emery, who had been close with the Bushes, remembers feeling unduly scrutinized by the Clintons. In the fourteen months he served them, he says, he was subjected to three drug tests and a background check that he was not due to have for several years. He says that some of the questions he was asked—including what church he belonged to—were unusually personal, so he refused to answer them. "I think they were just trying to find something to make it easier [to fire me]." He sighed. And, indeed, when Emery was fired from the White House in 1994, it was in part because of a favor he had done for former first lady Barbara Bush.

During the first Bush administration, Emery had been very helpful to Mrs. Bush. "We were very close. Chris taught me how to use a computer," she told me. After leaving the White House, she was working on her memoir when she lost a chapter, so she called on Emery for help. Emery was happy to oblige—but the favor fueled the Clintons' suspicion that the staff was too attached to the Bush family. When the Clintons saw the usher's call logs, Emery said,

White House butlers in between courses during a 1976 state dinner for French president Valéry Giscard d'Estaing.

Plumber Reds Arrington (*right foreground*) at work in the Plumber's Shop in the White House basement in 1952. Arrington had a nervous breakdown because of President Lyndon Johnson's never-ending demands concerning the White House shower. "If I can move ten thousand troops in a day, you can certainly fix the bathroom any way I want it!" the president screamed at Reds during one tirade.

Standing second from the right: Butler Lynwood Westray, serving at an outdoor picnic at the White House, July 29, 1970. Westray, now ninety-three, gets emotional discussing one evening when a member of the British royal family insisted on serving him a drink. "It blows your mind," he says about that night, a highlight of his thirty-two-year career.

Handsome young President-elect John F. Kennedy and President Dwight D. Eisenhower depart the White House for inaugural ceremonies, January 20, 1961. Preston Bruce, the impeccably dressed White House doorman who would become a close Kennedy family friend, holds the door open at the North Portico.

John Kennedy Jr. stands on the steps of his tree house on the South Lawn as his nanny, Maud Shaw, and Maître d' Charles Ficklin look on. One of the Kennedys' nine dogs, a Welsh terrier named Charlie, takes part in the fun.

On their last day in the White House, Jacqueline Kennedy and John-John say a tearful good-bye to residence workers, including Doorman Preston Bruce, standing to the left of Jackie.

Caroline Kennedy (*far left*) in the kindergarten classroom created for her in the residence's third-floor Solarium. The photo was taken less than a month after her father's assassination.

The Johnsons' longtime cook, Zephyr Wright, at a reunion for residence workers held at Smokey Glen Farm outside Washington, D.C., June 1983. Wright was one of the few people who could stand up to Lyndon Johnson. She said she knew she had to "talk up to him" well before he became president.

Lynwood Westray (*standing on the far left*) with fellow butler and friend Samuel Washington (*third from left*) at a holiday reception with President Johnson, December 16, 1964.

President Nixon with kitchen worker Frankie Blair. One evening they bowled until 2 A.M. "There may have been a bottle of scotch involved," recalls one staffer.

Steve Ford chatting with (*from right*) Butler Johnny Johnson, Executive Chef Henry Haller, Butler Eugene Allen, and Butler Alfredo Saenz (*standing on the left*) outside the family kitchen on the second floor of the residence.

Amy Carter and her nanny, Mary Prince, who had been in prison for murder when she met the Carters, playing on the South Lawn, February 1977. The two were inseparable from the moment they met.

Doorman Frederick "Freddie" Mayfield shaking hands with the legendary Muhammad Ali in the Blue Room after a state dinner for Jordan's King Hussein I and Queen Alia, March 30, 1976. Mayfield was so devoted to his job that he put off having bypass surgery because he didn't want to miss work. He waited too long—dying of a heart attack in 1984 at just fifty-eight years old.

President Jimmy Carter and First Lady Rosalynn Carter with White House workers at the state dinner for the Shah and Shahbanu of Iran, November 15, 1977. *Clockwise from top left*: Maid Viola Wise, Butler and Doorman Wilson German, Doorman Frederick "Freddie" Mayfield, and Frankie Blair, who worked in the kitchen.

they "came to the conclusion that I was sharing deep, dark secrets with the Bushes in Houston. Which I wasn't."

A short time later, Chief Usher Gary Walters called Emery into his office.

"Mrs. Clinton is not comfortable with you," Walters told him.

"What does that mean?" Emery asked, stunned.

"It means tomorrow is your last day."

Barbara Bush admits that her phone calls to Chris "caused trouble." Emery was scolded in public for "an amazing lack of discretion," in the words of Hillary's spokesman Neel Lattimore. "We believe the position that he had, as a member of the residence staff, requires the utmost respect for the first family's privacy."

Emery says he was devastated at the loss of his job, and his $50,000 salary. "I was out of work for a year," he says. "They ripped the rug right out from under me. You wonder what they'd do to someone who's really powerful." When he made it home that night, the first call he got was from Barbara Bush's assistant, saying that the Bushes had heard the news and wanted to help however they could. "The next call I got was from Maggie Williams's office [she was Hillary Clinton's chief of staff], saying that if I get any calls from the press I should direct them back to the White House. I immediately thought, 'Well, of course, that's what we always do.' I hung up the phone and I said, 'Wait a minute. They just fired me!'"

All these years later, Emery told me sadly, he understands why he was fired. "She was facing so many pressures," he says of Mrs. Clinton, "and unfortunately I was a victim."

But at least one former colleague of Emery's disputes his claims. This person, who spoke on the condition of anonymity, said that the Clintons were right to be paranoid about the residence workers, many of whom had served Republican presidents for twelve years. According to this source, "Everybody in the Usher's Office was upset when President Bush 41 was not reelected . . . and they showed it in front of the Clintons." Emery, in particular, was a "Republican from the top of his head to the tips of his toes," according to this source, and Emery himself says that he would have gone to California with the Reagans after they left office if they'd asked him.

Emery may not always have hidden his feelings around the Clintons. According to his colleague, as President Clinton came down from the second floor to attend an event one day, Emery said, "I can't understand why everybody has an orgasm when he's around." He made these kinds of comments loudly enough for Clinton aides to hear, his colleague said.

The Clintons may also have had good reason to be concerned about their security detail. They were still reeling from claims made by Arkansas state troopers assigned to protect Governor Clinton, who later told the press that they had helped facilitate Clinton's extramarital affairs in what came to be known as "Troopergate."

One incident particularly worried the Clintons. Late one night in 1994, while they were at Camp David celebrating Easter, Chelsea's former nanny and White House staff assistant, Helen Dickey, was in her third-floor room at the White House when she heard noises coming from the family's living quarters one floor below. When she went to see what was going on, she found a group of men dressed in black carrying weapons and rummaging through the Clintons' things.

"What are you doing? You have no right to be here," she yelled.

"We're Secret Service doing our job. Get out," they told her.

When Hillary returned, she asked Chief Usher Gary Walters for an explanation. He apologized for forgetting to tell her that the agents were sweeping the second floor to see if there were any listening devices. She was livid.

The Clintons cherished their time alone. In a 1993 interview, Hillary Clinton said she loved the second floor of the White House because it was the only place where the Secret Service didn't trail her family. "We can tell the full-time help that they can get off. We don't have to have them up there," she said. "That's a wonderful feeling, because everywhere else we are we've got people around us all the time."

By most accounts, Chelsea Clinton treated the residence staff with respect. Yet Ronn Payne believes that she had internalized some of her parents' animosity toward the Secret Service. In the very beginning of the Clinton administration, agents were stationed on the second-floor staircase landing, right by the president's elevator. Another Secret Service post was at the top of the Grand Staircase across from the Treaty Room on the second floor. (These posts were later moved to the State Floor at the Clintons' request.)

One day, according to Payne, he was walking through the second-floor private kitchen when an agent walked in behind him waiting to escort Chelsea to Sidwell Friends, the private school she attended in northwest Washington. Chelsea was on the phone.

"Oh, I've got to go," she told her friend. "The pigs are here."

The agent turned "crimson," Payne recalls. "Ms. Clinton, I want to tell you something. My job is to stand between you, your family, and a bullet. Do you understand?"

"Well, that's what my mother and father call you," she replied.

———

Doorman Preston Bruce said he had an ominous, prescient feeling that two of Richard Nixon's closest aides would one day betray the president. It was November 1968, and Bruce had already been the White House doorman for fifteen years. He knew something was unusual when, three or four days after Richard Nixon's election, a political aide kept showing up at the White

House. "I heard this man asking minute questions about the way things were run," Bruce said. "No detail seemed too small to escape his curiosity."

The man was Nixon's counsel and assistant for domestic affairs, John Ehrlichman. Chief Usher J. B. West led him on tours of the residence as Ehrlichman peppered him with questions.

Bruce had never seen anything like it. "We on the household staff already knew how to make the first families safe and comfortable—that was *our* job. What did this man plan to do?"

While Bruce was charmed that the Nixon family took the time to learn everyone's names—all eighty of them—he resented the way Ehrlichman and Nixon's incoming chief of staff, H. R. "Bob" Haldeman, treated him. "Hundreds of times they'd need the elevator. Each time they'd say, curtly, 'Take me to the second floor,' without so much as a please or thank you. They looked right through me as if I were invisible."

Nixon had an easy banter with Bruce, but Haldeman did things to make it clear that the residence staff were the help and nothing more. His office sent out a memo saying that anyone on staff who asked the president or any family member for an autographed picture or a favor would be fired immediately. "We all felt this was a cheap little shot," Bruce said. "We knew better than to approach the president with such requests."

Haldeman wanted no one standing in the hall outside the State Dining Room during state dinners—not even the Secret Service. It had been a tradition and a special treat for the butlers to listen in on the toasts from the hallway.

"There was something about Haldeman and Ehrlichman, that you could look at them and you knew that they would never have respect for a person like you," said Butler Herman Thompson.

Most of the presidential advisers were very protective of the president and wouldn't get involved in details of how the residence was run. "Even when we would be setting up tables, you would see Haldeman and Ehrlichman walking through," Thompson said, shaking his head. "The way they carried themselves, it was like they were fully in charge of everything."

Before Watergate, Nixon himself was well liked among the staff, although most staffers agree that he and his family were much more formal and stiff than their predecessors. Chef Frank Ruta tells a story about Pot Washer Frankie Blair, a congenial African American who was a fixture in the kitchen. One night Blair was cleaning up after the first family had finished dinner. President Nixon wandered into the upstairs kitchen and somehow they started talking about bowling—Nixon was such an avid bowler that he had a single-lane bowling alley installed in the basement under the North Portico. Nixon asked Blair if he would play with him, and the two of them bowled until two o'clock in the morning. "There may have been a bottle of scotch involved," Ruta added.

When they wrapped up, Blair turned to the president and said, "There is no way my wife is going to believe I was out this late bowling with you."

"Come with me," Nixon told him.

The two walked to the Oval Office, where the president wrote a note apologizing to Blair's wife for keeping him out so late.

Usher Nelson Pierce also remembered happy times with the Nixons before Watergate destroyed Nixon's presidency. When he found out that the president and first lady were traveling to the Seattle area, where he was born, he told the first lady how much he missed the snowcapped mountains of the Northwest. Not long after that, she asked him to join them.

"The president's secretary gave me the flight map," Pierce recalled, and he studied it carefully, "trying to figure out what I would see, what I would recognize. But the closer we got to Washington, the less I was seeing." Then, just as he was trying to get his bearings, "all of a sudden we make a sharp bank to the right and of course I saw Mount Adams, Mount St. Helens, Mount Baker, and Mount Rainier. . . . I knew that somebody had asked the pilots to go that way so I could see the mountains."

Pierce hadn't been back home since 1941, when he was sixteen years old. "I was so emotional when we made that sharp right and I knew what had happened. I just started sobbing."

Back at the White House, Pierce asked the first lady if she told the pilot to take that route just for him. "I wanted to see the mountains too," she replied with a wink.

The Nixons were formal with the staff, but they were kind— and their kindness made watching the president's slow unraveling so painful. The Watergate investigation dragged on for more than two years, and as each day passed, the president grew more and more exhausted. His shoulders slouched in defeat as he walked to and from the Oval Office each morning. Electrician Bill Cliber, who later became chief electrician, remembered Nixon having a very regimented schedule during his first term, waking up early to head to the Oval Office. But Watergate sent him into a deep depression; his whole routine "just broke apart."

At the height of the scandal, Pat Nixon and her two daughters also seemed to sink into despair. "Oh, Mr. Bruce," Nixon's daughter Julie pleaded tearfully to the doorman. "How can they say such awful things about my father?" Nixon's other daughter, Tricia, told me that she took comfort in the support of the residence staff. "You felt around you that positive spirit—that sense that we know who you are, we know who your father is, and we love you. We'll always admire your father." When you work in the residence you see "beyond politics, you see beyond the story," she says. "You see the true person."

BILL CLIBER

Backstairs, however, the tension that invaded the Nixon White House also infected the residence staff. Nixon may have discarded Johnson's industrial-strength shower, but he had his own bathroom eccentricities, asking for a calming whirlpool bathtub to be put in its place. "Finding ways to relax in general seemed to occupy much of the president's time at the White House," said Traphes Bryant. Nixon was so completely consumed by his own paranoia—right down to his famous "enemies list" of political opponents—that even residence workers never knew where they stood. For many staffers, including Usher Nelson Pierce, Watergate was more traumatic than even the Kennedy assassination, because it dragged on for so long. "You saw a man deteriorate day by day by day and there was nothing you could do to help him."

At nine o'clock on the evening of August 8, 1974, Nixon announced his resignation. He made the announcement from his desk in the Oval Office, and asked that the room be cleared as completely as possible, even asking his Secret Service agent to leave. "It was just one cameraman, one engineer from the TV company, two military people, and me. All of us had to be in there for sound and pictures," recalled Cliber, sitting at the kitchen table in his home in Rockville, Maryland. He remembers it like it was yesterday: "It was dead silence in that room. I mean, it was creepy silent."

After Nixon finished his subdued broadcast, Cliber left the Oval Office and walked down the colonnade. Nixon followed in silence. Cliber paused to let the disgraced president get ahead of him.

"Where you heading, Bill?" Nixon asked, on what must have been the hardest day of his life.

"Back to the residence," Cliber told him, sheepishly.

"Walk with me," the president said.

The two of them walked side by side down the columned outdoor hallway, which runs alongside the Rose Garden. Cliber stopped and turned to Nixon.

"You should feel proud of yourself. You did a fine job. The best you could."

"Yeah, I wish a lot of people felt that way," Nixon replied. His eyes were glassy; to Cliber, it looked like he was willing himself not to cry.

"It will catch up to them one day," Cliber told him.

They parted on the Ground Floor of the residence, neither saying another word. Nixon went to the president's elevator and Cliber went down the basement staircase to the Electrician's Shop.

That night Nixon stayed up until two o'clock in the morning, making phone calls from his favorite room in the house, the Lincoln Sitting Room. Outside, crowds could be heard chanting, "Jail to the Chief! Jail to the Chief!" He finally went to bed but slept restlessly, and when he woke up and looked at his watch, it read four o'clock. When he couldn't get back to sleep, he walked to the kitchen to get something to eat. He was startled to see Butler Johnny Johnson standing there.

"Johnny, what are you doing here so early?"

"It isn't early, Mr. President," Johnson said. "It's almost six o'clock."

In a 1983 interview, Nixon explained what happened: "The battery [in my watch] had run out, worn out, at four o'clock the last day I was in office," he said. "By that time I was worn out too."

Preston Bruce recalls seeing Nixon in the elevator in that last day in the White House. "Mr. President, this is a time in my life that I wish had never happened," Bruce told him. In the privacy of the elevator, Bruce recalls, they hugged each other and wept—just as President Kennedy's wife and brother had done with him after JFK's assassination, more than a decade before.

"I have in you a true friend," Nixon told Bruce.

———

PRESIDENT REAGAN WAS so friendly that, after a while, the maids, butlers, and ushers learned to slip through a doorway as they were walking down the Center Hall of the residence if they wanted to avoid getting trapped in a long conversation with him. He particularly loved talking about California, the state he governed for eight years. Cletus Clark remembers almost nightly visits when he was painting the president's exercise room. "One day he came down there and one of the painters was up on his treadmill. I was scared to death! I thought he was going to blow up. But he didn't, he said, 'Let me show you how that thing works.' He got up on it and started walking!"

Nancy Reagan didn't always approve of her husband's habit of chatting up the staff. "She'd keep him the way she thought he should be," Clark says. "She didn't want him to associate with the help."

At 2:25 P.M. on March 30, 1981, sixty-nine days into his presidency, John Hinckley Jr. shot a revolver six times at Reagan after he delivered a speech at the Washington Hilton. The attempted assassination shook the residence staff, who were still getting to know the easygoing president.

On the day Reagan was shot, Clark was in the Solarium. Nancy Reagan, her interior decorator, Ted Graber, and Chief Usher Rex Scouten were nearby. "I'll never forget that," Clark recalled. "Somebody came up there and whispered something to them, and the next thing you know they left. I was still up there trying to mix some paint to match some fabric."

The next day, while her husband was recovering in the hospital, Nancy Reagan suffered an injury of her own. When she got back to the residence, she went to the Game Room on the third floor, a cozy space with a pool table, to retrieve her husband's favorite picture to bring to him in the hospital as a surprise. With a car waiting for her downstairs, she climbed up on a chair to reach the picture and fell off, breaking several ribs. Only a few people on the residence staff knew about her accident; she never revealed it publicly, and the staff has never talked about it until now.

The Reagans' son, Ron, does not even remember the incident, though he was not surprised to learn about it decades later: "She would have been entirely focused on him at that point, and wouldn't have let broken ribs get in the way."

In that moment, Nancy Reagan conducted herself with the same resilience under pressure that the residence workers demonstrate every day.

CHAPTER VI

Sacrifice

That first day, I thought the Usher's office was a
twelve-by-twelve-foot madhouse. People ran in and out of the room
all day, the phone rang incessantly, and the buzzer buzzed.

—J. B. West, usher and chief usher, 1941–1969,
Upstairs at the White House: My Life with the First Ladies

Usher Nelson Pierce lived with his wife, Caroline, in a pretty white Colonial house in Arlington, Virginia, about four miles from the White House. Before he passed away, on November 27, 2014, he and Caroline liked to sit on the porch swing on summer days. During an interview, when I asked him how long they'd been married, he glanced over and asked her to remind him. She did not seem to mind his momentary memory lapse; in fact, she seemed to be used to taking a lead role in the relationship. Because of her husband's grueling schedule, Caroline spent much of their sixty-six years of marriage taking care of their four kids—two boys and two girls—almost singlehandedly.

One date Pierce did remember is the exact day he started at the residence: October 16, 1961. During his more than two decades at the White House, Pierce's hours were so long and unpredictable that it felt "strange" to his wife when he was actually home. The ushers' shifts changed so often that the Pierces kept a calendar on the table by their telephone so Caroline would know when he was working. She said her children have "lived the White House." Over and over, Caroline had to tell them: "'We can't do this because Dad has to work. We can't go today because he has to work.' Your life revolved around the White House." (She teased him that their children's friends never understood what Nelson did; given his title, they all assumed he was an usher in a movie theater. "That took him down a peg," she joked.)

But the privilege of working in the White House was never lost on Pierce. One day, Steve Bull, an aide to Richard Nixon, was leaving the West Wing just as Pierce was coming up the steps to start his shift. Bull made fun of him for wearing his White House ID around his neck on the driveway before he needed it out. Pierce told him earnestly, "Out of the two hundred and ten million people in this country, how many of us have the privilege of putting it on?"

Bull paused and replied, "I never thought of that."

In all his years at the White House, it was trying to keep up with Lyndon B. Johnson that put the greatest strain on his marriage. A nocturnal animal, Johnson often ate dinner after 10:00 P.M., slept a few hours, and woke up again at 4:00 A.M. (Carpenter Isaac Avery, who started at the White House in 1930, had never seen anything like it. "The Kennedys lived in a hurry," he said. "President Johnson lives in a race.")

The president's daughter Lynda recalls that her father "worked a two-day shift." She said he "would get up in the morning and work," and then about two or three o'clock, or whatever time he could take a break, he would come over to the mansion and eat lunch or a midday meal—sometimes it was pretty late in the afternoon, three or four o'clock. And then he would go to his bedroom, put his pajamas on, and sleep for thirty minutes or an hour. Then his second day started."

The residence staff adjusted their schedules to suit Johnson's demands. They worked in shifts, with ushers, maids, butlers, and cooks coming in at seven or eight o'clock in the morning and working until four or five o'clock in the afternoon, and another group coming in after lunch and working late into the night or early morning.

Every night, the navy chief would give President Johnson a massage in the president's living quarters. When Pierce was on night duty, he would wait downstairs until the navy chief came down to tell him the president had gone to bed, at which point he was free to leave. Every once in a while, Pierce recalled, the president would fall asleep on the table and the chief would have to sit down and wait until Johnson woke up so he could finish the massage.

"It was three, four, sometimes even five o'clock in the morning before we'd leave work," Pierce said, without a hint of resentment in his voice.

Johnson wasn't the only president who kept late hours. Pierce remembered a few parties thrown by the Kennedys that ran so deep into the night that he'd call his wife and ask her to tell their oldest son not to start his six-mile *Washington Post* paper route without him. He would rush home in time to drive him; sometimes it was the only time he got to see his son that day.

The ushers' workload amazes even top West Wing staffers. Obama's former personal secretary, Katie Johnson, was astonished at how efficiently they coordinated a last-minute celebration for the staff who worked on President Obama's historic health care legislation the night it passed on March 21, 2010.

"We didn't know if health care was going to pass until four in the afternoon, and of course the list of people who'd worked on health care was much larger than anyone had originally anticipated. So at four-thirty in the afternoon I'm calling over to the residence and telling them that we need to have food and drinks for a hundred people at eight o'clock," she recalled. She expected to hear some pushback. "They said, 'Oh, no big deal, we've got it.'" In a matter of hours they were able to pull off a memorable night for the West Wing workers, who drank celebratory champagne on the Truman Balcony.

For former White House spokesman Reid Cherlin, it was the only time he ever set foot in the living quarters. (The Obamas are especially private and only a few close friends, including Valerie Jarrett, are frequently seen upstairs.) Cherlin called the memory "vivid, because I knew I would never be able to go again."

While they were enjoying the champagne, speechwriter Adam Frankel asked Reggie Love if he could take a look at the Lincoln Bedroom. Soon everyone wanted to join in on the impromptu self-guided tour.

"Walk around," the president told the festive crowd.

That was all it took. "Everyone from the top people on down to the most junior people were just wandering around the bedrooms on the second floor. Everyone had the biggest smiles on their faces," Cherlin remembers. "The president was in a good mood."

"I can only get away with having you guys up here because Michelle is out of town," Obama told them. Pointing out the copy of the Gettysburg Address displayed in the Lincoln Bedroom, the president—who takes pride in his own handwriting—told the young staffers how much he admired Lincoln's beautiful penmanship.

For a politician sometimes viewed as standoffish, Obama often talks about the White House with a kind of boyish charm. Shortly after the inauguration, Frankel brought a new speechwriter to the Oval Office.

"Is this your first time here?" Obama asked.

"Yes, sir," Frankel's colleague replied.

"Pretty cool, huh?"

———

EXECUTIVE CHEF WALTER Scheib is quick to say how honored and grateful he is for the opportunity to work at the White House—even as he compares it to being in prison.

"You work for the same people every day, you don't have any personal life, family, social life, you work what we used to call 'White House flex time'—that is, you chose any eighty-five hours you want to work each week. You lose your family, lose your social life, lose your personal life, and in many cases even lose your professional life because you work with the same group of folks every day, day in and day out. So you have to find a new way to stay fresh."

Many of the butlers I interviewed were divorced, in part because of their work. Butler James Ramsey insisted he was never happier than since his 1995 divorce, even though he lost his house and his car in the process. "My life now, I come and go. I do what I want to do. I ain't got nobody to tell me what to do. I love my life." Having no one to answer to is helpful when working such unpredictable hours. Ramsey sometimes left the house at five or six o'clock in the morning and didn't return home until two o'clock the following morning if there was a state dinner.

Butler James Hall (nicknamed "Big Man" by Nancy Reagan) started at the White House in 1963 and was divorced nine years later. Hall was called to work state dinners and help the full-time butlers if they were short-staffed. He often got the call last-minute in addition to the full days he worked as a library technician in the National Archives.

Hall passed away around the time that his friend James Ramsey died. Before his death, I interviewed Hall at his tidy apartment in a retirement home in Suitland, Maryland, where his second bedroom was a shrine dedicated to his career. His souvenirs included letters from Chief Usher Rex Scouten, thanking him for his work at a dinner honoring prisoners of war from Vietnam, and for his help at Tricia Nixon's wedding reception. The letters hung next to a condolence note from President Clinton on the death of his father in 1995.

Hall harbored no resentment about his divorce or the late nights he spent working at the White House. He reminisced about the days during Nixon's presidency when the butlers used to wear tails and white vests: "They had us take the white vests off and wear black vests because they said we were 'sharper than the guests.'"

Of course, working on the residence staff didn't jeopardize every worker's marriage. In fact, some couples even found each other while working at the White House. After much cajoling, Head Housekeeper Christine Crans found time to fall in love with Engineer Robert Limerick in 1980. The two met when Crans was measuring Limerick for his uniform. Limerick's boss, the chief engineer, kept teasing them—until finally, Christine recalls, the two decided, "Okay, we're going to go out to make him happy." Less than a year later they were married.

When she told Nancy Reagan she was engaged, the first lady was thrilled. And relieved. "I think she was worried I might become a spinster," Limerick said, laughing. The housekeeper before her had married the pastry chef, and ever since then, "the joke is that housekeepers come in trying to find a husband." At their small wedding ceremony in Deale, Maryland, about forty of the sixty-five guests were members of the White House staff and their spouses, including Gary Walters and Rex Scouten.

Still, their busy schedules could be challenging. When the Clintons were in the White House, Limerick had to work every Christmas, and she and Robert eventually decided it would be better if he left his job as a White House engineer because the schedule was too grueling. Adding to the frustration of coordinating schedules, the Limericks couldn't talk much with each other about the incredible things they heard and saw on the job—even though they both worked in the White House. Limerick insists, "We didn't always come home and spill the beans."

————

USHER SKIP ALLEN, who worked in the residence from 1979 until 2004, knew one member of the staff who even gave his life for the job. Frederick "Freddie" Mayfield started as a houseman in 1962, vacuuming and moving heavy furniture. When he was promoted to doorman, he became something of an institution with his silver hair, white tie, and black tailcoat (he shared the same quiet dignity as his colleague Preston Bruce). As the doorman, he waited by the elevator at night to bring the president to the residence. "He had the greatest smile," said Luci Baines Johnson. "Every day was Christmas for Freddie Mayfield."

One day, Mayfield confided to Allen that his doctor told him he needed bypass surgery—immediately. Mayfield said, "I know I have to have it done, and the doctor said I had to do it right away, but I'll just wait until after the next presidential trip." By the time the next trip came around, it was too late. Mayfield had a heart attack on his way to work and died at just fifty-eight years old. "He never got his heart fixed because he kept saying, 'The president needs me now, I'll wait until he goes on this next trip and *then* I'll go to the hospital.' He never made it." It wasn't that Mayfield thought he was the only person who could do his job, Allen said. "It's just pride in station. It's 'I want to do my best for the president,' and they go out of their way to do that."

Nancy Reagan attended Mayfield's funeral on May 17, 1984, and was so affected by his loss that she said at the time, "It doesn't seem right here without him." Butler Herman Thompson remembers being moved when he saw her in the audience. "I thought it was very respectful." Decades later, she said she still remembers getting the call that he had died, and how "shocked and saddened" she was by the news. She knew right away that "it just wouldn't be the same without his smiling face at the elevator."

The staff are all like family to each other. Many of them played golf together back during Freddie Mayfield's day, and every Friday night a group of workers would gather in the Eisenhower Executive Office Building's small bowling alley to play against Secret Service agents and police officers. When Nelson Pierce's wife, Caroline, heard her old friend Freddie's name, her face lit up. "He liked turkey necks. I'd have to save the turkey neck every Thanksgiving to send to Freddie."

That camaraderie persists today. When one of the workers has a death in the family, or is having trouble paying medical bills, his or her colleagues pool together their money in a jar in the Butler's Pantry on the first floor to help with the costs.

"You could be having a bad day and a butler would come in that morning and say hello to you and get you laughing," Usher Nancy Mitchell recalled. "Somebody always comes in and picks you up."

Butler James Jeffries comes from a long line of White House workers. In fact, nine members of his family have worked at the White House. His mother's brother Charles Ficklin was the maître d' at the house, and another uncle, John Ficklin, was a butler and later became maître d' as well.

When Jeffries's mother died in 2012, he recalled tearfully, "practically everybody was at my mother's funeral except the president." His mother had never worked at the White House, but Butlers Buddy Carter and James Ramsey and Storeroom Manager Bill Hamilton all came to show their support for the Ficklin family. And his colleagues contributed almost four hundred dollars in memorial donations, though none of them were wealthy themselves. But Jeffries was even more amazed when the same thing happened after one of his uncles died. "My uncle, he didn't work at the White House. But he was a Ficklin, and he had passed away down in Amissville, Virginia, and we're going on and having the funeral, and all of a sudden I heard the door open in the church and Mr. West and the ushers and quite a few other people from the White House came to the funeral. I think they had a letter somebody read in the church from the president." He paused. "I started crying because I felt so good that people thought enough of us to come."

Jeffries still works a couple of days a week as a butler at the White House; he says he'll retire "when my legs don't want to let me stand up." When he arrives at the White House, the first thing he does is check a list on the cabinet in the pantry that gives him his assignment. He could be on first-floor pantry duty, bartending, or pickup (carrying a tray to pick up dirty glassware). He said he prefers working as a bartender or cleaning dishes in the back, because holding trays loaded with glasses is hard work for a man in his seventies with arthritis. He said his manager recently asked him if he was all right after he became breathless rushing between the Butler's Pantry and the East Room carrying two plates at a time. But he brushes off any such concerns—"I don't want to complain," he says—and these days his colleagues save him from doing much heavy labor, just as he did for the older butlers when he started, back in 1959.

"One time I remember the butlers had gotten so old that, when they were holding a tray with glasses or drinks on it, all of a sudden you could hear those glasses clanging because they didn't have the strength in their arms," he said. "I would go out there and take the tray from the guy and take his place so he could go on in the back."

Butlers often make a lasting impression on the first family and their aides. Desirée Rogers remembers the loss of longtime butler Smile "Smiley" Saint-Aubin, who passed away suddenly in 2009. Rogers called his death "one of the most poignant things of my tenure, and our team's tenure." Talking as though it were a loss in her own family, she said the Obamas held a service in his honor at the White House with his family.

"He was just an incredibly gracious man who was very, very good at what he did. That's why they call him 'Smiley'—always cheerful, always ready to serve, and always so helpful, whether it be something that our office needed or one of his peers needed," she said, adding, "I think for all of us it was an incredible loss so early on, at a time when all of us were just learning our way. It was a tough time."

The staff's sacrifices do not go unrecognized. Charles Allen, the son of Butler and Maître d' Eugene Allen, remembers a story his father once told him that shows the mutual devotion between the first family and their staff. Lady Bird Johnson was so worried about a butler's cancer-stricken wife that she kept pressing him about her treatment. When she did not like his answer, she called up two of the country's most well-regarded oncologists. That afternoon they flew in from New York and landed at Washington National Airport to meet the butler's wife.

In a similar display of love and respect, Electrician Bill Cliber remembers Secret Service agents approaching him after the birth of his son.

"Where's your wife at?" they asked.

"She's at Washington Adventist Hospital in Takoma Park," he told them. "Why?"

They said Lady Bird was thinking of sending her flowers. He pauses, tears beginning to fill his eyes so many years later. "No," he said, disbelievingly. "The first lady went and got flowers and she took them to her and gave them to my wife in the hospital." His wife, Bea, sat next to him as he spoke, but she just shook her head when I asked her to elaborate. It's a memory she wants to keep only for herself.

When Cliber thanked Lady Bird the next day, she told him it was the easiest thing she ever had to do as first lady.

CHAPTER VII

Race and the Residence

*For any American that understands the complex history of this country,
you feel it. Especially when you look at the drawings of how this home was
built and you see many slaves who couldn't enter the building working to
create the building. Some of those folks could be my ancestors and there
is a profound power and sense that comes with the fact that we are the first
African American family to occupy this residence over the years.*

—First Lady Michelle Obama

President Obama's historic 2008 election marked an important turning point in American history and was hailed by many as a crowning achievement of the civil rights movement. Not much more than forty years before his election, African Americans were legally discriminated against in the Jim Crow South; about a hundred years before that, slave pens were set up in Lafayette Square within full view of the White House. Now, the nation's first African American first family are being served by a mostly African American butler staff.

When they first moved in, the Obamas were circumspect around the residence staff. Some observers believed they may not have been entirely comfortable having butlers wait on them. The first couple are, of course, deeply aware of their unique historic status. Not only is Obama the first African American to be elected president, but—as he noted in a much-heralded speech addressing race during the 2008 primary season—he is also "married to a black American who carries within her the blood of slaves and slave owners." Michelle Obama's great-great-grandfather Jim Robinson was a slave; her great-grandfather Fraser Robinson was illiterate when he was a teenager, though he later learned to read. Indeed, some of Mrs. Obama's family members had jobs that were quite close to those of the residence workers—including her maternal grandfather, Purnell Shields, who was a handyman in Chicago, and one of her aunts, who was a maid.

Since his election the president has mostly tried to avoid getting mired in race relations, and his aides have had little to say about the relationship between the household help and the first family. But Chief Usher Stephen Rochon, who retired in 2011 as the first black chief usher, says that he noticed a special kind of understanding between the African American staff and the Obamas because "they're from the same culture." He cited the "sense of pride" among the residence workers "that this country had grown to this level to have a black president."

For Desirée Rogers—now the CEO of Johnson Publishing, publishers of *Jet* and *Ebony* magazines—being the first African American social secretary, for this particular first family, had a special significance. "On Inaugural Day, what was most compelling to me is that I looked at all these gentlemen preparing for the arrival of the first African American president—I could not help but be taken at how they looked. They reminded me, quite frankly, of my grandfather, who obviously was a pillar in our family." She said she wishes he could have been there to see it.

Rogers often heard the butlers say they never thought they would see the day when they'd be serving the first African American president. They may have even tried a little harder than usual. "I could just tell the pride that they had in preparing for this first family to come in. It was a very touching moment for me as we prepared the house for their arrival and as I saw all of these gentlemen working so diligently to make sure that everything was just perfect when they arrived from the parade."

Lonnie Bunch, the founding director of the Smithsonian's National Museum of African American History and Culture and a member of the Committee for the Preservation of the White House, said he would be surprised if Michelle Obama never talked to the African American staff at the White House about their special shared circumstances. He's quick to point out that the fact of the Obamas' race alone doesn't necessarily mean that their relationship with the African American staff is any closer or more personal than those of their predecessors. "But there's an obvious understanding and appreciation of who these men and women are," he said. "I think there's a feeling, as Michelle has said, this could have been me or this could have been members of my family."

Operations Supervisor Tony Savoy, who retired in 2013, insists that Obama's arrival at the White House did not affect how he conducted his job. "I'm going to give my best, all I can, to the person, regardless of who it is," he said. "I couldn't give no more to him than I'd give to a lady president or to another white president. It wouldn't make no difference. I would still give my 110 percent all the way across the board."

———

President Obama's two White House victories are especially remarkable given the troubled relationship between the White House and slavery. There was a thriving slave trade in Washington in the nineteenth century, though there were also many free people of color: by the time of the Civil War, census records show 9,029 free blacks and 1,774 slaves living in Washington, D.C. Back in 1792 when construction of the executive mansion began, the new capital city was a primitive swamp, far removed from any major eastern hubs—and carved out of the slave states of Maryland and Virginia. In November 1800, when John Adams moved in, one-third of Washington's population was black and most of them were slaves. African Americans—free and enslaved—helped build much of the nation's capital, milling the stones used in the pillars and walls of the White House and the U.S. Capitol. These workers were leased from their masters to work at government quarries in Aquia, Virginia, paid only in food (pork and bread) and drink (daily rations of one pint of whiskey each). Little is known about them beyond a list of first names—"Jerry," "Charles," "Bill"—that appears in government records.

It's hard to imagine what the grounds of the White House looked like as it was being constructed. A stone yard was erected on the northeast side of the mansion with dozens of large sheds housing worktables used for cutting stone. Close to the new walls of the house were two tall tripod rigs for hoisting the stone blocks into place. The rigs supported huge pulleys, some as high as fifty feet, which loomed over the massive construction site. Despite the grandeur of its architecture—it was likely the largest house in the United States until after the Civil War—the White House would remain a relatively unrefined place to live for decades after its first stone was laid.

Once the mansion was occupied, slaves were brought to work in the White House by every Southern president until 1860, including Thomas Jefferson, James Madison, and Andrew Jackson. In 1830, during Jackson's administration, the U. S. Census recorded fourteen slaves living on the premises, five of them under ten years old. "In essence, the African American fingerprint has been on the White House since its inception," Lonnie Bunch points out. Because the country's earliest presidents had to pay the residence workers themselves, they had much less help; Jefferson only had about a dozen servants. Of the dozen, only three were white; the rest were African American slaves from Monticello, Jefferson's Virginia home.

Many of the early Southern presidents tried to cut costs by replacing salaried whites and free blacks on the staff with their own slaves. President James Madison also relied on slaves from his home, Montpelier. His valet, a slave named Paul Jennings, eventually bought his freedom and went on to write the first ever memoir of life in the executive mansion.

President Andrew Jackson, a Tennessee slaveholder, decided to save money when he moved to the White House by replacing several white servants with slaves from his Tennessee home. The slaves who were visible to the public wore elaborate blue coats with brass buttons and yellow or white breeches. Most of them lived in crowded dorms in the basement or the attic, with its steep ceiling and poor lighting. The basement rooms were off of a forty-foot-long kitchen with giant fireplaces. During the first half of the nineteenth century, salaried servants and slaves slept on worn-out cots and mattresses.

By the time Zachary Taylor took office in March 1849, Northerners were expressing outrage about the practice of slavery. In a bid to save money, he supplemented the four servants he had on staff by bringing about fifteen slaves, some of them children, from his home in Louisiana, but he kept them largely out of view for fear of the public's reaction. Slavery was finally abolished in the capital city in 1862.

The roles of residence workers evolved gradually. In 1835, the principal gardener was the only person listed in a managerial role in the Federal Register. Congress created the official post of "steward" in 1866, when President Andrew Johnson hired William Slade, an African American who was a personal messenger for President Abraham Lincoln, making him the first official manager of the residence. The job description is in many ways akin to that of the modern-day chief usher, supervising all executive mansion staff and overseeing every public and private event. Because Slade was responsible for all government property in the mansion he was bonded for thirty thousand dollars—an astronomical sum in the nineteenth century. Slade's small office was located between two kitchens in the basement. It had freestanding cupboards full of silver and porcelain and big leather trunks with china and flatware dating back to James Monroe and Andrew Jackson that were still being used in dinner service after the Civil War. Slade personally kept the keys to the trunks and checked off each piece as it was washed and put away after formal dinners. The White House would not see another African American chief usher until Admiral Stephen Rochon took the post in 2007.

More than a century after President Jefferson trimmed his expenditures by replacing white servants with black slaves, Franklin D. Roosevelt brought white housekeeper Henrietta Nesbitt from Hyde Park to help control the first family's wild spending. Not long after the inauguration, Nesbitt helped the first lady reorganize the household staff. Eleanor Roosevelt made the decision to fire all the white household staff (with the exception of Nesbitt) and keep only the African Americans. Yet, given her generally outstanding record as an advocate of civil rights, her reasons were surprising: "Mrs. Roosevelt and I agreed," Nesbitt wrote in her memoir, "that a staff solid in any one color works in better understanding and maintains a smoother-running establishment."

Before this dismissal of the white staff, there were separate dining rooms for white and African American workers. When African American staffers accompanied the president to the Roosevelts' home in Hyde Park, New York, they were not allowed to eat in the dining room designated for the help, according to Alonzo Fields, an African American butler at the time. Instead, they were told to eat in the kitchen. Because of this practice, Fields wrote in his memoir, "I had my reservations concerning the White House as an example for the rest of the country."

————

As THE DECADES passed, African American staffers would capitalize on their prestigious positions. Even though they were servants, they were servants in the most important home in the nation. Lynwood Westray started his thirty-two-year career as a part-time butler at the White House in 1962. Born and raised in Washington, D.C., he remembers making just six dollars a week working as a grocery store clerk in 1939. Now ninety-three, he recalled his time at the White House as he sat in the three-bedroom bungalow in northeast Washington that he bought for $13,900 in 1955—a few years after he and his wife, Kay, were married. Outside, four lanes of traffic whiz by. ("People are crazy now, driving each other off the road!") In his entryway, framed pictures of Abraham Lincoln and Barack Obama hang side by side; a Michelle Obama doll sits on a side table. Two framed Christmas cards from the Johnsons and the Carters hang in the dining room.

Westray was a member of Private Butlers Incorporated, a group of African American White House butlers who helped one another find jobs in private homes on the nights when they were not busy at "the house." They were capitalizing on a growing need, Westray said. People in government would often call the maître d' at the White House and ask for names of butlers to work their parties, giving them a chance to have world-class service (and bragging rights) at private events. So when he wasn't working his full-time job at the postal service (he worked his way up from clerk to foreman), or working part-time at the White House, Westray served members of Congress, ambassadors, and other Washington power brokers at Georgetown dinner parties.

"They were tickled to death. They would introduce you, not as Sam, or John, or Charles, but as 'mister.' I was *Mister* Westray!"

Westray says that serving as a butler has traditionally been considered "a black job." He said his friends didn't realize how impressive his position was "until they found out that we were making all [that] money outside!" Because of their White House connection, Westray said, "The butlers had it made in this town!"

During one of our first interviews, Westray's eyes lit up when his wife, Kay, walked slowly into the room supported by her walker, wearing bright red lipstick and a blue pantsuit. Their affection for each other was contagious; they teased one another constantly. When asked what their secret was to such a long marriage, Kay said: "You love a little, you cuss a little, and you pick up and you start all over again."

Lynwood chimed in, beaming, "The first fifty years are the hardest."

Kay passed away in May 2013, after sixty-five years of marriage, and now Westray says he hardly knows what to do without her. He talks about kissing her forehead right before she passed away, not with sadness but with a sort of wonder. "Death is a part of living," he says. He keeps a laminated copy of her obituary in his shirt pocket and her ashes in an urn on the fireplace mantel, above her Christmas stocking, which was still hanging there on a spring day a year after her death. But he's doing his best to move on. "I'm learning how to be single. I'm cooking, washing clothes, cleaning, all of those things I never did," he says sadly. When he cooks for himself, he makes Kay's favorite recipes, like fried apples, to prove to his family that he can manage on his own. But he won't even consider dating: "I'm too old!"

For the first ten years, Lynwood Westray worked at the White House part-time, supplementing the income from his main job at the post office. After retiring from the post office in 1972, the chief usher invited him to join the regular force. "My wife didn't want me to because of the hours." But the Westrays' only child, Gloria, said that her father's job "opened up doors for them." She loved telling people that her father worked at the White House—and found that it added to her own self-esteem. "I had standards that were higher," she says now. "I couldn't be out being mischievous."

As a teenager, Gloria says, she once came home from school to find the FBI waiting for her. "My mother was livid. Apparently this guy that I had been dating, he was a little older, and he was involved in something that wasn't good and the FBI was questioning me, and I was like, 'I honestly don't know anything.' You could imagine when my dad came home." She promised her father that she would never see the man again; his reputation—and their family's livelihood—were at stake.

She said she was often asleep when her father came home from work, but she would press him the next morning at breakfast about the glamorous dinner he had served the night before. Usually, the most she could get out of him was the menu.

Though Westray kept his secrets throughout his career, as he aged, he began sharing his stories. During one interview, he went to a closet to retrieve mementoes, including photos of himself serving drinks at a 1970 picnic on the South Lawn, a photo of him with Reverend Billy Graham after one of his Sunday prayer sessions at the White House, and even a jewelry box containing a small piece of hardened vanilla cake from Tricia Nixon's wedding.

Westray happily recalls one night in 1976 when something extraordinary happened. It took place in the Red Room, with its ornate carved furniture and walls lined with gold-embroidered scarlet twill satin, nestled between the Blue Room and the State Dining Room on the State Floor. On the night in question, Queen Elizabeth II and Prince Philip were guests at the White House, there to celebrate the bicentennial of the American Revolution. Westray, dressed in his tuxedo uniform, and his friend and frequent working partner Sam Washington, happened upon Prince Philip sitting alone late at night in the Red Room.

"Your Majesty, would you care for a cocktail?" Westray asked, presenting a tray of cocktails to the prince.

"I'll take one . . . only if you let me serve it," Philip replied.

Westray glanced at Washington. "He couldn't believe it. No one had ever asked us that before." Westray and Washington accepted the invitation, pulling up chairs, in shock, and allowing him to serve them a drink. He can't remember what they talked about or what they drank, but that night the Duke of Edinburgh wanted to feel normal, if only briefly.

"He wanted to be one of the boys, that's all." Westray paused for a moment. "I was served by royalty. It blows your mind."

In 1994, more than three decades after he first walked through the mansion's imposing wrought-iron gates, Westray retired from the White House. He might have stayed longer, but after learning he needed triple bypass surgery, he did what he thought was best for the dignity of the executive residence and for the staffers who make it tick: "I would have been a disgrace to the men serving in the White House if I dropped a platter on someone," he said. "It would be better for me not to be there."

———

Westray wasn't the only butler to see a less-than-formal side of the Duke of Edinburgh. Alonzo Fields, who served as a butler and maître d' from 1931 to 1953, described a similar encounter a quarter century earlier. It happened while he was serving the royal couple and their entourage breakfast at Blair House, where most foreign dignitaries stay. After then-Princess Elizabeth and her staff were seated, no one waited for her husband's arrival to start eating. After the royal party had "nearly finished their melon," the duke rushed in, saying, " 'I'm afraid I am a little late.' "

"He was in his shirtsleeves with his collar open and he grabbed a seat before anyone could seat him," Fields, who died in 1994, recalled in his memoir. "The princess did not stop eating her melon, although the others stood while the duke was taking a seat. Seeing the duke there in his shirtsleeves with his collar open gave me the feeling that this was the behavior of a commoner and not what you would expect from royalty. And I admired his audacity, for I know what a blasting I would have got if I had been visiting with my wife and had come out in my shirtsleeves. . . . It was pleasing to find the duke to be a human being who, no doubt, felt more comfortable in his shirtsleeves."

Prince Philip wasn't the only member of the royal family who surprised the White House staff with an endearing moment of informality. Once Queen Elizabeth II shocked the staff by undressing herself after a state dinner—and leaving her diamond tiara, a hefty diamond necklace, and other priceless jewels strewn about the room.

————————

A GENERATION YOUNGER than Fields, Herman Thompson was destined to work at the White House. Though he worked full days as a supervisor at the Smithsonian Printing Office, his father worked at "the house" as a part-time butler (and one of the founders of Private Butlers Incorporated) and his uncle worked there as a houseman. He was friends with Maître d' Charles Ficklin, and with Eugene Allen, who lived nearby. He even used to get his hair cut by Preston Bruce, who worked as a barber when he wasn't escorting dignitaries to meet the president. "All of them knew me before I knew myself," Thompson says of the close-knit group of African American butlers.

The staff watched each other's backs, both personally and professionally, Thompson recalls. "Everybody wanted to support Charles, then it was John, then Eugene," he said. "The main objective was to help out the maître d', because we had black maître d's and you wanted to make sure they looked good." In turn, the maître d's kept a Rolodex of reliable part-time butlers, chosen because they knew how to do everything from setting a table flawlessly to making a world-class martini.

"You didn't have to teach them anything, you didn't have to tell them what to do," said Thompson, who started working at the White House in 1960 and left at the end of President George H. W. Bush's term. Now seventy-four, Thompson still sets the family table for dinner every night for his wife of more than fifty years.

At state dinners Thompson was in charge of serving wine—with a different vintage selected to accompany each new course. He had to make sure each bottle was open and ready to pour when the food was served. "That might sound like something simple," he said, but not when you had ten people to a table "and you had to keep that going throughout the night." Christmas parties, he recalls, were especially difficult—in part because it fell to him to carve a huge steamship round roast.

But Thompson always considered the job a privilege, and one that could disappear in an instant. If a butler chatted too much with the guests—after all, you never knew who you were talking to—or scraped the plates too loudly in the adjoining pantry, he might never be asked back. Guests "were supposed to be given the best service that you could get in the United States," Thompson said. "There were people from all over the world watching."

———

EVEN MARY PRINCE couldn't believe how her luck had changed. Less than a year after being handed a life sentence for killing a man in the small town of Lumpkin, Georgia, the African American inmate, who was in her midtwenties, was trading her Georgia penitentiary cell for the governor's mansion, where she would be responsible for taking care of Governor Jimmy Carter's three-year-old daughter, Amy.

"When I first got the call to go to the governor's mansion, I didn't know what to expect," Mary Prince told me. "After I went there, Amy and I—we hit it off the very first day. I mean we *really* hit it off the very first day. From that day on, it was me and Amy."

Prince was part of a prison trustee program that assigns prisoners to work at the governor's mansion in different capacities: some do yard work, others cook, and some even take care of the family's children. Prince had no idea at the time that her close ties with Amy would catapult her to an even more bizarre reality: four years living and working in America's most famous house.

Prince's troubles had begun one night in April 1970 when her cousin got into a fight with a man and another woman outside a bar. According to Prince, she was trying to wrestle the gun away from them when it accidentally went off. But another eyewitness said that Prince grabbed the gun and deliberately killed the man in defense of her cousin. Prince stands by her innocence. "I was in the wrong place at the wrong time," she insists. "I got caught up in a situation that I did not understand. It took six years and ten months for them to clear my name."

At the time, Prince was ill-served by the justice system. She met her court-appointed attorney for the first time when she entered the courtroom for her trial. He advised her that if she pled guilty, he would get her off with a light sentence, but the plan didn't work. Mary Fitzpatrick, as she was known at the time, was sentenced to life in prison. (She took back her maiden name in 1979 after officially separating from her husband.)

Yet before the year 1970 had come to an end, Prince had been selected by Rosalynn Carter to care for her daughter at the governor's mansion. Mrs. Carter was convinced that the young woman had been unjustly convicted. "She was totally innocent," Rosalynn Carter says. Forever loyal to their daughter's nanny, the Carters have practically adopted her as a member of their family. "She had nothing to do with it," Rosalynn said firmly, sounding agitated by the question decades later.

When Jimmy Carter won the presidential election in 1976, Prince's work release was terminated and she was sent back to prison—her good luck seemingly coming to an end. But Mrs. Carter was so confident in Prince's innocence that she wrote to the parole board and secured her a reprieve so that Amy's beloved nanny could work for them at the White House. Even more remarkably, the president had himself designated as Prince's parole officer. Ultimately, after a reexamination of her case, Prince was granted a full pardon.

The former first lady, who has been by her husband's side as he's pursued so many humanitarian projects during America's longest post-presidency, says that Prince was convicted because of her skin color. "It was tough days, it was tough at home," she said. When President Harry Truman desegregated the armed forces, she recalls, "we came home to the desegregated South"—but racism was by no means obliterated. "You just didn't mention the race issue. It was easy to see why Mary was picked up." President Carter, who took heat for the decision to bring Prince to the White House, agreed with his wife's assessment. "Hers was a story all too common among the poor and the black before some of the legal reforms were imposed on our nation," the president wrote in one of his memoirs.

During her first six months as the country's most famous nanny, Prince said she got about fifty letters a day, and people pretending to be long-lost relatives called to plead with her to ask the president for favors. "I was worldwide news," she said, not sounding too upset by her stardom at the time. "Going from prison to the White House." But the press couldn't believe that the Carters would let a convicted murderer take care of their little girl, and not all the attention was kind: the story got so much traction that *Saturday Night Live* even devoted a skit to it, with actress Sissy Spacek playing a young Amy Carter and comedian Garrett Morris in drag playing Mary.

The media firestorm couldn't have been easy, but Prince took solace in her faith. "I'm a Christian and I prayed about everything," she told me. "I asked God if I did anything wrong to please let me know and forgive me. And I guess that's why the good Lord blessed me with the good life that I had since then. It was a real blessing for a prison inmate to go to the governor's mansion and get close to the family."

Even within the White House, things weren't always easy. Prince had a hard time making friends with the residence staff, who viewed her as an outsider—and one with a controversial past. Some of them resented her because she was brought in by the president and got to live in her own apartment on the third floor. Others, evidently, envied her position of power: if Prince decided she wanted to cook a Southern-style dinner for the first family, she could send all the cooks home at a moment's notice. She didn't have to play by anyone's rules as long as she kept the Carters happy. And they loved her. One evening when she was walking by the pool on the south side of the West Wing, she happened upon the first lady doing laps. "Come on in!" Mrs. Carter shouted. Prince wasn't in a bathing suit. "Just dive in in your uniform!" the first lady said, laughing. So she kicked off her shoes and jumped into the pool in her starched white nanny uniform and showed the first lady what she had learned in her swimming class. (Amy loved to swim so she started taking lessons herself.) Prince says that evening, "just me and the first lady together out there swimming," is her favorite memory of her time in the White House.

But rumors flew backstairs and some former staffers even believed she was guilty of murder. "That's a good way to get rid of your husband," one worker joked, unaware that she'd never been accused of killing her husband.

Prince paints a different picture of her time in the residence and says that the luxuries of living in the White House never fazed her. "None of that was exciting to me." Instead she focused on her work, and on getting her two sons settled after relocating them from Atlanta to an apartment in Suitland, Maryland, a working-class suburb of Washington. When she was done taking care of Amy at night she took a taxi to see her boys, who were looked after by her sister during the day. She'd help them with their homework, make sure their school clothes were ready, and take a taxi back to the White House late at night so that she could be up early with Amy the next morning. She never asked the Carters if her sons could move in, even though she missed her boys terribly.

"I never thought it was appropriate for me to have my family living in the White House under their roof. That was *my* job. I was able to pay for them to be close to me and have their own place." She valued the boundary between her work life and her life at home with her boys. When she was through working, she says, "I could always go home to them."

She never thought race was much of an issue in the White House until an usher came to her with a message that made her furious. "My kids are always dressed neatly," she says, "because I made sure of it." But one of her sons worked at a Georgetown tennis club, and sometimes when he visited Prince at the White House he would arrive still wearing his tennis shorts. One day, an usher approached her: "Mary, I got a phone call that your kids were coming in here with raggedy clothes on," the usher told her. "But don't worry about it. It's gossip. I've never seen those kids come here not dressed neatly."

To Prince, it was a dual insult: calling her African American children unkempt, and implying that she wasn't doing her job as a parent. "I guess they thought I was dirt," she said. She never found out who it was that lodged the mean-spirited complaint. "I think it was somebody who was just prejudiced against the idea that President Carter got me out of prison and brought me to the White House."

But Prince rose above it all, finishing her time at the White House with dignity and maintaining her warm relationship with the family that saved her from prison. Today she lives just three blocks away from the Carters in Plains, Georgia; she still sees them almost every day when they're in town—and takes care of their grandchildren.

————

USHER NELSON PIERCE knew he had a problem—and it had to be fixed immediately.

When he first got to the Usher's Office as a young man, in 1961, he was responsible for bringing residence staff personnel files up to date. This meant looking at what every worker was paid. "I was amazed at the salaries," he said. The African American staff were making significantly less than their white colleagues.

The timing of the revelation was terrible. In his first State of the Union address, President Johnson declared "an unconditional war on poverty," at a time when the poverty line was accepted to be around $3,000 a year or less (around $23,550 in today's dollars). "Our joint federal–local effort must pursue poverty, pursue it wherever it exists—in city slums and small towns, in sharecropper shacks or in migrant worker camps, on Indian Reservations, among whites as well as Negroes, among the young as well as the aged, in the boomtowns and in the depressed areas," the president said in his January 8, 1964, address before a joint session of Congress.

It turns out that poverty existed right under the president's nose. The higher-paying jobs at the White House—ushers, florists, executive chefs, head housekeepers, carpenters, and plumbers—were viewed as more professional, and were given to white workers. The traditional domestic jobs, like butlers and maids, were filled mostly by African Americans and paid far less. (As a young usher, Pierce was making almost six thousand dollars a year, twice as much as the underpaid new hires.) Everyone on staff was paid less than they would have been at an equivalent job in the private sector, but overall the white staffers fared far better.

On January 9, Pierce told Chief Usher J. B. West that they needed to talk. The president had hired two new people who fell below the poverty line. "Before the press finds out that we have poverty cases working in the White House," Pierce said urgently, "you better up the salary of the two new maids we just hired at $2,900 a year."

West knew the salaries—in fact, he'd hired the maids himself—but it hadn't occurred to him that the media could seize upon this information to label the president a hypocrite. West raised the two maids' salaries immediately.

It wasn't lost on Pierce that it took a public relations scare to force West's hand. "The residence staff, as dedicated as they were to every president that they worked for, it was amazing to me that they weren't paid more than what they were paid."

Curator Betty Monkman wouldn't have been surprised by the pay discrepancy. Almost as soon as she came on board, in 1967, she recalls, she sensed an undercurrent of racism—"this Southern thing," she called it—beneath the surface bonhomie of the White House. For example, she could not believe that everyone called Doorman Preston Bruce by his last name. "He was a very distinguished man, he had a great presence about him," she said. "When I first came there everybody would call him 'Bruce,' so I just thought 'Bruce' was a first name. Then, after a while, I realized it was his last name. I just was appalled that I had been calling him that."

———

STOREROOM MANAGER BILL Hamilton insists that *he* was the one who led the revolt to get equal pay for the underpaid African American staff. That runs contrary to the impression created by *Lee Daniels' The Butler*, the film loosely based on Butler Eugene Allen's life, which shows the title character going into the head Usher's Office demanding a raise. By most accounts, Allen was too shy and too respectful of the institutional hierarchy to be so brazen.

Hamilton, however, is neither. He was born eight blocks from the White House. His mother stayed at home to raise her ten children. After living on Capitol Hill, she told him, she never wanted to live in a white neighborhood again. Hamilton was just twenty years old when he started as a houseman, during the Eisenhower administration. The Eisenhowers ran the White House like a military operation. He remembers vacuuming after the tours ended for the day, trying to erase any footprints from the rugs before Mamie Eisenhower could see them. When a guest walked through the Ground Floor, the houseman would turn the vacuum off and turn his face toward the wall. (When President Kennedy saw the workers behaving this way, he asked a staffer, "What's wrong with them?") Hamilton worked nine to five in the storeroom to support his seven children (at one point four of them were in college at the same time), then drove a cab after work until eleven o'clock at night. "I worked like a dog," he said. "But I always made sure I was home for the weekends."

Whenever a new president takes office, Hamilton says, his political advisers tend to treat the residence staff with disdain. "The West Wing staff just think they are better than you. Then they learn their lesson after they get there: it takes all of us to run this show for the president." But Hamilton resented being mistreated, and he had to find a way to express his frustration.

"I'll never forget when we went up to see J. B. West," Hamilton recalled at his home in a quiet, middle-class retirement community in Ashburn, Virginia, about an hour outside Washington, D.C. He made his move in the late 1960s, around the time of Martin Luther King Jr.'s assassination and the days of riots that followed. Washington was on fire as angry protestors, enraged by

King's murder and the inequality they saw around them, tossed Molotov cocktails and looted stores. Some came within just two blocks of the White House.

Inside the gates, Hamilton was furious. Everyone else seemed to be getting a raise, he said, except for the African Americans on staff. Inspired by the civil rights protestors, he gathered a handful of his fellow housemen—the workers in charge of vacuuming and heavy-duty cleaning—and made an announcement.

"They're having a state dinner tonight and we're not working."

There was a long pause as his colleagues mulled it over. They had already agreed to help that evening. (Staffers from the different shops were often asked to help out at events, as they had already been cleared through security.)

"What do you mean we're not working? We're going to lose our jobs," one of them said.

"This is what I'm trying to tell you all. If we all learn to stick together, there's nothing they can do."

"They can't bring somebody in off the street" to work the event, he argued, because they wouldn't have clearance.

Hamilton finally convinced his coworkers, and together they went to see Chief Usher J. B. West.

West was furious. "Are you the spokesman for the group?" he asked Hamilton.

"You could say that," he replied.

West was as "red as a beet," Hamilton remembered, laughing. For once, he had his boss over a barrel.

"You expect me to put on that little black bow tie, white shirt, and suit? If somebody drops something I'll go pick it up?" West asked the group.

Hamilton did not waver: "Sir, I don't give a damn what you do when I leave here."

Contrary to the portrait in *The Butler*, it wasn't the butlers who questioned the salary discrepancies; according to Hamilton, they "didn't make any waves." In fact, Hamilton was disappointed that they didn't join him—it was the butlers who had the real power among the White House staff because they worked in the closest proximity to the first family. If they got up the courage to tell the president and the first lady that they were being underpaid, Hamilton was sure something would be done to correct it. But not only did the butlers refuse to join him in protest, some were angry at him for potentially putting their own jobs at risk.

"We were not active in the civil rights movement. Our role was to serve the president and his family. Period," said former Butler and Maître d' George Hannie. In 1963, Hamilton said he was the only residence worker who went to hear Martin Luther King Jr. deliver his famous "I Have a Dream" speech at the Lincoln Memorial during the March on Washington. He describes the experience as "thrilling." But by following his conscience and demanding action years later he was angering his colleagues. He says, "I had more of *my* people mad with me" for demanding a raise. "But I had kids to take care of. I'm going to make sure my kids are going to be better than what I am. I didn't care what it takes, it was going to happen. I went home and told my wife one day, 'I'm tired of these people [white management paying African Americans less]. I might not have a job, but from now on I'm taking no stuff from nobody down there.'"

When Hamilton and his fellow residence workers finally stood up, however, justice prevailed. Two days after they sat out that state dinner, the black staff members got their raise. Hamilton thinks it was because J. B. West could see the writing on the walls beyond the White House. "He knew, with everything going on on the outside, he couldn't get out of it. I knew I had him when I had him. Wasn't no doubt in my mind."

Even though he's still angry about the blatant racism at the White House, Hamilton talks about his fifty-five years serving eleven presidents with a sense of awe. "When I walked into the White House for my interview, it felt like the first day of my life," he said. He had never been to the White House, even for a public tour. "I just couldn't believe it, and my parents couldn't believe it. It just doesn't happen!"

————

EUGENE ALLEN WAS certainly more careful about rocking the boat than Bill Hamilton.

When Allen's only son, Charles, was in Vietnam, he dreaded the prospect of fighting on the ground. "The only time I ever asked my father to do me a White House favor was when I asked him to ask President Johnson to get me out of this," he recalls.

In his letter he begged his father out of sheer desperation: "Go to the man, get me out of the infantry. I will stay in the war, but just get me out of the infantry. We're walking ten to twenty miles a day. I'm starving to death." Charles added: "I'm not a physical coward, Dad, but can you see if Mr. Johnson can get me in an aviation unit?"

When Charles heard back from his father, it was not the response he was hoping for. "He wrote me back and said something to the effect that if the Kennedys were still in power he thought he could do something. If Bobby was still around." But the Johnson White House was a different story. "I don't know these people that well," he said. "So you're going to have to stick it out."

————

WHITE HOUSE BUTLERS, maids, pot washers, and housemen were considered to have good, solid jobs in Washington's African American neighborhoods in the 1960s and 1970s. "There was always a sense of elegance, a sense of recognizing that this is a special occupation," Lonnie Bunch said. He attributed the sense of pride and professionalism in these trades to the fact that many families passed the work on from generation to generation: "The father teaches the son who teaches the grandson."

For generations of black Americans, a job at the White House was more than just a job. "They recognized that their service was about more than them. They really felt that they were carrying a double burden. They had to work hard to keep their jobs, [but] they were also carrying [certain] expectations and attitudes toward their race. They wanted to make sure that they were at the top of their game."

The fact that the White House butlers were mostly African Americans sometimes raised questions. Usher Chris Emery remembers when Soviet political leader Mikhail Gorbachev made his historic visit to the White House in 1987 and they had to scramble at the last minute to protect the two world leaders from a sudden downpour on the South Lawn.

"[Chief Usher] Gary Walters saw all the butlers standing there with umbrellas and said, 'I can't have all these African Americans holding umbrellas for these world leaders. It will look terrible.'" So Walters asked Emery and another white usher to go outside and hold umbrellas over Reagan and Gorbachev so that the White House would not look like "the last plantation," as Emery put it.

Butler Herman Thompson, a member of the first fully integrated high school class in Washington's public schools, was on the front lines of desegregation. The discrimination and outright hatred he saw in his white classmates made him "very rebellious as a person," he said recently over lunch at a downtown Washington restaurant not far from where he grew up. "It was not pleasant."

Thompson saw the same kind of racism in the White House that he did in the rest of the city, and he tried to fight it, but more surreptitiously than Bill Hamilton. "Many times, when African American people were there as guests, we would make it a point to make sure that they were looked after, that they would have the same type of attention as everyone else had," he said. As late as the

Nixon administration, butlers still wore tails for state dinners. As more black musicians like Duke Ellington and the Temptations started playing at the White House, however, and more African American guests appeared, the butlers were told to stop wearing tails to avoid exacerbating the appearance of a social divide between the workers and the guests.

"We used to joke that they changed the tails because the world was changing. A lot of times people who would come in, they wouldn't know who the butlers were and who the guests were." He chuckled. "You had some very distinguished-looking gentlemen working there and people would make predecisions about who was who." Thompson said he was mistaken for a guest a few times.

Even though he had seen things slowly improve, he was shocked when he met Admiral Stephen Rochon, the new chief usher, at Eugene Allen's funeral. "You figured it would be a cold day in hell before any black person would get the job!"

Rochon, who was born in 1950, grew up in New Orleans at a time when 10 percent of Americans still couldn't eat at Woolworth's counters. He still vividly remembers an incident that occurred when he was thirteen, when a red 1957 Chevrolet with a big Confederate flag in its back window pulled up to him while he was walking to a Boy Scout meeting. The car was full of white teenagers who shouted "nigger" and threw a Coke bottle at him. Because of that painful experience, he said, he told his White House staff he would always listen to their concerns about discrimination. "I didn't want someone else to hurt the way I did."

He did occasionally hear charges of racism. The only African American working in one of the shops came to Rochon one day and told him he thought he was being talked down to because of his skin color. Rochon immediately got the man's supervisor in his office and told him he wouldn't stand for it. "Word travels fast at the

White House," he said. "If it was with one department, believe me, every department knew about it."

There's a divide between workers like Bill Hamilton and Herman Thompson, who saw clear racism at the White House and felt compelled to combat it, and Eugene Allen, Lynwood Westray, and James Ramsey, who made do with the way things were.

Butler Alvie Paschall, now ninety-three years old, is a lot like his friend Lynwood Westray. He was just four years old when he started picking cotton in Henderson, North Carolina. He and his six brothers and sisters worked straight through the Great Depression, and he says his parents taught them to be respectful of authority. Reluctant to share too much, he represents an older generation of African Americans who were taught not to be "mouthy," he says, because that could cost them their jobs. "You're there for a particular thing: you're there to serve. Your job comes first."

Dressed nattily in suspenders and a cream-colored silk tie, Paschall told me that he carried that lesson with him all the way to the White House, where he started his career during the Truman administration. When there was a fight, or a private conversation he knew he wasn't supposed to hear, he had to decide quickly whether to leave the room discreetly or stay and pretend he hadn't noticed. "I did all of those things!" He laughed.

Westray is incredibly forgiving. The segregationist Alabama governor George Wallace, whose "segregation now, segregation tomorrow, segregation forever" speech was a black mark on the politics of the 1960s, sought to redeem himself in the eyes of the public after surviving a 1972 assassination attempt. Westray recalls that he also tried privately to win over the African American residence staff during visits to the White House. "After George Wallace got shot you would think he was one of our buddies," Westray said, shaking his head. "Every time he'd come down to the White House, the first thing he'd do was come back and want to be back there with us, back there in the Butler's Pantry." The assassination attempt "changed him completely," Westray said. "The Lord works in mysterious ways. It took a bullet to straighten him out."

Instead of snubbing Wallace, the African American butlers sat around and joked with him. It was not about holding grudges or about forgetting past offenses, it was about doing their jobs—which sometimes meant biting their tongues.

Butler and Maître d' Eugene Allen's son, Charles, said that his father experienced more racism at the high-end Kenwood Country Club in Bethesda, Maryland, outside Washington, D.C., where he shined members' golf shoes, than he ever did at the White House. Not because the racism didn't exist, but because no one wanted to get on the bad side of the president.

"People are going to be careful about the way they treat you because of the way these first families feel about these people. You can see yourself sailing out of the gate if you're disrespectful."

Lynwood Westray agrees. The White House "was one place where you didn't have all that foolishness," he says. "Even though we were all black butlers, people thought more of us because there we all were meeting kings and queens."

Outside the White House was a different matter. Westray loves to recount a story about his old friend Armstead Barnett, who worked and lived in the White House when Franklin Roosevelt was president. "One day he caught a cab to go home and he told the guy, 'Take me to 1600 Pennsylvania Avenue.' It was a white cabdriver and he didn't want to take him. 'There are no blacks living at the White House,' the driver told him. But he finally took him, and when they got to the gate Armstead got out to go in, everybody knew him, he didn't even have to show his identification." Westray smiled. "When he went in the gate and didn't come out, the cabdriver was still sitting there wondering, 'Where in the hell is that guy going?'"

President Kennedy shared a crowning moment of the civil rights era with Doorman Preston Bruce. Less than three months before his assassination, Kennedy asked Bruce to join him in the third-floor Solarium and listen to the throngs of people gathering to hear Martin Luther King Jr.'s historic speech at the Lincoln Memorial. They could hear the crowd singing the civil rights anthem, "We Shall Overcome," as they stood there together—Bruce the son of a sharecropper and Kennedy the scion of America's royal family. The president gripped the windowsill so hard that his knuckles turned white. "Oh, Bruce"—he turned to his friend—"I wish I were out there with them!"

The respect Kennedy had for the African American residence workers was returned. Eugene Allen never missed a day of work in thirty-four years and never complained about his coworkers or his bosses, the president and first lady. His son, Charles, said the only time he ever saw his father cry was when he was putting his coat on to go back to work at the White House after Kennedy was assassinated. "It depressed him terribly at that moment," Allen said thoughtfully of his father. "But, to use military terminology, he was a soldier. You buck up. The only tragedy that he didn't recover from was when my mother passed. He couldn't pull himself back up from that."

Allen, who passed away in 2010, was the last person who would have ever wanted a movie made about his life. By all accounts he was a shy and gentle man who would never have agreed to talk to the media were it not for prodding from Helene, his wife of sixty-five years. She said she wanted people to recognize Eugene's service to the country.

"When he walked in that door, he never complained about his coworkers, he never talked about the principals he worked for in a bad way. He kept that stuff close to his vest. That was our livelihood."

James Ramsey was another residence worker who shared that attitude. He grew up working in tobacco fields in North Carolina, sometimes helping to serve lunch in his high school cafeteria "just to give me a plate of food to eat." He came far in life and was grateful for the opportunity to work in "the house." Ramsey said he hated to hear stories of butlers going directly to the chief usher to complain about working conditions or their peers. "We didn't have no problem. All of us stuck together."

He also said that he never saw any racism, or he chose to rise above it. "People have been very nice to me since I've been coming up. Because I used to do the part-time catering and meet a lot of people. Segregation?" he asks. "It's over with—done."

One thing that may have helped Ramsey weather the indignities of segregation was his healthy sense of humor. Chef Frank Ruta remembers Ramsey joking openly about race, poking his head into the second-floor family kitchen to ask Ruta, who is white, how he wanted his coffee: "Do you want it like me, or do you want it like you?"

Yet James Ramsey conducted himself with pride and dignity, and he recognized the momentous change that the 2008 election brought to the White House. What was it like to be a black man working for the first African American first family?

"It was beautiful. It was beautiful."

————

ZEPHYR WRIGHT WAS truly a part of the Johnson family. Hired by Lady Bird Johnson when she was still a home economics student at a Texas college, she cooked for the Johnsons for twenty-seven years in Texas and in Washington, D.C., where the Johnsons brought her to live with them at the White House.

As they drove through the segregated South on their way to Washington, Lady Bird stopped the car at a hotel to look for a place to stay the night. She refused to stay in a hotel if Zephyr could not also stay there.

"Do you have rooms for tonight?" Lady Bird asked at one hotel.

"Yes, we have a place for you," the woman behind the desk told her.

"Well, I have these other two people," Lady Bird replied, gesturing toward Zephyr and another African American who worked for the Johnsons.

"No. We work 'em but we don't sleep 'em," the woman replied.

Lady Bird was disgusted. "That's a nasty way to be," she said over her shoulder as she stormed out.

After that humiliation, Wright wouldn't drive back to Texas until a decade later. The journey was one factor that informed the president and the first lady's zeal for civil rights legislation. After President Johnson pushed the Civil Rights Act that overturned so-called Jim Crow laws through Congress in 1964, Wright agreed to visit the state where she was born. "It's very different now," Johnson reassured her. "You can go any place you want to go; you can stop any place you want to stop." LBJ was proud that the historic legislation that he spearheaded would have a direct impact on his friend's life.

Johnson looked to Zephyr Wright as a kind of sounding board for his efforts on behalf of civil rights. During his vice presidency, he asked her for her feelings about Martin Luther King Jr.'s March on Washington. As president, when he appointed Thurgood Marshall as the first African American Supreme Court justice, he rushed to tell Wright the news. Johnson was persistently insecure about whether African Americans appreciated the reforms he enacted on their behalf, and sometimes complained to Wright about it: "I can't see how they can't see what I'm trying to do for them." Since his death, it has been alleged that Johnson used the word *nigger* even as he fought to pass civil rights legislation. One Johnson aide told me that the president did use the racial slur when he was expressing his frustration with certain African American civil rights leaders who wanted bolder reforms. "They were just being so wretched, making it harder for him," the aide said. For some, incremental change was not enough.

One frequent White House guest of Johnson's was Georgia senator Richard Russell, a mentor of Johnson's in the Senate but also a leading opponent of the civil rights movement. At first, Zephyr Wright knew him only as a visitor. "He was a very nice person" behind closed doors, she said. As the civil rights battle played out in public, however, she saw Russell more clearly. "When I read about and heard about the things he was doing and saying in Congress, then I got a different feeling about him." But she never let her feelings show. "I felt, 'Here I am; I'm working for Lyndon B. Johnson. These are his friends. I must accept them the way they are because he accepts them. There is nothing else I can do about it.'"

Many of those who worked closely with the Johnsons had no idea that he would be announcing his decision not to seek reelection on the night of March 31, 1968. Social Secretary Bess Abell found out when she turned on the TV. Wright was at home too, and she cried when she heard her longtime boss say he would be leaving the White House. She knew this would mark the end of her time with the Johnsons: Washington was home to her now, and she wanted to stay.

Wright admired Johnson, both for his civil rights reforms and for the sheer effort it took to push them through Congress. "He had always been such a fighter," she said. Politics was his "whole life," she recognized, and she was convinced that he gave it up because he felt his presidency's greatest accomplishments were being overshadowed by the albatross of Vietnam.

Johnson's frustrations were no secret among the residence workers. Once, around the time of his announcement, Dog Keeper and Electrician Traphes Bryant walked into a room just as Johnson was railing about the war. "They shot me down. The only difference between the Kennedy assassination and mine is that I am still alive and feeling it," he lamented.

To Wright, Johnson seemed at peace with his decision to leave Washington. "At last we are going home," he said to Wright the day after his announcement. "Are you going with us?"

"No, I'm staying here," she told him.

He was stunned. "It won't be the same without you," he said, sadly.

Wright was sad too, and in a way she felt abandoned by the president's decision. "To me it was just like losing a family. But it was what he wanted to do."

After he went back to his ranch in Stonewall, Texas, Johnson suffered from major heart problems and he fell into depression. His daughter Luci would call to check on him and see if she could help. "There's nothing you can do," he told her. "I just miss some of my creature comforts." He especially missed the custard that his mother and Zephyr made for him.

"Maybe I could help," she offered.

"No, you can't. Your mother doesn't cook. My mother's dead, and Zephyr got uppity and left me," Johnson complained.

"Zephyr got *uppity* and left you?" Luci repeated back to him, aghast. It seemed absurd for her father, who was a champion of the civil rights movement, to be angry at Wright for pursuing her dreams and staying where she felt most at home. "You spilled your life's blood trying to give her more opportunities in life, and then when you left Washington she chose to stay in that community because she found them and discovered them and was able to enjoy a great deal more opportunity in Washington, D.C., than she would have in Texas."

Her father recognized that he was being selfish, but he said he still missed her custard and comfort food. Luci offered to help.

"Daddy, Zephyr told me that I could either get out of her kitchen or learn how to cook. So what is it that you want that she used to make for you? Because I can make it and I'll drive down from Austin every day."

The former president went through a litany of foods, asking if she could make each one. When she said yes, "all of a sudden I went up in the world. It meant a lot to me. Though I'm sure it didn't mean much to his cardiologist."

————

IN 1959, JAMES Jeffries was just seventeen years old when he joined a family tradition and started working in the White House kitchen. His uncles Charles, John, and Sam Ficklin were never far away if he needed them. "When I went to work down there, they used to give me a five-gallon bucket of ice cream every day and I ate ice cream all day long. They were trying to fatten me up!"

His job was to put out the desserts: "They didn't have all of these fancy desserts back then, they only had vanilla ice cream and we'd sprinkle some chocolate on top. I had fun working." He worked in the kitchen for about a year before he moved upstairs to become a pantry helper.

Jeffries, now seventy-four, was born in Virginia. His mother had to drive from their home near Warrenton to give birth to him at the Freedmen's Hospital, which provided medical care to the African American community in the area. He was aware that the lingering racism of the time also existed inside the White House. "Back in the day white folks always thought they were superior to black folks," Jeffries said during an interview in his Washington row house. "I would not let nobody talk to me any kind of way."

At the end of each week, Jeffries had to give Executive Chef Henry Haller a voucher with his hours to sign so that he could get paid. "Some part-time chef came in and he looked at my sheet and saw that I was making more money than he made," Jeffries said. The newly hired white worker went to Chief Usher Gary Walters and asked how an African American pot washer could be making more money than he was.

Jeffries was furious when he learned about the complaint. The answer was simple: "I was putting in more hours. There were a lot of times when I'd be working two or three hours after they'd all gone home." He approached Haller and said, "Henry, how would you feel if you had a young guy come in starting at the same salary as you? I've been working here years before this guy was even thought of. I don't want to watch my pay go backward."

Haller replied: "You're right about that."

Jeffries remembers the scene from decades ago vividly. "It was funny, that day we had some mats on the floor that were about an inch thick or so and he stood on the edge of the mat rocking back and forth and said 'Jimmy, let me think about this.' He walked over to where the oven was and he said, 'Jimmy, how do you figure you have the right to talk to me like you're talking to me?'"

"I put my pants on the same way you put yours on. Why shouldn't I talk to you? I'm telling you the way I feel," Jeffries replied.

Haller looked at him and said, "Jimmy, you aren't going to ever have to worry about your money. Not as long as I'm here." And he was as good as his word.

———

THE WHITE HOUSE has long been used to showcase American talent. The Kennedys invited the American Ballet Theatre to perform in the East Room, and when the Clintons were in office, Eric Clapton, B. B. King, and Yo-Yo Ma all performed there.

In 1969, twenty-three-year-old Tricia Nixon invited the Temptations, the chart-topping Motown group, to perform. Jeffries remembers how the members of the band lingered in the Old Family

Dining Room with the serving staff when they weren't onstage, because "they could relate to us and have a personal conversation."

"I got to see them, I got to shake hands and party with them," Jeffries says. "They didn't stay out in the parlors, they came in the back because at the time most all of us in the back were black," he said. "James Brown and the [Famous] Flames—they all came back there." The residence workers made the stars more than welcome: "Whatever food we'd have back there, they'd have that food and drinks and stuff." That night in 1969, while they were chatting, the band invited Jeffries to bring his children to come play at the pool at their hotel in the Washington suburb of Rockville, Maryland. "I didn't, that's the only thing I regret. I just got busy."

Otis Williams, the last surviving original member of the legendary Motown group, told me that they made it a rule not to talk politics when they performed at the White House. "Our mind-set is just to entertain. We don't go there with politics in our mind. We strictly go there to perform."

Williams does not remember the specifics of that night in 1969—he has performed at the White House at least half a dozen times—but he does remember watching the African American staff at work. "They didn't show any disgust about the way they were treated. They were consummate professionals." While he and his bandmates had certainly experienced racism outside the White House, the singer recalled, he never felt it when he performed there.

Williams says that performing in front of President Obama was a special honor: "We never would have imagined—in our lifetime anyways—[that we would] see a black man be president."

For Jeffries, having the Obamas in the White House makes him want to keep working: "That just makes me feel like, 'Okay, I'll go to work as often as I can.'"

CHAPTER VIII

Backstairs Gossip and Mischief

I'm loyal to doing my job for the family, but I'm going to go back and say,
"Do you know what they did today? I can't believe they said that!"

—BILL HAMILTON, HOUSEMAN AND STOREROOM MANAGER, 1958–2013

The staff is discreet, but they're also human. They naturally swap stories over lunch, not only sharing important information but also bonding over the incredible events they witness and, sometimes, the inherently funny situations they get into.

One of Social Secretary Bess Abell's favorite stories involved the White House china. In 1966, the Johnsons decided to order a new china service. Lady Bird worked closely with designers from Tiffany & Company and the manufacturers Castleton China to create designs that reflected her commitment to the beautification of America's roadways and parklands. The dinner plates feature an eagle, and the borders of each plate were decorated with different American wildflowers. The dessert plates showcased the state flower of each of the fifty states.

When the china finally arrived it was breathtaking, Abell recalled—except for the dessert plates. The state flowers were ugly and unformed. "They looked like puppies had squatted in them." She laughed, as though she'd seen them just yesterday. At the time, though, it was not so funny. She was horrified. Abell ran to show them to J. B. West. (West was a favorite of both Abell and Jacqueline Kennedy. "He was divine," Abell recalls. "He made the best frozen daiquiris—one of the reasons he and Mrs. Kennedy got along so well!")

West's daiquiris, she said, "fueled one of the great little extravaganzas" at the White House. Because standards required that anything that was not perfect would have to be destroyed, a set of replacements were ordered—and then the staff found a clever way to destroy the faulty plates. Instead of throwing them in the Potomac River (a longtime graveyard for broken White House china), they decided to have some fun. Abell, West, and a few others went down to the bomb shelter with the plates—and a pitcher of daiquiris. They hung bull's-eyes on the wall with the names—and in some cases caricatures—of their least favorite West Wing staffers and threw the plates at them.

"It was better than a Greek wedding."

———

IN 1975, FORMER residence worker Traphes Bryant became one of the first insiders to expose Kennedy's now-famous philandering in a book. Most of the workers had known about it at the time, but they had resolved to keep the secret to protect the institution of the American presidency. According to the Kennedys' press secretary, Pierre Salinger, the workers were explicitly asked "not to engage in publicity which might adversely reflect on the White House as a national monument." And, though he said he never signed a non-disclosure agreement, Carpenter Milton Frame remembered: "We were told not to talk to the press or the news media when I was hired." Another staffer was asked to sign a piece of paper the day he retired that said he wouldn't write a memoir until a grace period had passed—the White House suggested a whopping twenty years.

As Bryant's book revealed, President Kennedy took advantage of his wife's long absences. She spent as much time away from the confines of the White House as possible, preferring to retreat to Glen Ora, a four-hundred-acre farm they leased in Virginia's horse country. (They later built a house nearby that she named Wexford after the county in Ireland where the president's ancestors came from.)

When she was away, the president liked swimming nude in the heated indoor White House pool, built in 1933 as part of President Roosevelt's therapy regimen to treat his polio. Kennedy often rendezvoused there with his female paramours, some of whom worked as secretaries in the White House. When he noticed male residence workers peering in at the pool through the glass door, he demanded that the door be frosted. (The president would ask the cooks to prepare some food and drinks—small sausages with bacon and daiquiris—and then dismiss them for the rest of the day. The sausages were kept in a portable warmer and the daiquiri pitcher was chilled in the refrigerator so guests could help themselves. "I can take care of it," he'd tell the kitchen staff.)

Once, a staffer was asked by an usher to fix a problem with the pool. Since that kind of work was usually saved for times when the first family wasn't around, the residence worker assumed that no one would be there. When he opened the pool door, he was shocked to see Kennedy adviser and close friend Dave Powers sitting by the pool—naked—with two of Kennedy's secretaries. The mortified staffer ran out and immediately assumed he would be fired. Nothing was ever said about the incident, however, and the story would remain a family secret for years.

The residence workers knew that when Jackie Kennedy was away the second floor was off limits. One night, though, it slipped

Bryant's mind when he took the elevator to the third floor to check on an appliance. The elevator stopped at the second floor accidentally. "I could hear lovey-dovey talk," he said. Another colleague saw a naked woman walking out of the kitchen when he went upstairs to see if the gas was turned off. "When Jackie was away, riding the elevator was hazardous duty," Bryant recalled.

Everyone backstairs raised an eyebrow when they heard one female political staffer giving her family a tour of the second floor. When she got to the president's bedroom, she "pretended she didn't know where it was and had never seen it before." In fact, she'd been there many times.

Bryant never told anyone outside of the White House—not even his wife—about Kennedy's affairs while the president was still in office. But downstairs they couldn't help but gossip. They needed to know how to conduct themselves, and sharing stories helped them figure out which hallways to avoid.

Johnson too generated gossip among the staff. He liked to corner the prettiest girl in the room at a party and try to kiss her on the cheek. By the end of the night he'd often have lipstick marks on his face. An embarrassed Lady Bird, who was sometimes in the same room, would plead with her husband, "You're wanted over there, Lyndon. You're neglecting some of your friends."

Rumor had it that Johnson even "inherited" two female reporters from Kennedy. "He would mention one or the other to me as 'all woman' or 'a lot of woman' and even accord them the ultimate compliment he ordinarily reserved for his favorite dog, Yuki, telling me they were 'pretty as a polecat,'" Bryant wrote. In a sign of the times, Lady Bird stoically stood by as her husband flagrantly humiliated her in public.

Ironically, Johnson was a possessive husband. One day Bryant, who was originally hired as an electrician, was told to go to Lady

Bird's room and install an extension cord for her manicure table. The outlet was behind a dresser where the first lady happened to be sitting. Bryant had to lie on the floor almost underneath her to plug in the cord.

Johnson walked in just as he was getting up off the floor. The president's mouth was "wide open" and he had the expression of "a jealous husband." Bryant stammered: "Mr. President, I was just putting in an extension cord for Mrs. Johnson's manicure table."

Lady Bird seemed to enjoy turning the tables for once.

————

SOMETIMES WHITE HOUSE guests want to bring a piece of history home with them.

Usher Skip Allen worked during state dinners, monitoring the south end of the State Dining Room to make sure no one's wineglass was empty. He always had a service of silverware and extra napkins at the ready, so that if someone dropped a fork he could appear almost instantly with a new one. And every now and then he noticed a guest surreptitiously slipping something into a handbag.

The help never asks someone directly whether they have taken a piece of china or silverware. They usually shame them into handing it over by playing dumb and asking politely. "When you pick up the plate, you ask for the knife and the fork, and if it's not there I say, 'Oh, maybe you dropped it.' We look around on the floor and they usually say, 'Well, here it is!'"

As Jackie Kennedy's wardrobe assistant, Anne Lincoln helped schedule hair appointments and buy clothes before she was promoted to head housekeeper and assigned to the impossible job of keeping food costs down. During the Kennedy administration, she says, stealing a piece of Camelot was common. By the end of one luncheon, she recalls, they were missing fifteen silver teaspoons, two silver knife dishes, and four silver ashtrays. "People come here with the idea that this is their property, so they just help themselves." She remembers one occasion when the soft-spoken first lady got aggressive. "One night she saw one of the guests slip a vermeil knife into his pocket," she said. After dinner, but before the guests had left, she asked Maître d' Charles Ficklin to count the vermeil silver services. When Charles reported that a knife was indeed missing, Mrs. Kennedy went right up to the stunned guest and asked for the knife back. He handed it to her without hesitation.

Jackie knew how a dinner table should be set and how a gourmet meal should taste, but she had no idea how to cook herself; Lincoln never saw her go into the kitchen to fix dinner or a late snack. President Kennedy was also hopeless in the kitchen. "The president loved soup before he went to bed and we have a can opener up there on the second floor—and I think it took him about eight months to learn how to use it," Lincoln said. "I don't think [the first lady] knew how to use it either." The butlers would laugh about it with Lincoln the next morning: "Oh, the poor president had trouble with the can opener again last night."

In mid-October 1963, a few weeks before her husband's assassination and shortly after the loss of a son named Patrick who was born prematurely that summer, Jackie called the chief usher into her bedroom. "Oh, Mr. West," she whispered in her childlike voice. "I've gotten myself into something. Can you help me get out of it?" She had invited a princess to stay overnight on the second floor, but she and the president decided they wanted some time alone instead. The devastating loss of their son had brought them closer together than ever. "Could you help us cook up something so we can get out of having her as a house guest?" she begged.

Jackie devised an elaborate ruse to get out of hosting. She told

West to make it look as though the Queens' and Lincoln Bedrooms—
the only two fit for royalty—were still being redecorated, so that her
guest couldn't possibly stay at the White House.

"Her eyes twinkled, imagining the elaborate deception," West
wrote.

West called Bonner Arrington, Reds's brother, who worked in
the Carpenter's Shop, and gave him the game plan:

"Bring drop cloths up to the Queens' Bedroom and Lincoln
Bedroom. Roll up the rugs and cover the draperies and chandeliers,
and all the furniture. Oh yes, and bring a stepladder."

Next he called the painters and asked for six paint buckets for
each room, including two (empty) buckets of off-white paint in each
room. And he asked for a few dirty paintbrushes. He also brought
in ashtrays full of cigarette butts so that it would look like a crew
had been hard at work. In a testament to the White House residence staff's hierarchy and mutual trust, no one involved in the
intricate scheme asked questions.

When she arrived, the princess was treated to a tour of the residence by the president. JFK pointed to the paint cans and drop
cloths in the Queens' Bedroom, "This is where you would have
spent the night if Jackie hadn't been redecorating again," he sighed
dramatically.

The next morning the first lady called West, giggling, to thank
him. "The president almost broke up when he saw those ashtrays."

————

The Arringtons were just shy of their sixtieth wedding anniversary when Reds passed away in 2007. "We had a good life," his wife,
Margaret, says fondly.

The stories he told her span his thirty-three years as a White
House plumber working for seven presidents; she clearly loves recounting them, as they help her to keep his memory alive. Some

of them involve presidential quirks—such as JFK's habit of asking Reds to fill his bathtub up with water the night before so that the next morning he could save time by just topping it off with hot water. Or the time when the Kennedys' nanny, Maud Shaw, called Reds in a panic after accidentally flushing John-John's diaper down the toilet.

Before his death, Reds did an interview recounting the time when he almost caught the wrath of Lyndon Johnson—and his job was saved only thanks to the intervention of Johnson's valet. One night Reds was working late on LBJ's infamous shower pumps, fixing them with pipe dope, a material used to tighten and seal pipes. The next morning he got a call from Johnson's valet.

"Reds, you and your men better get up there and clean the showerheads out. When the president got out of his shower this morning, he had blue pipe dope all over his back." He added, "I haven't said a word to him. I just took a towel and kind of patted him dry." But the president liked to get a massage every morning, so his valet had to call his masseuse to warn him not to say anything when he saw the president's blue-stained back. "Don't ask him, 'What's all this stuff' on his back," the valet instructed. "Just take something, alcohol or something, and just kind of clean him up. Because if he knows that there's pipe dope on his back, all the plumbers are going to be fired." Reds was thankful that Johnson never found out, and he went on to work several more years at his beloved White House.

Reds told his wife that when Queen Elizabeth II came to visit, the plumbers had to build a chair that would fit over the toilet seat for her majesty—almost like a throne. "Reds just said that was really a 'royal flush!'" She giggled.

When the queen came to visit Washington in 1976 she was already such a frequent guest that most of the residence staff were completely unfazed by her presence. Just before the white tie state dinner, the Fords, following tradition, met the queen and Prince Philip at the entrance to the Diplomatic Reception Room. They

Usher Chris Emery was asked to step in for an African American butler and shield President Reagan from a sudden downpour on the South Lawn during Soviet political leader Mikhail Gorbachev's historic visit to the White House in 1987. Chief Usher Gary Walters didn't want the White House to look like "the last plantation," Emery said.

Nancy Reagan examines a Christmas arrangement as President Reagan and White House florists Nancy Clarke (*third from right*) and Ronn Payne (*second from right*) look on, December 1987. Mrs. Reagan was a perfectionist who could be hard to please. One incident in particular led a beloved staffer to resign.

The Reagans in the Oval Office saying good-bye to Eugene Allen on his last day in 1986. The longtime butler and maître d' was the inspiration for the 2013 movie *Lee Daniels' The Butler*.

President George H. W. Bush and Houseman Linsey Little playing horseshoes on the White House lawn, June 24, 1990. Bush set up a horseshoe pitch next to the White House's outdoor swimming pool, where he'd play against residence staffers several times a week. Barbara Bush says she was especially sad to leave the White House because she knew the Clintons wouldn't continue the tradition.

Barbara Bush admires an arrangement in the Flower Shop with Florist Ronn Payne in 1989. Mrs. Bush would often stop by the shop in the early morning hours wearing only her robe over a bathing suit as she made her way to the White House pool for her daily swim.

Hillary Clinton does a last-minute touch-up in the Blue Room before the 1996 National Governors Association dinner as longtime butler James Jeffries stands by. The Clintons, like the Kennedys and the Johnsons before them, loved to entertain, which took a toll on the staff. Jeffries remembers telling a weary Bill Clinton, "You need to take a break."

The Clintons had an especially complicated relationship with the staff. Here President Clinton meets Executive Housekeeper Christine Limerick outside the linen room on the third floor of the residence on Inauguration Day, January 20, 1993. Maid Anita Castelo looks on.

Executive Pastry Chef Roland Mesnier with Hillary Clinton, March 8, 1996. Mesnier was there through the Lewinsky scandal, and he knew to expect a call from the first lady requesting her favorite dessert when she was having a particularly hard day.

Butler James Jeffries and his mother, Estelle, who is the sister of legendary White House butlers John and Charles Ficklin, at a White House Christmas party with President George W. Bush and Laura Bush, December 19, 2006.

President George W. Bush and his family loved Butler James Ramsey. And Ramsey loved them back. "If I live to be one hundred," Ramsey said, "I'll never forget his family."

President Obama confers with Chief Usher Stephen Rochon during one of their daily walks from the residence to the Oval Office, March 6, 2009. The president uses the time to register any household complaints. "If the water pressure wasn't right, or the Wi-Fi's not working, you've got to talk to somebody about it, right?" says former Obama aide Reggie Love.

Butler James Ramsey speaks with Sasha and Malia Obama in the State Dining Room as their grandmother Marian Robinson looks on. The Obamas have a unique relationship with the mostly African American butler staff.

More than fifty years after his first day at the White House, Doorman Wilson Jerman escorts the Obamas to the residence in the White House elevator, May 4, 2009. Jerman can remember standing underneath the White House's North Portico and hearing the *click, click* of horses' hooves as President Kennedy's flag-draped casket was taken from the White House to lie in state in the Capitol Rotunda.

escorted the royal couple to the elevator, on their way to spend a few minutes in the residence to chat before dinner.

As they waited for the elevator to take them upstairs, it suddenly opened to reveal the president's twenty-four-year-old son, Jack Ford, in jeans and a T-shirt—hardly appropriate attire for a royal greeting. Without missing a beat, the queen turned to Betty Ford and said: "Don't worry, Betty, I have one of those at home too." She was of course, referring to her son Prince Charles.

———

On December 21, 1970, in a scene that could never happen in today's age of heightened security, an unlikely guest stopped by the White House for a surprise visit. That was the day that Elvis Presley asked for an impromptu meeting with President Nixon (he had a bizarre request: he wanted to be sworn in as an undercover Federal agent), and ended up in the middle of a small office party by mistake.

Bill Cliber and a group of other staffers were singing "Happy Birthday to You" to one of the curators when he looked up to see Elvis and his bodyguards standing in the doorway of the tiny Ground Floor office.

"I just wanted to say happy birthday!" the country's most famous entertainer said.

The room went silent, mouths agape.

"Everyone was dumbfounded," Cliber recalled, still shaking his head in disbelief.

A minute later, a White House police officer tapped Presley on the shoulder and asked if any of his bodyguards was carrying a gun.

"Yeah," Presley replied.

"Could you leave it with me while you go see the president?"

"Sure," Presley said casually. "Ralph, give him your gun." Somehow Presley snuck in a Colt .45 pistol, which he gave the baffled president as a gift.

IVANIZ SILVA

Maid Ivaniz Silva spent most of her time in the family's inner sanctum on the second and third floors of the residence. Usually things ran like clockwork, with the maids keeping track of when the president and the first lady were off the second and third floors so that they could go in and work without disturbing them. But one evening things did not go as planned.

Usually the White House assigns around four maids to work in the residence: two in the morning and two in the evening. One day, Silva, now seventy-six, was in President Reagan's bedroom after 5:30 P.M., turning down the bed and closing the curtains. But when she went into the bedroom's sitting room, she couldn't believe what she saw: the president, sitting there reading the newspaper, without a stitch of clothing.

"I walk in the sitting room and there he was, naked, with the papers all around him!" she said. She rushed out of the room blushing before the president had time to say a word. He must have been as surprised as she was.

Later, she passed him in the hallway. Reagan looked at her with a twinkle. "Hey, who was that guy?" he asked.

"I don't know, sir," she said, laughing shyly.

Silva is still bemused by the incident. "He knew I saw him naked, so he had to say *something*."

Reagan may have been a bit embarrassed, but by most accounts he was fairly comfortable being naked, even when it may have unnerved the staff. About a month after Reagan's inauguration, Usher Skip Allen had finally completed his training and was cleared to work alone. On one of his first solo shifts he received an eyes-only package that had to be brought up to Reagan immediately for his signature.

Allen went up to the second floor in search of the president. He was nowhere to be found so he tracked down Reagan's valet to ask where the president was.

"He's in there," the valet said, pointing to a closed door. Allen knocked.

"Who is it?" Reagan shouted.

"It's Skip Allen from the Usher's Office. I have an eyes-only package for you."

"Come on in."

When he opened the door, Allen realized it was the president's bathroom. Reagan was just coming out of the shower.

"All he had on was a skim of water!" Allen remembers.

"Bring it over here," Reagan told him. The president signed his name and Allen went back downstairs.

Not long after, at around nine o'clock that same night, another eyes-only package came for the president. Allen was told that the president and first lady usually went to bed at nine o'clock, but he had no choice; he had to interrupt them.

He nervously went upstairs to track down the president again. This time he saw lights on in the Reagans' bedroom. His hands shaking, he knocked on their door.

"Who is it?" Nancy Reagan asked.

"It's Skip Allen from the Usher's Office. I have a package for the president."

"Come in."

Just then, the president was coming out of his dressing room wearing only his underwear.

"Oh, Ronnie, you could at least put on a robe," Nancy scolded him.

The president looked at her. "Oh, Mommy," he said, using his pet name for her, "don't worry about it. He's already seen me naked once today. We're old friends." They all burst out laughing.

The Reagans' son, Ron, said that his parents' relaxed, unselfconscious nature around the staff probably made working there easier. The Reagans were used to having housekeepers around, and they never worried about what the help thought of them. "It's hard to be in the position of a butler, or someone like that, if the person who you're trying to serve is very self-conscious about the fact that you're there. But my parents were not."

Ron also acknowledges, however, that his parents' nonchalance could be interpreted as dehumanizing the staff. "It says they don't count, because they aren't worth making someone feel self-conscious." There does seem to have been a distinction between the Reagans' cavalier attitude toward the staff and George and Barbara Bush's equally comfortable but more respectful attitude toward them. When President Reagan stopped and chatted with workers, it was usually to talk about himself or to make a joke. The Bushes would ask workers about their families and express concern about the amount of time they spent with them at home, recognizing that they enjoyed a life beyond the White House gates—a gesture that may not have occurred to the Reagans.

Some White House stories take on a different light in retrospect. Toward the end of Reagan's presidency, one butler recalls, he saw the president unaware of what was happening around him at a crucial time. "The movie star was the president," he said, "and I was working down in the kitchen. The next thing I know, I looked around and smoke was coming out of the vents." A butler working on the fireplace had forgotten to open the damper, so smoke was billowing back into the room Reagan was sitting in. "I heard the fire truck and people came rushing in and ran upstairs to the second floor."

Not long thereafter, one of the firefighters, a woman, came back downstairs, laughing. "What's so funny?" the butler asked her, surprised that she wasn't more concerned.

Barely able to answer through her laughter, she told him: "Do you know the president was sitting up there as if nothing was going on? Just watching TV, reading his newspapers."

"He didn't even realize," the butler recalled.

At the time, no one knew that the president may already have been suffering from the beginnings of Alzheimer's disease. In the moment, it seemed like just another quirk of a president who was rarely flustered in the eyes of the staff.

———

SOME OF THE most enduring gossip comes from staffers who cannot get along with each other. Working at the White House can sometimes create big egos and foster big personalities. Many of the staffers who get hired, especially as chefs, are highly accomplished professionals who consider themselves the best at what they do. This kind of competitive spirit can lead to professional rivalries—the most glaring recent example being the open feud between Executive Chef Walter Scheib and Executive Pastry Chef Roland Mesnier.

Eleven years of working side by side did nothing to diminish the animosity between the two men, which they feel just as acutely now, a decade after they both left the White House. Mesnier, now seventy years old, was hired by the Carters; Scheib, ten years his junior, was hired by the Clintons. They disliked each other so much that they often refused to discuss the dishes they were preparing. Scheib would simply hand Mesnier the weekly menus so that Mesnier could plan accompanying desserts. Scheib admits that he's less gregarious than Mesnier and runs his kitchen more like a military commander. ("If I wanted friends," he says, "I'd go volunteer at a youth group.") Mesnier, who presents his creations with gusto, is an artistic Frenchman who gave all of his colleagues a cake of their choosing each Christmas, making dozens and dozens of fruit cakes, stollen, and pound cakes each year. ("The staff were not just other workers for me," he says, "they were my family.")

Scheib scorns Mesnier for his books and television appearances, which he sees as spotlight-hugging. "He has made himself bigger than the families, and this is unfortunate." Mesnier claims that the comparatively trim Scheib (who looks more like a business executive than a chef) was hired because he's attractive and articulate, a good spokesman for Hillary Clinton's campaign to promote healthy American cuisine. "Walter and I, we did not get along because I knew he couldn't cook," he says dismissively.

"The ushers would joke that if Roland and I were spotted having a beer somewhere everyone should fall down on their knees and pray because the apocalypse is clearly upon us," says Scheib.

Mesnier did show great affection for Scheib's predecessor, French Chef Pierre Chambrin, but the Clintons fired Chambrin after he refused to exchange his heavy French menu for a healthier one featuring American cuisine. Hillary Clinton wanted to promote healthy American food, especially as she embarked on her effort to revamp health care. But Chambrin said the real reason he was let go was about appearances, not cuisine. "I am French, I am fat, and my English is terrible. I didn't fit the profile they wanted to show to the American people."

For the Clintons, Chambrin told me, "food was fuel" and nothing more. "From the beginning, I knew I was doomed with the Clintons. I did what they wanted. I even tried to please them with no butter, no fat, make the menu without French words. But how do you say sauté without using the word *sauté*, for instance?"

Chambrin hated the Clintons' casual relationship with food. Unlike the Bushes, the Clintons wanted to eat in the kitchen. "When we changed from the Bushes to the Clintons, we went from the rich to the grits."

When Scheib was hired as Chambrin's replacement, the cramped Ground Floor kitchen became an incredibly uncomfortable place to work. Chef John Moeller started working at the White House soon after Mesnier got his own small pastry kitchen and says without a hint of humor, "If he had stayed in that main kitchen and worked with us side by side, there might have been blood."

CHAPTER IX

Growing Up in the White House

I ask you to consider the effect of saying good night to a
boy at the door of the White House in a blaze of floodlights with a
Secret Service man in attendance. There is not much you can do
except shake hands, and that's no way to get engaged.

—Margaret Truman

When twelve-year-old Chelsea Clinton moved into the White House in 1993, Steve Ford sent her a letter. His advice: make friends with the Secret Service, as they might become your only link to the outside world. He says that he had it relatively easy, with so many siblings to share the experience. For Chelsea, an only child, living in the White House would be harder. And of course that ended up being the case when she had to endure the embarrassment of her father's very public indiscretions without any siblings to help shoulder the burden. "I thought she always had a much, much tougher situation than the other families that usually had two or three siblings." Looking back on Chelsea's time in the White House, though, Ford says now, "I just thought she handled it wonderfully."

When children move into the White House, the residence staff wants to protect them. They have seen what it's like for other children growing up in the residence and they want to help them live their childhoods as normally as possible. Along with the extra responsibility of looking after children, though, the staff often relishes having a rambunctious toddler or a fun-loving high schooler around. Presidential children can bring a degree of warmth and innocence to a household, lightening the often-stressful atmosphere of the executive mansion.

Storeroom Manager Bill Hamilton watched generations of presidential offspring learn to live in the bubble of the White House. The younger the children were, he says, the easier it was for them to adjust to their claustrophobic new lives. Caroline and John-John Kennedy found it relatively easy to be themselves within the mansion's walls; they were so young when they came to the White House that they didn't really know anything different. For Chelsea Clinton, and for Sasha and Malia Obama, being a teenager in the White House means coping with adolescent angst while living in the spotlight. And older children, like the Fords, Luci and Lynda Johnson, and Barbara and Jenna Bush, may have had it hardest of all, in Hamilton's view, when they realized they would have to give up a level of freedom they were used to, and would not have it back again until their fathers left office.

"Once you're up in that college age where you've been out there drinking beer, running with guys, going to parties and all that, it makes a big difference," he said.

George W. Bush's daughters—affectionately described as "wild little girls" by their grandmother, Barbara Bush, when they were younger—were already familiar with the residence by the time their father was elected; they had played hide-and-seek when their grandparents lived there, and spent time in the Flower Shop making arrangements. During their father's presidency, they confided in Usher Nancy Mitchell about their boyfriend problems. (Jenna would later admit to a "little hanky-panky" on the White House roof.) Staffers say the girls acted like typical nineteen-year-olds, and Jenna grew so attached to the residence staff that she asked Head Florist Nancy Clarke to do the flowers for her Texas wedding.

Still there will always be certain constraints that come with life in that particular bubble. "It's a miserable life for a teenager," said Usher Nelson Pierce. "It was very difficult to be confined, knowing that you couldn't do anything without [the Secret Service] right on your tail."

––––––––

Not since the Kennedys' departure have such young children lived in the White House. When the Obamas moved in, Malia was ten years old and Sasha was only seven. Now sixteen and thirteen, the girls have spent six years growing up with a slew of maids, butlers, and chefs, in a house with its own private movie theater, tennis and basketball court, and swimming pool. And that's just their day-to-day life: that does not include the elegant dinners and catered parties they sometimes get to attend, or the private Jonas Brothers concert on the night of their father's first inauguration.

Barbara and Jenna Bush, who graduated from high school the year their father was elected, gave Malia and Sasha a full tour before they left, including stops in the movie theater and the bowling alley and even a few secret hallways. Clearly enjoying the idea of another younger pair of sisters taking their place, they told them to slide down the banisters every once in a while, advice that Sasha Obama, the more bubbly of the sisters, no doubt enjoyed.

Like the Kennedys, the Obamas are committed to having their children lead normal lives. Florist Bob Scanlan, who retired in 2010, describes seeing a scene that plays out in so many American house-holds on Sunday mornings: air mattresses splayed out on the floor of the Solarium from a sleepover the night before.

The girls get dessert only on weekends, but when their grand-mother, Marian, is in charge, they splurge, eating ice cream and popcorn. She "really gives the family their privacy. She lives on the third floor for the most part, [and] in the time that I was there took her meals separately. The girls eat with their mother and father in their own space on the second floor and Mrs. Robinson eats on the third floor," Scanlan said. "I'm going home," Marian would say before dinner as she walked upstairs to her private suite, giving her daughter time alone with her husband and children.

"She had fresh flowers put in her living room and her bedroom. She was always very kind, very gracious, very appreciative of ev-erything that she got." When Scanlan came in to replace a floral arrangement, she would often tell him not to bother. "That's fine, but the other flowers still look good to me," she'd say.

Michelle asked the florists to label all the flowers in the arrange-ments in their living quarters so that she and her daughters could learn the different names. The first lady also asked beloved long-time butler Smile "Smiley" Saint-Aubin, who was from Haiti and spoke beautiful French, to speak in his native language when serv-ing her daughters so that they could start learning the language. (He passed away in 2009.)

Scanlan wanted the Obamas to have a special first Christmas season at the White House (they spend the holiday itself in Hawaii), so he made boxwood Christmas trees and put one on Malia's dresser and one on Sasha's mantel.

Malia especially liked hers. When Scanlan went into her room to check on the tree he found a sticky note waiting for him: "Florist: I really like my tree. If it's not too much to ask could I please have lights on it? If not, I understand." Her sign-off was a heart. Scanlan took the note off the dresser and brought it down to the Flower Shop. "Now you tell me, how could I *not* put lights on that tree?" He laughed.

Staffers provide extra nurturing because they know what scrutiny these children face. In 2014, Sasha and Malia came under attack from a Republican House staffer during the annual White House turkey pardon ceremony. "Dress like you deserve respect, not a spot at a bar," wrote Elizabeth Lauten in a Facebook post. Lauten, who was communications director for Republican representative Stephen Fincher at the time, was referring to the girls' short skirts. Her disparaging comments came under criticism from Democrats and Republicans alike who mostly agree that the children of sitting presidents should be off-limits. Lauten resigned because of the media firestorm; the episode reinforces the incredible strain of growing up in the White House under constant surveillance. The glare of the spotlight has only intensified with an endless news cycle and the rise of social media.

———

Caroline and John-John Kennedy, in turn, were the youngest children to live in the White House since Theodore Roosevelt's brood famously wreaked havoc there at the turn of the twentieth century. Caroline was three years old, and her brother just two months old, when their parents moved into the residence. Jackie Kennedy desperately wanted to raise unspoiled children; she made them sign thank-you notes when they were invited to other children's parties (young John-John merely scribbled) and always brought them down to the kitchen after their birthday parties to thank the staff. Caroline and John-John learned the meaning of "no" at just two years old, said Letitia Baldrige; when introduced to Secretary of Defense Robert McNamara's wife, they looked her straight in the eye and said, "How do you do, Mrs. McNamara?" (Though in John-John's case it may have been more like "Mrs. Nama.")

"It was 'How do you do' day and night, not only to Mommy and Daddy's friends but also to the ushers, butlers, maids, policemen, Secret Service, and gardeners, and the people in the kitchen and in the butler's pantry—whomever they happened to pass," said Baldrige.

Unlike first ladies before her, Jackie Kennedy didn't allow her children to address the butlers by their last names only; she considered that rude, especially since they were speaking to older, dignified gentlemen, most of whom had been working in the mansion for decades. "It was, 'Mr. Allen,'" said Curator Jim Ketchum, referring to Eugene Allen. "They called Preston Bruce 'Mr. Bruce.' She was not about to have them say 'Bruce' or 'Allen.'"

Sometimes, though, when Jackie wasn't around, Caroline and John-John treated the staff with a familiarity that their mother might not have approved of. Usher Nelson Pierce's favorite memory in all of his twenty-six years working at the White House involved simply reading a story to John-John. "Mrs. Kennedy's stereo wasn't working right, and I had to escort one of the Signal Corps men upstairs to work on it," he recalled. "John-John picked up a book and brought it over to me and told me he wanted me to read it."

Pierce did as he was told and sat on the edge of the sofa. He thought there was no way such an active little boy would sit still long enough to actually make it through the book. "I thought he'd stand beside me while I read the book, but no. He got up and then got down and pushed me in the chest and said, 'Sit back, sit back!' So I put my arm around him and we read the book. As soon as I read the story he jumped down, took the book, and put it back where it was." For Nelson, spending time with the Kennedy children was a welcome break and a reminder of his four children at home.

One evening, the Kennedys' nanny, Maud Shaw, called down to Pierce for help. She was in the Family Dining Room on the second floor and John-John hadn't quite finished dinner. Meanwhile

Caroline, who was already done eating, was down on the floor trying to do a somersault—to no avail. She looked up at Pierce when he walked in.

"Mr. Pierce, I have a terrible time. My legs either go to the right or they go to the left."

"Caroline, think very hard about making your feet go straight over your head," he told her.

Her next attempts were much improved.

"Mr. Pierce, do somersaults with me!" she begged.

Pierce laughed at the memory, "Fortunately, Maud Shaw came to my rescue so I didn't have to do somersaults with Caroline on the dining room floor!"

Decades later, Chef Walter Scheib explained how the staff viewed the first family. "While a state dinner is the most high-profile thing you do, at the same time, the day of the state dinner, you might get a phone call from the residence saying Chelsea or one of the Bush twins wants a bowl of oatmeal or blueberries or something, and suddenly that becomes your priority. It isn't about cuisine, it's about offering first families a little island of normal in a very, very crazy world."

Sometimes, what the first family wants is mundane and frustrating for the skilled chefs, especially when there are kids living in the residence. John Moeller remembers one morning when he and a newly hired chef were making pancakes for Chelsea Clinton. The new hire spotted real maple syrup in the refrigerator but Moeller told him that Chelsea prefers the imitation maple syrup that most kids eat. The new chef fought him, insisting that the real thing is always better. Eventually, Moeller relented and sent the butlers up with the high-end syrup. Two minutes later it came back with a request from the first daughter for the fake stuff. The first family's preferences override everything else.

Residence staff must provide a safe place for the president's children to be themselves. Johnson's eldest daughter, Lynda Bird Johnson Robb, remembered finding solace in the residence staff at a time when outsiders could never be fully trusted. "The people who worked there, they were just wonderful. I'm sure everybody who's lived there has appreciated them and thought how lucky we are to be surrounded by people who want to help us and who are not trying to get anything from us. They were not going to go sell us out."

Lynda met her husband, Charles "Chuck" Robb, when he was a military social aide at the White House. His job was to make sure the president's guests were comfortable at receptions and dinners, chatting with partygoers who were nervous to meet the president and first lady, and directing them to their seats. No one outside the staff knew that Lynda and Robb were dating. After he was done working, Robb would rush up to the Solarium to play bridge with Lynda. The butlers saw them, of course, but they guarded her privacy absolutely.

Robb was first in his Marine Corps officers Basic School at Quantico, Virginia; he earned a Bronze Star in Vietnam, and later went on to become governor of Virginia and serve two terms in the Senate. When Robb was deployed, Lynda was pregnant with their first daughter, Lucinda. While she was lying awake at night, sick with worry about her husband, she could hear the shouts of Vietnam War protestors outside her bedroom window.

Lynda had Caroline Kennedy's former room, facing Pennsylvania Avenue; there was nowhere to hide. Her younger sister, Luci, lived in what was once John-John's bedroom. Between them was the small room that had belonged to Maud Shaw, which they converted into a walk-in closet for their out-of-season wardrobes.

President and Mrs. Johnson's room overlooked the South Lawn, so they didn't hear the shouting quite as clearly, but Lynda and her sister shuddered at the angry protests. "It was distressing to Luci and to me when you could hear the people yelling from across the street all day and night about the war, particularly since both of our husbands were over there. They were sacrificing, and I was pregnant, and they would say things that were very hurtful about my father. I knew how much he wanted to end the war."

Curator Betty Monkman remembers gathering in the Usher's Office and looking out at the protestors. She'd turn to her older colleagues and say, "Those could be your children standing in the park."

"You can't escape what's happening around you there," she said. "It feels like you're in a little cocoon, but you're very aware of everything that's happening outside." On a bitterly cold day, President Johnson—desperate to quell the protestors' rage—even asked the butlers to bring them all hot coffee.

"I was quite young then, in my late twenties," Monkman recalls, "and I would go to parties and I would not tell people where I worked, because if I did the reaction to me would be so negative. So I would say, 'I work for the Park Service,' because they'd want to vent to me about their politics. Maybe I felt the same way, but I didn't want to hear it!"

On Tuesday through Saturday, parts of the Ground Floor and the State Floor of the White House were open to the public, and during those years of constant public protests, the lack of privacy grew unbearable for Lynda. "Even after the assassination we didn't have the kind of security [we should have had], and so the tourists would be there right under our window early," she said. "They would be right under my window and they would be saying, 'Stand over here, Myrtle,' and I would be trying to sleep!"

Texas first lady Nellie Connally once told Lynda that she'd often thought about dropping a water balloon on tourists from the window of the governor's mansion.

"I laughingly said I wanted to do the same," Lynda says. "I never did."

It wasn't the affable tourists who were the real problem, however; it was the protestors outraged by the continuation of the war who made life in the White House so difficult. Usher Nelson Pierce remembered once when "kids" on a public tour dumped vials of their own blood in the State Dining Room of the residence workers' beloved house. "We had to dry-clean the drapes." Sometimes visitors even unleashed cockroaches inside the White House. "We had to train the housekeeping staff on what to do if some of these situations occurred," Monkman said.

A pivotal moment for LBJ came when Lynda went to him in the middle of the night, in tears after seeing her husband off to Vietnam, and asked why Robb had to go to war. The president faltered, realizing that he had no answer. It wasn't long afterward that Johnson announced he would not be seeking reelection.

———

STEVE FORD WAS just a couple weeks away from starting his freshman year at Duke University in August 1974 when his father was suddenly thrust into the presidency.

"All of a sudden we all got ten Secret Service agents, and life changed. Trust me, at eighteen years old, that's not really the group you're hoping to hang out with."

Ford decided to forgo college and moved to Montana to work on a ranch and avoid the spotlight. Still, he spent two months at a time staying with his parents in a room on the third floor, where his three siblings also had rooms.

"The White House really belonged to the staff, because they were the ones who were there for four, five, six different administrations," he said. "The lease on the house was very temporary.

For some of us shorter than others!" (Ford's father spent fewer than three years in the White House, leaving in 1977.) But Ford remembers those years vividly. "It was truly like living in a museum," he says. "Everything dates back to Lincoln or Jefferson. I can remember moving in there—at home usually I put my feet up on the table where we lived in Alexandria, but Mom goes, 'Don't put your feet up there! That's Jefferson's table.'"

For the Ford family, moving into the White House was an earth-shattering change. For almost twenty years, while Gerald Ford was in Congress and even while he was vice president, they had lived in a four-bedroom, two-bathroom redbrick Colonial on a quarter-acre lot on Crown View Drive in Alexandria, Virginia, across the Potomac from the White House.

When Ford became vice president in December 1973, after Spiro Agnew's resignation, their two-car garage became home to his Secret Service detail, and bulletproof glass was installed in their master bedroom. (It wasn't until 1977 that the U.S. Naval Observatory became the vice president's official residence.)

Chief Usher Gary Walters later recalled how approachable the Fords were. Once he got a phone call from President Ford asking him to send someone to look at the shower in his bathroom in the White House because there was no hot water. It had been like that for a couple of days and he was just using the shower in his wife's bathroom. But no rush, Ford told him.

The Fords had to wait to move into the White House for seven days after their father became president because the Nixons needed time to move their things out. When they finally moved in, the president and first lady brought their favorite chairs from home—his was a comfortable leather chair—for the private sitting room off their bedroom.

Susan Ford, the youngest of President Ford's four children,

remembers begging her parents to let her redecorate her room and switch out the blue shag carpet. They wouldn't let her because the cost would come out of their own pockets. "My father didn't believe in mortgages; he was truly a Depression baby," she told me.

Like most normal kids, the four Ford children, all in their teens or early twenties, could not wait to cause trouble. On the day they moved into the White House, Steve Ford called his best friend, Kevin Kennedy, who lived around the corner from him in Alexandria. "Kevin, we finally moved in. You gotta come over—you gotta see this place."

He cleared his friend through security and gave him a tour, showing him his room on the third floor and taking him to the Solarium, with its rooftop access. They took out a stereo and blasted Led Zeppelin's "Stairway to Heaven" on a turntable on the roof of the White House. "That was my first night in the White House," Ford said. "Eugene, the butler, knew what we did, and I was so thankful that he never ratted me out to my parents. The staff knows everything you do."

But they try not to judge, Ford said. In part because they greatly sympathize with all the children who do some growing up in the residence. "There were no moral billy clubs."

———

FOR GENERATIONS OF presidential children, living in the White House was both a blessing and a curse. Margaret Truman called the executive residence "the great white jail," and some other children even took pains to escape.

Susan Ford recalls sneaking out, making her famously softhearted father furious. In a practical joke gone wrong, Ford somehow managed to make a run for her car, which was sitting at the semicircle on the South Lawn ("You always left your keys in the car in case they have to move it," she said) and drove straight out of the White House gate. The Secret Service agents assigned to her couldn't shut the gate or chase after her because her mother's car was driving in at the same time.

Susan picked up a friend and went to a Safeway parking lot, where they shared a six-pack of beer. Eventually she went to a pay phone and told the Secret Service agents she would return to the White House by 7:00 P.M. (She had to come home to pick up Hall & Oates concert tickets.) As soon as she returned, her father wanted to see her.

"The fun is over," she remembered thinking. "Now reality sets in."

The president said he was disappointed in her. He must have been furious, knowing that the radical Symbionese Liberation Army (the group that had kidnapped heiress Patty Hearst) had threatened to take her hostage. Susan was the only Ford child to have Secret Service protection before her father became president. What was a lighthearted adventure could have turned into a national crisis if she had been kidnapped. (Susan clearly didn't mind the Secret Service that much; later she would marry a former member of her father's protective detail.)

Like his sister, Steve Ford tried to live a normal life. It didn't always work. "When we moved in, I had a yellow Jeep that I drove," he said, laughing at his own naïveté. "I used to pull in and I'd park it in front of the diplomatic entrance on the driveway. I'd go upstairs and I'd look out my window and it would be gone." The staff didn't think a Jeep was an appropriate car to park in front of the White House. "Every time I'd come home they would move it around back and kind of hide it. I'd get frustrated and I'd go down and move it out front again and they'd move it back."

———

AMY CARTER, WHO was nine years old when she moved in, left her mark on the White House—literally. Her name is written in Magic

Marker on the wall between the elevator shaft and the second-floor service elevator. "Amy opened the door and stuck her hand between the elevator shaft and wrote her name," said Operations Supervisor Tony Savoy.

Amy wasn't content staying upstairs in the residence, Savoy recalled. She wanted to explore. "She was curious. You have this great big house, all these doors, let's look in 'em."

The Carters famously sent their daughter to public school in Washington, D.C. It was hard for a girl trailed by Secret Service agents to fit in, especially when her teacher kept her indoors during recess in a misguided effort to protect her. By the time they got to the White House, her mother Rosalynn recalls, Amy—their fourth child and only daughter—was used to being an outsider. "It was what she knew, because she was three when we moved to the governor's mansion. It was not different for her. Mary came to be with us. It was just her life."

Nanny Mary Prince helped Amy feel more comfortable with it all, Rosalynn said, but the freckle-faced girl knew that her life was different. Back in the Georgia governor's mansion, she'd had even less privacy: there, just getting to the kitchen meant braving a wave of tourists. But Amy was a self-possessed child, so much so that she sometimes seemed oblivious to outsiders. "When she was three years old," her mother says, "everybody made a big fuss over the baby when they saw her and she'd just walk straight through and look straight ahead. I remember when she went to school the first day in Washington everybody was so distressed because Amy looked so lonely. That was just her normal life."

When they first moved into the White House, Rosalynn says, Amy sometimes went downstairs to the State Floor during the public tours, but "people made such a fuss over her" that she stopped. When the tours were done for the day, she returned—and went roller-skating through the East Room.

Members of the residence staff were fond of the feisty little girl. Mary Prince often called Nelson Pierce at his desk to see when he would come over to the mansion to tune Amy's violin ("Music and baseball were the things I lived for," Pierce said.). Butler James Jeffries said Amy would sometimes ask him for help with her homework when he was upstairs in the family kitchen. Life lived in government housing—albeit elegant government housing—was all Amy knew, and the staff were like family to her. One day she went to all the different shops in the residence with her Secret Service agent to ask the staff for money to help sponsor her in a walk, said Curator Betty Monkman. "We were her neighborhood. She was coming to solicit. Then we pledged a certain amount—and then she came back to collect!" said Monkman. "She couldn't go out in the street and do that."

The Carters tried to provide some sense of stability and normalcy for Amy. Monkman remembers passing the China Room near the Curator's Office one day when she saw Amy and her friends carving pumpkins—and "there was President Carter, down on the floor with them."

Mary Prince insists that Amy was not tainted by her celebrity— contrary to some who said she insulted foreign guests by reading a book during a state dinner. "She was not a spoiled brat. She really never tried to get her way. She was just a young kid having fun."

Chef Mesnier describes Amy as a whimsical little girl who was not overawed by the majesty of the White House. After school, she sometimes ran down to the kitchen to ask him to send up the ingredients for her favorite sugar cookies, which she liked to make herself in the small kitchen on the second floor and bring to school the next day. Often, though, after putting them in the oven, she would start roller-skating or playing in her treehouse and completely forget about them; when the smell of burned cookies wafted through the hallway, at first a slew of Secret Service agents would run to the

Pastry Kitchen thinking that that was the origin of the problem. Mesnier would look at the harried agents and just point upstairs. They would then go racing up to the second floor to open the windows and rescue the ruined cookies. The next morning Amy would usually come to the kitchen and tell the chef that she was supposed to take cookies to school and she didn't know what to do. When Mesnier asked her what happened to the ingredients he sent her the day before she would reply, blushing, "There was a small accident." (He got so used to this routine that, when Amy wandered into the kitchen the next morning to ask for some cookies to take to school, he would have a backup batch ready to go.)

The Carter children lived a charmed life even before coming to the White House—their father was a successful farmer who had served two terms as a Georgia state senator and one as Georgia's governor. Sometimes they seemed totally disconnected from the real world, especially from the people who served them every day.

One butler remembers chatting with one of Carter's sons, who was in his twenties at the time. He was sitting in the family kitchen reading an article in the newspaper about rising rent prices in Washington. He looked up from the paper at the butler and said: "I'm glad that I'm allowed to stay here in the White House."

The butler turned to him and said: "Yes. That's one reason I'm in here, working two jobs because the rent costs so much. I'm struggling." Carter's son was shocked. He couldn't believe this dignified man had to work two jobs just to pay the rent.

"You come outside and live with me and you'll see," the butler told him.

———

THE CLINTONS FIERCELY guarded their daughter Chelsea's privacy, and asked the media to limit their coverage of her to public events only. For the most part journalists complied. But the media had other ways of plunging her name into the news. In a 1992 "Wayne's World" skit on *Saturday Night Live*, Mike Myers, playing the goofy Wayne, jibed that adolescence "has been thus far unkind" to Chelsea, adding "Chelsea Clinton—not a babe." The skit enraged the Clintons, and the remarks were edited out of rebroadcasts. Meyers even wrote a letter of apology to the Clintons.

Like the Obamas and the Kennedys, the Clintons felt it was important not to let their children become spoiled in the White House. In fact, Chelsea often told the chef not to worry about cooking for her. She'd be making her own dinner: Kraft macaroni and cheese.

By and large, Chelsea was adored by the residence staff. Maid Betty Finney said she was like their own child—they felt protective of her. "Teenagers, you're thinking rudeness. That was never, ever Chelsea. I had never seen her be rude in the entire stint I had there," Finney said. "She wrote me a note thanking me for my services. That's just the way she was."

Still, Chelsea was a "normal" teenager in some ways. For starters, she hardly ever made her bed. And like all teenagers, she liked hanging out with her friends.

Well before *Downton Abbey* showed Lady Sybil getting cooking lessons from downstairs cook Mrs. Patmore, Chelsea Clinton and some friends from her posh private school, Sidwell Friends, did a sort of informal internship with the residence staff. (Years before, Jackie had taken five-year-old Caroline to the White House kitchen to bake tiny pink cupcakes from a toy baking set Caroline had gotten for her birthday.) Chelsea and her friends spent part of the day in each department, learning from the best how to cook, clean, and arrange flowers. She proudly showed her parents her flower arrangement—which was displayed in the Red Room—and made them try some of the meals she learned to prepare.

"Mrs. Clinton had decided they wanted Chelsea to be a little bit more self-sufficient and didn't necessarily want her going to the dining hall and out to restaurants each night," Executive Chef Walter Scheib recalls. "So I got a call from Mrs. Clinton asking if I would teach Chelsea how to cook." There was another factor at play: Chelsea was a vegetarian, and her mother wanted to make sure she would be able to prepare healthy food for herself when she was in college. The summer of her senior year in high school, before she went off to Stanford University, Chelsea wandered down to the kitchen to learn the beginning and intermediate levels of vegetarian cooking.

"She was an extremely quick study, and as everyone knows now she is very, very bright," Scheib said. Even at seventeen, Scheib said, she was acutely aware of the staff's sacrifice. "She's a very intense person who didn't take this opportunity lightly. She respected us tremendously in terms of us offering her our time."

At the end of their lessons, he gave her a chef's coat inscribed: CHELSEA CLINTON, FIRST DAUGHTER. The White House calligraphers even made her a diploma: "Walter Scheib's White House Cooking School." Later, Chelsea sent Scheib a note: "Thank you very much for letting me take your time. I hope I wasn't too much trouble."

"I think back to what I would have been like had I been the first son at seventeen," Scheib says now. "I was a bit of a jerk; she was so modest and understated and so thankful for all of the things we did. I remember Chelsea would call down for breakfast and say, 'If it's not too much trouble . . .' And I would say, 'Chelsea, it's not too much trouble. It's my job.'"

The butlers later told Scheib they'd overheard Chelsea talking with her mother about what she'd learned from him that day in the kitchen. "Mrs. Clinton and Chelsea were very, very close. The first lady would change her schedule if Chelsea was available for a meal."

The residence staff often saw this softer side of Hillary, counter to her hard-charging public persona. "In private she was a doting and caring and truly loving mother. She thought Chelsea was the be-all and end-all."

For Scheib, it was that kind of access to the first families that made his grueling job special. "This is what working at the White House is. Some will talk about, 'I made this cake,' or 'I made that soup,' or 'I arranged these flowers.' That's not what the job is. The real beauty of the job is getting to see these relationships. It was never about us. It's not about the pastry chef, it's not about the chef, it's not about the florist, it's not about the groundskeeper. It's about families."

———

No matter how friendly the staff become with the children of the residence, the line between the help and the family was always clear. "For all the fancy titles, we're domestic staff, we need to remember our place," said Scheib. During the Bush years, he said, "Our only job was to be sure that Jenna and Barbara had exactly what they wanted for lunch or that the president's meal coming back from church on Sunday was exactly as he wanted it."

They always wanted to impress the first family. For Hillary Clinton's fiftieth birthday, Mesnier created an over-the-top cake made of blown sugar balloons—with a hand-painted reproduction of her best-selling book *It Takes a Village*.

For Chelsea's sixteenth birthday, he struggled to think of something that would wow her and her parents. He did not know what to make for her and emphatically refused, in his heavy French accent, to "make a cake with flowers on it for a sixteen-year-old. I want something with meaning!"

Two days before her birthday, Mesnier still hadn't settled on the right idea for her cake. Then, on his commute to work, he heard on a radio show that Chelsea wanted a car and a driver's license for her birthday. That settled it. He made a handmade Washington, D.C., driver's license and a car made out of sugar. But the Clintons were celebrating her birthday at Camp David in Maryland's Catoctin Mountain Park about sixty miles north of the White House, so the cake had to be sent all the way out there—and Mesnier was so worried about the trip that he loaded the cake into the van himself and gave the driver strict instructions on how to handle it. "If you don't listen," he said, "you're going to have a problem." Then he made the driver promise to take a photo of the cake once it arrived.

———

IT MAY BE hard for some presidential children to adjust to life in the White House, but the residence staff is always happy to see them. They bring a levity and joyousness that is otherwise absent in the staid and elegant rooms. The second and third floors are cheerier when kids are running up and down the hallways. "Everybody was old when I got there," says Bill Hamilton, who started during the Eisenhower administration. When the Kennedy family arrived, however, the difference was like night and day. He remembers seeing Caroline and John-John playing with their menagerie of animals, including a pony named Macaroni that Caroline would ride on the South Lawn. "It was just so nice to see. You didn't think this would ever happen in the White House."

CHAPTER X

Heartbreak and Hope

I still can't talk about it.

—WENDY ELSASSER, FLORIST, 1985–2007,
ON WORKING IN THE WHITE HOUSE ON SEPTEMBER 11, 2001

Pierce, hurry up and get to the office. The boss has been shot," a panicked Secret Service officer barked at Nelson Pierce as he walked through the White House gates to start his shift on the afternoon of November 22, 1963.

More than five decades later, Pierce remembered every minute of that day in 1963. Once he got through the gate he raced to the residence and rushed to the Usher's Office, where a group of horrified staffers were gathered around the TV.

Unlike the rest of the country, Pierce had no time to mourn. He had a job to do. Like most of the residence staff, he showed very little outward emotion that day. Everyone on the household staff went on "automatic pilot," said Curator Jim Ketchum. "I think most of us were intent on carrying on."

As the usher on duty that terrible day, it was Pierce who got the official word from a Secret Service agent calling from Parkland Hospital in Dallas confirming the president's death.

Pierce was steering the ship in unchartered waters. No modern president had ever been assassinated, and never before had there been footage of the event with the violent images playing over and over.

It was the beginning of a long and emotionally draining week. Pierce walked through the White House gates on a Friday and didn't leave until the following Wednesday night. There was so much work to be done. The first thing he did, in a state of shock, was to call the engineers and order them to lower the flag on the roof of the White House to half-staff. He let himself break down only once—when he saw that flag being lowered. After composing himself, he called the General Services Administration Control Center to notify all U.S. embassies and ships at sea to lower their flags in kind.

Within ten minutes of leaving Dallas, Mrs. Kennedy's personal secretary, Mary Gallagher, called Pierce from Air Force One and told him that Jackie wanted her husband's funeral to be as much like President Lincoln's as possible. Pierce wasn't sure what that would entail, but he immediately set to work. "We had no training for anything like that. It was just something you fell into automatically —we were doing what the first lady wanted," he said. He quickly got in touch with the Curator's Office, and they in turn worked with the Library of Congress to figure out how best to replicate Lincoln's lying in state and funeral.

Curator Jim Ketchum found an old engraving of the East Room draped in black for Lincoln's funeral. To re-create the effect, West called Lawrence Arata, the White House upholsterer, who proposed using black cambric, a thin black material stretched across the bottom of chairs to disguise their springs. As it happened, Arata had ordered a new hundred-yard roll just a few days before.

Arata and his wife quickly got to work, hanging the fabric exactly as instructed by the president's brother-in-law, Sargent Shriver, who supervised funeral preparations at Robert Kennedy's request. The Aratas hung the black cloth over chandeliers, windows, and doorways. They worked with the help of their grief-stricken colleagues from late in the evening until the president's body returned in the early-morning hours.

"A lot of people thought it was silk material, but it was plain black cambric. Mrs. Kennedy wanted it very, very humble, the same as Lincoln's funeral. Nothing fancy," Arata said. "I pinned the cambric on the draperies and tried to drape the material to give it a custom appearance."

A grief-stricken Preston Bruce directed friends and family who were arriving in shared disbelief to begin preparations for the president's funeral. He helped drape the black fabric on the main floor of the White House as the first lady instructed. In the East Room, Bruce and Maître d' Charles Ficklin placed giant tapers—long, slim candles—next to the platform that would support the president's casket. From the moment Bruce arrived at the White House at 2:22 P.M. on November 22 until the hearse pulled under the North Portico after four the next morning, Bruce said he had "only one idea in my mind. I would wait for Mrs. Kennedy. I wanted to be there when she came back to the White House."

Chief Usher J. B. West was at home when he heard the news on the radio, and he rushed to the office. He writes in his memoir about the following hours: he directed the butlers to prepare coffee and the maids to start readying all the guest rooms, "little meaningless gestures, but a signal that our work must go on."

"We were told originally that the president's body would arrive at the White House about 10:00 P.M. Well, we got the call at 10:00 P.M. that they didn't know what time it would be so it was about 4:25 A.M. when the president's body arrived at the White House,"

Pierce said with sadness sweeping over his face. "We were up all night and all the next day."

Pierce helped the butlers settle Kennedy family members into their rooms at the residence. Over the next four nights, he and the other ushers slept on folding cots in the basement. There was an area there that they used to change into tuxedos for state dinners, and there was at least a bathroom and a shower for them to share.

When Pierce saw Jackie for the first time in the early morning on November 23, he nearly froze. "When Mrs. Kennedy and Ted and Robert came around the corner from the hall to the elevator I was wondering what I would say to Mrs. Kennedy. Our eyes met as she came around the corner and we had a rapport that I had never had with anybody that I knew—I didn't have to say anything," he recalled, tearing up when he talked about seeing her suit caked in her husband's blood. The traumatized first lady was only thirty-four years old. "We lost a friend, a very close friend," Pierce said as he thought back to the mood among the residence workers that fateful day. Social Secretary Letitia Baldrige remembered being asked by Robert Kennedy to select a coffin; she decided on a midpriced casket, since it would forever be hidden underneath the American flag.

"Hundreds of people were walking around those corridors silently, numbly," she recalled. "They used to be such happy, bustling, noisy corridors. Now people moved slowly, bowed, and when they spoke, they whispered, as if afraid their emotions would burst forth."

Within fifteen hours, by the time the president's body was back at the White House, the staff was able to arrange for the casket to rest on the same catafalque used for Lincoln nearly one hundred years earlier. President Kennedy's body was returned after hours at Bethesda Naval Hospital, where the president's autopsy was performed while Jackie paced the halls smoking cigarettes. Representatives of each of the armed services carried the coffin up the North Portico stairs. Father John Kuhn of St. Matthew's Church offered a short prayer. Only after the flag-draped coffin was in the East Room did the first lady leave her husband's side. In the coffin she placed a letter she wrote to her husband, a pair of gold cuff links she had given him, the presidential seal carved on a whale's tooth, and a note from Caroline and John-John to their slain father.

For Mrs. Kennedy, the president's loss was compounded by the couple's renewed intimacy after the devastating death of their baby, Patrick Bouvier Kennedy, on August 9, 1963, less than four months before the president's assassination. About ten days before Patrick's premature birth, Jackie wrote Head Housekeeper Anne Lincoln and asked her to go out and buy some baby hangers. Lincoln was putting off the errand, since the baby was not due for several more weeks.

The boy died just two days after he was born five and a half weeks early. "The whole room was fixed up, and I know the second when Patrick died [that] we got up there just as fast as we could and took everything out and put it all away," she recalled. They didn't want the president and first lady to be reminded of their gut-wrenching loss when they returned. J. B. West called the Carpenter's Shop immediately upon learning of Patrick's death, and ordered them to get rid of the rug, crib, and curtains in the blue-and-white nursery. Now Jackie was being forced to endure another life-changing death.

Bill Cliber had just started as an electrician at the White House that year. He helped drape the black cloth over the chandeliers, and when Jackie Kennedy came to review her husband's body, he quietly walked to the opposite side of the room to give her privacy.

"We knew how to disappear," he said. And this was a moment when the residence staff were especially aware of the first lady's need for privacy.

For twenty-four hours, the president's family and friends paid their respects in the East Room. After a small mass that Saturday,

Jackie walked up to Chief Usher J. B. West and threw her arms around him. "*Poor* Mr. West," she whispered.

"I couldn't speak. It was all I could do to stand," West said. "I just held her for a moment."

Knowing that she and her children would have to leave the White House soon, Jackie asked him to take her to see the Oval Office one last time. Shockingly, it was already being taken apart. Model ships, books, and the president's rocking chair were being carted away by the residence staff. "I think we're probably in the way," she murmured, trying to take in every last detail of the room.

She walked the short distance to the Cabinet Room and sat at the imposing mahogany table. "My children. They're good children, aren't they, Mr. West?" she asked the chief usher, who had become a friend.

"They certainly are."

"They're not spoiled?"

"No, indeed."

"Mr. West, will you be my friend for life?" the first lady, who had seemed to have it all just a day earlier, pleaded.

He was too upset to speak. He could only nod. The Sunday after the assassination, the flag-draped coffin was carried on a horse-drawn caisson, the same one that had carried the bodies of Lincoln, FDR, and the Unknown Soldier, to the Capitol Rotunda where it laid in state for twenty-one hours. The procession mirrored Lincoln's so closely that there was even a riderless black horse just as there had been almost a hundred years earlier. Two hundred and fifty thousand people went to pay tribute to the president. The state funeral was held on Monday, November 25.

"We were standing out on the North Portico, and it was just a quiet day, couldn't hear nothing but those horses—*click, click,*" longtime residence worker Wilson Jerman vividly recalls. "It was a very sad day."

Shortly before the funeral, Usher Rex Scouten called Preston Bruce into his office, where Robert Kennedy was waiting for him. Kennedy told Bruce that Jackie wanted him to walk in the funeral procession to St. Matthew's Cathedral. A car would drive him to the cemetery for the burial.

The funeral service "went by like a dream," Bruce recalled. He remembered seeing John-John salute his father's casket, and remembered that that night Jackie had arranged for cake, ice cream, and candles to go with the little boy's dinner to celebrate his third birthday.

The great-grandson of slaves, Bruce had never gone to college, so he was astounded to find himself standing feet away from General Charles de Gaulle and Ethiopian emperor Haile Selassie, dressed in their full regalia, at the president's funeral at Arlington National Cemetery. They were just some of the dignitaries from more than one hundred countries who came to Washington to share in the nation's grief. For Bruce, Jackie Kennedy had done him the honor of a lifetime: positioning him alongside heads of state and including him among the president's family and closest friends.

JIM KETCHUM HAD just left the Oval Office, where he had been working all morning with a crew from the Smithsonian. It was less than a year before the 1964 presidential election, and Kennedy was already making plans for his presidential library in case he was defeated. The president insisted that his library have an accurate copy of the ornate *Resolute* desk that was carved from the timbers of a British Arctic Exploration ship named the H.M.S. *Resolute.* Kennedy was the first president to have it installed in the Oval Office, and it became world-famous because of a playful photo of John-John peeking his head out from a built-in panel underneath it as his father worked. That morning Ketchum and the team from the Smithsonian were examining every square inch of the iconic piece of furniture.

As soon as he sat back down in his office, he heard a police officer talking in the hallway. "We just had word from Dallas that the presidential motorcade has been hit and we think the president was involved."

Ketchum and two other people in the Curator's Office took the elevator to the third floor and rushed to find a guest room with a TV to watch the news. Not long after, Ketchum got a call from Mrs. Kennedy herself, on board Air Force One. She repeated the order her secretary gave to the ushers: she wanted him to find books describing how the East Room was decorated during Lincoln's funeral.

Around dusk that evening, helicopters started landing on the White House lawn in quick succession. Looking back on that terrible day, Ketchum told me that he could only liken the sight to a scene from the epic Vietnam film *Apocalypse Now*, released years later. The copters were coming from Andrews Air Force Base, carrying some of the people who had been on the flight back from Dallas and others whom Johnson had asked to come meet him to discuss the transition. Ketchum spent the next several hours preparing the East Room. He didn't leave to go back to his northern Virginia apartment until Sunday morning. After getting a few hours of rest at home, he got a phone call at around six-thirty on Monday morning, the day of the president's state funeral. It was Mrs. Kennedy. "She was obviously getting next to no sleep," he said. She was calling about a small detail, showing her almost obsessive focus on appearances even as she faced the enormity of losing her husband.

"She was going to receive most of the visiting dignitaries in the Red Room, but she wanted to have people like [French president] de Gaulle and a handful of other individuals who would really be considered the top of the ranking, in the Yellow Oval Room just above the Oval Blue Room," he said.

Jackie was worried that they would see the painting by French post-Impressionist painter Paul Cézanne in the Yellow Oval Room. "I'd really like to have something more American to share with these people," she told Ketchum resolutely. "Would you, and could you, as soon as possible, get into the White House and take down the Cézanne?" By 8:15 that morning, the Cézanne had been replaced by a newly acquired series of large prints of American cities. "They were the perfect substitute," Ketchum said proudly.

Ketchum was surprised that Chief Usher J. B. West, who was so close to Mrs. Kennedy, didn't show more emotion after the assassination. West explained to the grief-stricken Ketchum: "I came to the White House in 1941 and my president [Roosevelt] died in April of 1945. If the first president under whom you've served in the White House dies, it is a much more trying experience than those that come after."

When President Kennedy died, Ketchum says, he finally understood what West meant. There was a degree of composure that was always expected from the domestic staff. And with the widowed first lady setting a stoic tone, everyone else fell in line. If the president's wife was able to keep herself together, a curator at the White House who barely knew the president should certainly do the same.

West was surprised that the campaign-averse Mrs. Kennedy had wanted to accompany her husband to Dallas, but he remembered how close the couple had grown since Patrick's death that August. Later, Jackie told West she was glad she had been there in her husband's final moments: "To think that I very nearly didn't go! Oh, Mr. West, what if I'd been here—out riding at Wexford [their house in Virginia's horse country] or somewhere. . . . Thank God I went with him!"

Mrs. Kennedy was so fond of West, and grateful for his kindness in that dark time, that when he passed away in 1983 she asked Nancy Reagan if he could be buried at Arlington National Cemetery, even though it is reserved for career military personnel and their families. The Reagans obliged.

———

IT WAS NANNY Maud Shaw who broke the news of the president's death to the children. Caroline was five days short of her sixth birthday when her father was assassinated. John-John was just three days from his third birthday. As helicopters noisily landed on the South Lawn, Caroline pointed at each one and asked if that was the helicopter carrying her father back from his trip. Shaw chose her words carefully. "There was an accident and your father was shot," Shaw said haltingly, almost unable to control her own grief. "God has taken him to heaven because they just couldn't make him better in a hospital."

Shaw told Caroline that she would be reunited in heaven with her father and their baby brother Patrick, but in the meantime he would be watching over her and her mother and her brother. Caroline was just old enough to start crying.

John-John was so young that Shaw tucked him into bed without telling him anything. He soon learned enough, though, to say: "My poor mommy's crying. She's crying because my daddy's gone away."

———

AT FIRST, LADY Bird Johnson thought someone was setting off firecrackers. That would have been entirely in keeping with the festive air of the day, as children waved signs and people threw confetti and leaned out of office building windows to wave at the gorgeous first couple.

The Johnsons were riding two cars behind the Kennedys on

November 22, 1963. Their lives, like those of the Kennedy family, would be forever changed by the events of that day.

Mrs. Johnson couldn't believe that the president had been shot until they pulled up to the hospital. She glanced over at the Kennedys' car and saw "a bundle of pink, just like a drift of blossoms, lying on the backseat. It was Mrs. Kennedy lying over the president's body."

When she went to see the first lady outside the operating room, she was amazed at how alone she looked. "You always think of someone like her as being insulated, protected," she wrote in her diary. Lady Bird hugged Jackie and whispered, "God, help us all."

On the flight back to Washington, with President Kennedy's casket in the plane's corridor, Lady Bird went to see Jackie again. Jackie told her the same thing she later told West: that she was glad she'd been with her husband in his final moments. "What if I had not been there?" she wondered aloud.

When Lady Bird asked if she could find someone to help her change out of her bloodstained suit, she refused "with almost an element of fierceness—if a person that gentle, that dignified, can be said to have such a quality." The gory sight was deeply moving. It was a shock to see that "immaculate woman exquisitely dressed, and caked in blood."

"I want them to see what they have done to Jack," Jackie told her defiantly. (The strawberry pink suit was an exact replica of a Chanel design, made by a small U.S. dressmaker; the first lady had chosen it to avoid criticism for wearing too many expensive foreign labels.)

The country was consumed by grief and panic. For Luci Baines Johnson, sixteen years old at the time, there was a deep fear that the news reports she was hearing secondhand were incomplete and that her parents had also been hurt. She was sitting in Spanish class at Washington's National Cathedral School when her teacher announced the news. "No one ever said a word about my father or mother," she recalled. Class was swiftly dismissed and she wandered into the school's courtyard alone and in a daze. "I looked over and saw that the Secret Service had very thoughtfully sent a man I knew, one of my father's detail—and I turned and ran in the other direction as if I could run away from the inevitable. And of course, I wasn't capable of outrunning a Secret Service agent." The agent grabbed her and said, "I'm sorry. I'm so sorry, Luci." She beat on his chest and screamed, "No!" He never said that the president was dead, she says, "Because the words were just unsayable." It wasn't until she asked him, "And Daddy and Mother?" that she found out that her parents were unharmed.

Ninety-nine minutes after President Kennedy was pronounced dead, Vice President Lyndon Baines Johnson was sworn in on Air Force One. When Johnson stepped off the plane at Andrews Air Force Base, this time as president, he told the waiting press: "We have suffered a loss that cannot be weighed. For me it is a deep personal tragedy. I know that the world shares the sorrow that Mrs. Kennedy and her family bear. I will do my best. That is all I can do. I ask for your help—and God's."

The specter of tragedy would haunt the Johnsons those first few months in the White House. Their transition was made worse because some members of the Kennedys' loyal staff would never trust the new president, whom they considered a loud, uncouth bully. (Even Jackie Kennedy had referred to Johnson during the campaign as "Senator Cornpone.")

Caroline Kennedy's life may have been changed forever, but her mother wanted her routine to stay in place for as long as possible. At Mrs. Kennedy's request, Lady Bird Johnson allowed the little girl to continue to attend kindergarten with a group of her friends in their third-floor Solarium classroom until the end of the first semester in mid-January. Little Caroline was dropped off at the South Portico every morning and picked up every afternoon. The elevator took Caroline and her classmates to the linoleum-floored classroom, complete with chalkboards and cubbies. The other students were the children of longtime friends of the first couple. Caroline's ballet class sometimes still practiced on the South Lawn, "fluttering like little pink birds in their pink leotards, tulle tutus, and ballet slippers," recalls Social Secretary Letitia Baldrige.

After her father's death, Caroline never stopped to see her old room on the second floor or bounce on the trampoline, J. B. West said. "Except for a few sentimental servants, she was generally ignored. Lynda and Luci [the Johnsons' teenage daughters] were the new Princesses."

For Nelson Pierce, seeing Caroline every day brought a sense of solace, not sorrow. "We were so glad that she was continuing with school and her friends," he told me. "Of course, she was young enough so that the loss of her father, when it was school time, it was forgotten. She blended in with the kids and had a good time." (Once Caroline finished the semester, Luci and Lynda made the Solarium into a teenage hideaway, complete with a soda bar, a big TV set, and two record players.)

In the wake of the assassination, security at the White House was enhanced. Butler Lynwood Westray recalls that the residence staff were all subjected to a new clearance check by law enforcement— their backgrounds scrutinized and their friends and families interviewed. "One or two of the guys couldn't make the grade after having been found okay" before, he said. "They were just cut off from working there after that." Westray said his phone was tapped after the assassination. "They wanted to make sure people there were doing what they were supposed to be doing."

Kennedy's death changed the course of history and it had a deep, personal effect on the residence staff who loved him so much. A certain innocence would be forever absent from the halls of the executive mansion.

———

NEARLY FORTY YEARS later, a very different kind of traumatic event shook the White House. On a late summer morning, under a cloudless azure sky, the mansion was buzzing with activity. The Bushes were hosting the annual picnic for members of Congress and their families. One hundred and ninety picnic tables adorned the South Lawn. Executive Chef Walter Scheib was working with Tom Perini, a favorite caterer of the first family's from Buffalo Gap, Texas, to create a festive, Texas-style cookout for the fifteen hundred expected guests, complete with chuck wagons and a green chili and hominy casserole.

Warm weather and clear skies were forecast for the afternoon barbecue. Maids were cleaning the Queens' Bedroom on the second floor, where George H. W. Bush and Barbara had spent the night before. The former president and his wife left at 7:00 A.M. for an early flight. President George W. Bush was in Florida, visiting a Sarasota elementary school.

Even with all the activity swirling around her, Laura Bush seemed alone in the White House on the morning of September 11, 2001. She was getting dressed in silence in the Bush's second-floor bedroom, rehearsing the statement she was set to make before the Senate Education Committee that morning. She was nervous about her visit to Capitol Hill, where she would be briefing the committee about an early childhood development conference she'd organized earlier that summer.

The first lady and the residence staff—from the maids, butlers, and florists, to the cooks prepping for the annual picnic—were all lost in the events of a typically busy day. But that day was anything but typical. "Had the TV been turned on, I might have heard the first fleeting report of a plane hitting the North Tower," Laura Bush said.

A few minutes after 9:00 A.M. Laura got into her waiting car at the South Portico to head to the Russell Senate Office Building, less than two miles away. The head of her Secret Service detail told her that a plane had slammed into one of the World Trade Center towers. Chief Usher Gary Walters, standing beside him, was also hearing the news for the first time. *How could a plane fly into the World Trade Center on such a clear day?* He wondered aloud.

"Gary, you need to go inside and watch the television," the agent told him.

The first lady's motorcade sped up Pennsylvania Avenue to the Capitol to make the hearing. Walters headed back inside to the Secret Service room on the Ground Floor, located behind the president's elevator, where he knew there was a television. But the room was crowded with people in front of the TV, so he went to the Usher's Office, where he ran into some household workers. He gave them quick instructions on the setup for the picnic, still unaware of the extent of the devastation.

When he got to his personal office, which is separate from the Usher's Office, it too was packed with people huddled around the TV. He walked in just as the second plane flew into the South Tower.

"How in the world did they get that on television?" he asked, stunned.

"Because that's the second plane," someone responded.

Once Walters realized that the event wasn't an isolated accident, he called the Bushes' social secretary, Catherine Fenton. They decided to cancel the event, and Walters went back to the South Portico, where he had just seen Laura Bush off moments before. There was so much confusion and uncertainty but he couldn't waste a moment.

Just as they had after President Kennedy's assassination, the residence staff delved into their work with a single-minded focus. Walters coordinated with the National Park Service, in charge of the White House grounds, to determine who would be moving the picnic tables and cleaning up the chuck wagons.

"As I walked out of the South Portico, I saw the terrible smoke and flames at the Pentagon," Walters recalled. It suddenly struck him: the White House could be next.

Even as people started to evacuate the White House, Walters knew he would be staying: "As far as I was concerned, my responsibility was there at the White House."

His job was to make the house run at all costs, even if it now felt like he was working in the center of a giant bull's-eye. He couldn't do it alone. He asked the uniformed division of the Secret Service to allow Executive Chef Walter Scheib, who had already been evacuated, to return. He grabbed a few others, including Chief Electrician Bill Cliber, and told them they needed to stay and help clear the picnic tables, even as the Secret Service was screaming for everyone to drop everything and run for their lives. "I got the word that everybody was evacuating, but we had something that we needed to do," Walters said.

Meanwhile Walters's daughter, a student at Boston College, was anxiously watching the news, terrified for her father after someone mistakenly told her that a plane had crashed into the White House, not the Pentagon. Walters and his small crew were too focused on clearing space for the president's helicopter to call their families.

Cliber's wife, Bea, was home watching TV with relatives. She didn't know whether her husband was going to be all right. "It was panicsville," she recalled. "We just sat and waited." She didn't hear from him until eight o'clock that night.

On his way up the driveway—and, potentially, back into harm's way—Scheib yelled at the colleagues streaming toward him out of the mansion to leave the grounds as fast as they could. He shouted at the president and first lady's staffs, already racing out of the West and East wings, warning them that the police were saying another plane was heading for the White House.

"Everyone who worked for me in the East Wing—they were mainly young women who expected a very glamorous job at the White House—were told to kick off their high heels and run," Laura Bush recalls. "Can you imagine what it would be like to all of a sudden have a job where you were told to run?"

Walters and the others cleared 190 picnic tables, weighing hundreds of pounds each, from the South Lawn. "My knees banged together," Walters said. "It sounded like a bass drum." Rumors of further attacks kept coming in, but they blocked them out. "We've got a job, we've got to do it," Cliber said.

Even then, when the world felt like it was turned upside down, the residence staff focused on keeping their beloved house running and not spilling any secrets. As some reporters noticed them feverishly working to clear the South Grounds, they asked whether the president was coming back to Washington right away. "Haven't heard a word," Cliber told them, even though he knew they were working to help speed up the president's return.

The first lady's car was driving up Pennsylvania Avenue to Capitol Hill when she learned that a second plane had hit the other World Trade Center tower. "The car fell silent; we sat in mute disbelief," she wrote in her memoir. "One plane might be a strange accident; two planes were clearly an attack."

———

When Maid Betty Finney started working at the White House in 1993, she had no housekeeping experience except for taking care of the home she shared with her husband and their two daughters. She was working at a steakhouse in Myrtle Beach, South Carolina, when her husband died suddenly. She needed a job—fast. As with most White House positions, hers came through a connection: her daughter knew Executive Housekeeper Christine Limerick, who brought her on board.

BETTY FINNEY

Eight years after she was hired, she found herself fearing for her life.

Finney was cleaning the second floor Queens' Bedroom, where the president's parents had spent the night on September 10. When they left for the airport, the Bushes had forgotten to turn off the TV. Finney and a couple of other terrified maids gathered around it, watching as the second tower was hit. Like so many other tragedies that affected the presidency, even as they were standing at the heart of the story, the residence workers were left to learn the news from the TV.

"I ran down the hall to the Yellow Oval Room and looked out the window, and you cannot see the Pentagon from there, but I saw smoke," she says. "I went back to the Queens' Bedroom and then I had to run upstairs for something."

Before she made it to the third floor, she heard one of the Secret

Service agents yelling "Get out of the house! Get out of the house!" She never made it upstairs; instead she ran downstairs. "I didn't know what was going on. I didn't know they had started the evacuation. We got out and everybody was on the streets. It was really scary. Everybody just went in a different direction, wherever they could get out."

On Capitol Hill, Laura Bush got out of the car to meet with Senator Edward Kennedy, chair of the Education Committee, both knowing that there would be no briefing that day. He escorted her to his office.

Oddly, even as an old TV in the corner of the room was blaring the devastating news out of New York, Kennedy wouldn't look at the screen. Instead he gave the first lady a tour of the family memorabilia in his office, including a framed note that his brother Jack had sent their mother when he was a child. It said, "Teddy is getting fat."

"All the while," the first lady said, "I kept glancing over at the glowing television screen. My skin was starting to crawl, I wanted to leave, to find out what was going on, to process what I was seeing, but I felt trapped in an endless cycle of pleasantries." Later she wondered if Kennedy had simply seen too much death in his lifetime and couldn't face another tragedy, especially one on such a massive scale.

After they made a statement to the press telling them there would be no briefing and expressing concern about the attacks, Bush walked toward the stairs to go back to her car and the White House. The lead Secret Service agent stopped her and her staff abruptly and told them to run to the basement. Deeply worried about her husband's safety, she waited with her friend Senator Judd Gregg, the ranking Republican on the Education Committee, in his private interior office in the lower level of the Capitol. There, they huddled together and called their children to make sure they were safe. Reports were coming in from everywhere, some less reliable than others—including one rumor that Camp David had been hit and another that a plane had flown into the Bush ranch in Crawford, Texas.

Moments after the second plane hit the South Tower, Christine Limerick ran to the linen room on the third floor and told her staff to drop everything and leave. Immediately.

She heard American Airlines Flight 77 crash into the Pentagon. "It sounded like an explosion," she recalled.

When she returned to her office, she realized she couldn't account for maid Mary Arnold. She tried to go back upstairs into the residence to search for her, but the Secret Service wouldn't let her. She was told she had two minutes to get out of the White House and that a plane was on its way.

"Nobody questions them when it's on lockdown," she said. Arnold somehow got out of the White House and had enough money on her to get home.

Limerick remembers being haunted when she realized that not everyone would be allowed to evacuate the potential target. "The look on the faces of the Secret Service agents who were told that they had to stay," she said. "I will never forget that."

Workers say the Secret Service told everyone to head north because they thought the plane would come from the south—a less obstructed flight path to the White House. Cooks, butlers, carpenters, and maids fanned out, running for their lives. Some members of the Pastry Shop walked across Arlington Memorial Bridge, crossing the Potomac together and gathering at the nearest person's home.

Finney and half a dozen of her colleagues went to one of the florists' houses on Capitol Hill, where they huddled around the television in disbelief. They had all run out so fast that hardly anyone had time to collect their purses, leaving them all without wallets. That night they walked miles to their cars back at the White House and drove home, many still in shock.

Some staffers didn't make it out in time to evacuate at all. There were butlers on the second and third floors who were working on setting up the bars for the picnic—peeling lemons and making lemon wedges—who didn't get the word that something was going on until nearly an hour after the house was evacuated. A few engineers were stuck in the basement for hours, oblivious to the panic upstairs and the danger they were in.

Amid the chaos, one butler ran down to his locker in the basement to change his clothes before riding home on his motorcycle. The gate slammed behind him, trapping him, and he couldn't get out until a Secret Service officer recognized him and finally opened the gate.

———————

A LITTLE AFTER ten that morning, a few minutes after the World Trade Center's South Tower collapsed and about twenty minutes before the North Tower followed, the first lady was collected from Senator Gregg's office by Secret Service agents and an Emergency Response Team dressed in black wielding guns. "GET BACK!" they shouted to Capitol Hill staffers as they raced the startled first lady to a waiting car. At about the same time, United Airlines Flight 93 crashed in a field near Shanksville, Pennsylvania, when a group of brave passengers tried to wrestle control of the plane from the terrorists. If they hadn't acted, that plane would likely have headed straight for the Capitol or the White House. Many White House workers credit the passengers on that plane for saving their lives.

There was a lot of discussion about where to take the first lady during those confusing hours. The Secret Service eventually decided to move her to their own headquarters, a few blocks away from the White House. She sat there for hours, in a windowless basement conference room, watching the video of the twin towers falling over and over.

Phone lines were jammed that day as petrified family members tried to make sure their loved ones were safe. Even the president had trouble reaching his wife from Air Force One after he took off from Florida. A little before noon, after three unsuccessful attempts, the Bushes finally managed to connect. She told him she'd reached their daughters and that they were safe.

Meanwhile dozens of residence workers dressed in their uniforms gathered in Lafayette Square across Pennsylvania Avenue from the White House. Chef John Moeller described the aftermath of the Pentagon attack: "I could see huge plumes of smoke swirling in the sky—it was a beautiful day—it was as black as black can be. They were just swirling, swirling, swirling into the sky. I've never seen an explosion that big in my life." Finally, a group of workers decided to walk to the nearby Capital Hilton in search of bathrooms, landlines, and a television.

Nearby, the busy Connecticut Avenue commercial district was in chaos. Drivers had gotten out of their cars and gone running down the street, worried that they would be caught in an attack. "Mass hysteria had taken over," Walter Scheib recalls. "I remember walking by a BMW 700 series sitting in the middle of Connecticut Avenue with the doors open and the engine running and nobody in it."

Laura Bush saw none of this. After hours of sitting in the windowless conference room, she was finally brought to the President's Emergency Operations Center beneath the White House. Vice President Dick Cheney and other top officials had been gathered there since that morning. Built for President Franklin Roosevelt during World War II, the command center is accessible only through a series of unfinished underground hallways with pipes hanging down from the ceiling. There she would wait to be reunited with her husband.

Florist Bob Scanlan was putting the finishing touches on the picnic table arrangements in the small Flower Shop underneath the North Portico when a friend called and told him the news. Stunned, he wound up at nearby Freedom Plaza, several blocks from the White House.

As he walked there with several colleagues, he heard the piercing noise of American Airlines Flight 77 slamming into the Pentagon. "We decided that we couldn't stay there," he said. "We were like lost souls." He and a coworker walked more than two miles together to reach their homes on Capitol Hill.

————

AFTER HELPING CLEAR the picnic tables, Scheib and a group of residence staff worked in the kitchen from two o'clock in the afternoon until nine o'clock that evening, serving food (much of it prepared earlier for the barbecue) to the Secret Service, National Guard, D.C. police, and White House staff who had to stay behind. Leftovers were sent to the relief effort at the Pentagon. "Four of them [residence workers] served over five hundred meals to the staff that were in and around the White House," Walters said.

When people thanked him for the food, Scheib replied, "Just keep whatever the hell's on the outside on the outside, will you?"

Once the lawn was cleared, Cliber and a handful of others finally tried to leave the White House, only to find themselves locked in by security doors. A plane had been spotted overhead, and the Secret Service ordered them down to the bomb shelter, a corridor running west to east under the White House. They stayed down in the old shelter until around eight o'clock that night. (The plane overhead turned out to be a U.S. military aircraft.)

When they learned of the death toll—all told, nearly three thousand people lost their lives that day—all anyone who works at America's most famous house could think was, *That could have been us.*

That evening the first lady finally got to see the president when they were reunited in the President's Emergency Operations Center.

The Secret Service recommended that the Bushes sleep on an old bed in the basement, but they refused. "I've got to get some sleep, in our own bed," the president said. To the Bushes, the White House was home. They were even more fiercely attached to it now that it had narrowly missed total destruction.

———

AFTER THE ATTACKS, the Secret Service wanted to close the White House to tours. Early on the morning of September 12, Chief Usher Gary Walters approached the president as he walked to the Oval Office and lobbied for the public tours to remain open. "Mr. President, last night you said everybody should go about their normal activities. One normal activity that will be watched very closely is that the White House is open for tours."

The president paused and replied, "You're right."

In the wake of the attacks, however, the decision was made to close them. The September 11 attacks weren't the only cause for concern; just a week later, letters containing anthrax spores arrived at the offices of several news media figures as well as two Democratic senators. Walters said that some members of the residence staff were put on preventative drugs in case they were exposed to anthrax.

Bill Cliber would never be the same after 9/11. He knew how it felt to be scared as he walked into work every day; after all, his White House career had started shortly before Kennedy's assassination. But this was different.

"It shook me. I had my time in," he said, referring to the years of service that government workers need in order to qualify to get a significant portion of their pay in retirement. Still, he wouldn't leave because he had promised himself that he would work at the White House for forty years, so he kept on going.

After September 11, though, the mood changed at the White House for everyone. The Curator's Office deposed members of the staff, asking them to talk about what they went through that day for their records. The glamour of working at the White House was overtaken by fear. Pastry Chef Roland Mesnier said that he and his staff were completely unaware why they were being evacuated so urgently, because they didn't have a TV in their kitchen. Afterward he demanded that one be installed. After 9/11, most of the workers decided to keep a bit of cash and their White House pass on them at all times in case they needed to leave quickly.

Betty Monkman, who was in charge of preserving and cata-loguing all of the important artwork and furniture in the White House, had to worry not only about saving her own life but also which historic pieces must be salvaged in case of an emergency. The Lansdowne portrait of George Washington in the East Room and the Gettysburg Address in the Lincoln Bedroom are among the top priorities.

Reflecting on that horrible day, she says she is still furious that there was no clear evacuation plan for the building. "This young woman who worked in the Usher's Office came running through our office saying, 'Get out, get out, get out!' and then the White House police said 'Go south!' and then some people said 'Go north!' It was so chaotic."

Monkman had decided to go to the bomb shelter that morn-ing, but when she got halfway down she thought, *Oh my God, if they bombed us we'd be buried under the rubble.* So she headed back upstairs and went to Lafayette Square, where ambulances and fire trucks blazed past her on their way to the Pentagon.

Scheib said the household workers are not the priority in a crisis and shouldn't expect the Secret Service to worry about them. "We are domestic staff, we are not the thrust of anything," he said. "If you're going to be there, you have to understand there's a target on the back of every person who works at the White House."

Scheib was sad to see the enormity of the attacks weigh on the president. Bush seemed as if he "literally had the weight of the world on his shoulders." Always aware of how food affects moods, Scheib went from creating more contemporary cuisine to preparing pure comfort food for the president and the countless world leaders who came to show their sympathy and to strategize in the weeks following the terrorist attacks. "I went back to my mother's table," Scheib said.

Counselors from Bethesda Naval Hospital came in to talk to the workers about the trauma they had experienced. Cliber spoke with a counselor, but no one had any time-tested advice for the staff: "Nobody had ever been through that."

Florist Wendy Elsasser says she still can't talk about that day without crying. For months, Mesnier had panic attacks taking his morning shower. His wife and son begged him not to go back to work, and he listened when Gary Walters gathered the staff about a week after 9/11 and said they should leave if they couldn't stand the pressure.

But just like Bill Cliber, Mesnier couldn't bring himself to go. "You have to understand, I believe this job was made for me," he said. "It's where I belong."

First Lady Laura Bush was comforted that no one quit out of fear. She told me that watching the residence staff go back to work made her feel better about living in the White House. "We knew we were going to be there and we were confident that we would be safe, but on the other hand they could have chosen another job or just said, 'You know, this is just too much stress now. I'd rather go on,'" she said. "They didn't. None of them did."

Epilogue

★

Oh my God, she would be so proud of me.

— Butler James Ramsey on how his mother would have reacted to his White House career if she had lived to see it

It was ninety-eight degrees, another sticky Washington summer day. A window unit is working overtime in the three-bedroom redbrick row house in northeast Washington that Butler James Jeffries bought in 1979. He quickly and unnecessarily apologizes for his half-painted living room walls. "This would have all been painted before Easter, but I'm seventy-two and I get tired quick."

With the History Channel blaring in the background, and his lanky teenage grandson wandering in and out ("I used to look just like him"), we sit at a table covered with photographs of his children and grandchildren, and Jeffries tells the story of how the White House came to define his family's legacy. In a slow and deliberate voice, he explains how he was either related to or knew most of the people who ran the residence over the last fifty years. His name might be Jeffries, but he's a Ficklin; nine members of his family have worked there.

Even the members of the staff who he wasn't actually related to became like family. Eugene Allen, who took over as maître d' after Jeffries's uncle John Ficklin retired, "was just like an uncle too." Doorman Preston Bruce lived in the same housing complex as his aunt, and Jeffries says Bruce was a father figure to him.

"Mr. West, Mr. Scouten, they stayed in the background. My uncle [John] ran the White House," Jeffries says, proud of the close-knit circle of African Americans who made the residence tick. Family folklore has it that his uncle Charles got the family a foothold in the White House by impressing President Franklin Roosevelt while working on a military ship in the navy. Roosevelt asked him to draw a table setting, and he sat down and drew it expertly. Years later, Charles was asked to come to the White House for an interview.

Jeffries is continuing his family's tradition. He started working at the White House when he was just seventeen years old, in 1959. He remembers the exact date: January 25. His son is a butler there now, and even though Jeffries himself is long past retirement age, he still works at "the house" part-time. The job pays twenty-five dollars an hour. "They help me out down there, they don't have me doing any hard lifting or nothing."

Jeffries is a witness to American history. He is one of a handful of people still alive who remembers what it was like working in the Kennedy White House, when a new generation and new technology brought the residence into America's living rooms. He remembers a side of the first lady that few people ever saw.

"I remember Mrs. Kennedy would come downstairs, she might ask us to put a chair over there or even have us take the chair out of the room, and maybe fifteen or twenty minutes later she wanted us to bring the chair right back." He laughs. "Another guy and myself, we were the youngsters, and all the older guys would disappear! I never felt like I had to run, I wanted to be right there with her. I just stood by and did whatever she asked me to. If I could move it by myself, I moved it."

One Saturday night, years later, he was told to stop washing dishes and go upstairs to the second floor to help Betty Ford with something. When he got upstairs, Ford asked, "Where are the butlers?" She was looking for the full-time butlers.

"They just went downstairs. I can go get them for you," he told her, pushing the elevator button to go back down.

"All I need is a man," she called to him, impatiently, from the Family Dining Room.

He laughs with a wink. "I said to myself, *Wait a minute,* what *is this lady getting me into?* So I went to see what she wanted and all she wanted me to do was take the nineteen-inch television into the bedroom!"

Like so many of his colleagues, Jeffries fondly remembers President George H. W. Bush's kindness. "Old man Bush made me feel like I was just a person, just the same as he is. I was so glad I had watched a football game, because the next day, or one day during the week after the football game, I happened to walk in to take the orders for drinks up on the second floor and he was talking to the other guests and he asked me, What did I think about the game? I managed to talk with him about it. I took the orders and went on back and when I came back he said something else to me about the game."

Jeffries remembers serving drinks to the Clintons and their friends one night before a formal dinner, and running into an exhausted President Clinton on his way into the Solarium. Clinton confided in him, "If Robert Mitchum weren't a guest I wouldn't even bother going downstairs tonight."

Jeffries felt sorry for the weary president. "You need to take a break," he told him.

They are a dying breed, these people who actually hold dear

personal memories of the Kennedys and Johnsons, the Nixons, Fords, Carters, and Reagans. Their recollections paint these iconic figures in a rare and intimate light. In the small moments that make up a life, the residence workers catch a glimpse of the humanity in the presidents and first ladies whose true personalities are rarely known beyond the walls of the White House. Just like anyone else, America's leaders have moments of indecision, exhaustion, frustration, and joy.

All too often, now, the veteran residence staff see each other only at retirement parties and funerals. They try to keep up over Facebook and e-mail, but the older staffers, who aren't perpetually plugged in, sometimes find out about a colleague's passing long after the fact.

During the course of our conversations, I hated it when a pained expression would sweep across one of their faces when I mentioned that a colleague of theirs had passed away, unaware that they didn't know already.

There were delightful moments too. In the course of researching this book I sometimes had the happy occasion to reconnect people who had long lost touch. I gave Usher Chris Emery Head Housekeeper Christine Limerick's e-mail address. Nelson Pierce asked me for Bill Hamilton's phone number.

"I've got to call that turkey," James Ramsey said, eyes twinkling, when he asked me for his old friend Chef Mesnier's number.

Residence workers look on patiently as each new family learns to live within the confines of the White House. They know it's only a matter of time until their loyalty and discretion become lifelines for the president and the first lady. They are, after all, the only people there with no motivation other than to serve and comfort.

The first family and their aides rely on the residence workers, in part because they know so much about how first families live their lives. "When it comes down to it—and this is not just for me but for most of the people who went to work there—there's no track record, there's no institutional knowledge that you have" that can help you learn the job, said former Obama aide Reggie Love. "You basically are showing up with a clean slate and no instruction manual."

Despite the archival research I conducted before setting forth on these interviews, I had no idea what to expect when I began sitting down with the residence workers—many of whom generously opened their homes to me. I was so happy to discover that what you see really is what you get. Most of them are not cynical or competitive, like so many people in and around Washington politics; their desire to contribute small but integral roles in the functioning of America's democracy is genuine. They may not influence policy, but their jobs are arguably as important as those of many political appointees. Without them, the White House would be uninhabitable.

From preparing quiet meals for the first family to serving celebrities, members of Congress, and world leaders, they represent the best in American service, while practicing their own unique brand of diplomacy. And, implicitly or explicitly, their efforts are rewarded with the gratitude of the most powerful men and women on earth.

———

ADMIRAL STEPHEN ROCHON became chief usher in 2007, just a couple of months before one of Queen Elizabeth II's many state visits. "We impressed the queen enough that she invited me and a couple of my staffers to Buckingham Palace to see how the Brits do it."

When he arrived at Buckingham Palace, Rochon was astonished when the queen walked through their version of the State Floor and made her way right up to him. "Who are you, young man?" she asked him.

"Well, Your Majesty, I'm Admiral Rochon, the chief usher of the White House," he told her. "We entertained you for your state visit."

The queen's face lit up and she started waving across the room to her husband, "Oh Philip, oh Philip, come quick!"

One reason the residence workers leave such a lasting impression is that they make it all look effortless. "Butlers scurry around providing service that is both smooth and subtle. You get your food without being quite sure how you got it," recalled Betty Ford's press secretary, Sheila Rabb Weidenfeld, about attending her first state dinner. "Everything is perfect and everyone is beautiful and elegant, because they are part of the most beautiful and elegant setting in the world."

When crisis or tragedy strikes, the staff is at their best. During the Iran hostage crisis, First Lady Rosalynn Carter told me, "They were especially attentive during that time because they were concerned. They were concerned about *us*."

Residence staffers are completely in tune with the family they serve. They would do almost anything for them—often sacrificing their own marriages, countless hours with their children, and in the sad case of Freddie Mayfield, even their lives. "They are the greatest con artists in the world," Luci Baines Johnson joked. "They make every administration feel they love them best."

And it's true: Butler James Ramsey knew when President George W. Bush was in need of a good laugh. Executive Housekeeper Christine Limerick knew to bite her tongue during one of Nancy Reagan's tirades. And Chef Roland Mesnier knew exactly when Hillary Clinton could use a slice of her favorite mocha cake.

Ramsey did not seem near death when I interviewed him. He knew he was sick, though—he had colon cancer that was spreading to his liver—and he kept putting off my persistent requests to meet for lunch. ("You're a nice lady, baby. We'll do it. I'll call you.") Always jovial, he never let on how much pain he was in. Ramsey was hopeful about life and his future, animatedly describing dinner dates with a new girlfriend and talking about a trip he was hoping to take to Las Vegas with Storeroom Manager Bill Hamilton.

His daughter would later tell me that he had turned to herbal medicine to help fight the cancer that was ravaging his body.

When he passed away, on February 19, 2014, the families he loved so much returned his affection: Laura Bush spoke at his funeral, attended by dozens of his White House colleagues, and letters from President Obama and President Clinton were read at the service. His pallbearers were fellow butlers.

"He always seemed to know when we needed a little boost of his humor, which happens a lot in the White House," President Clinton wrote. "Hillary, Chelsea, and I all have our Ramsey memories. The man could tell a story, and his opinions on unfolding events, from politics to sports, were often hilarious." The Obamas praised Ramsey's "unwavering patriotism."

"James witnessed great moments in our nation's history," they said.

Laura Bush brought her daughter Jenna to the service, which was held at Trinidad Baptist Church in northeast Washington, D.C. The former first lady eulogized the butler who brought her husband much-needed moments of levity when it seemed the world was crashing down around him. ("She brought tears to my eyes," says Ramsey's daughter, Valerie.) Ramsey was more than just a staffer, Mrs. Bush said, he was a devoted friend. And, like all his colleagues, he possessed qualities of loyalty, devotion, and discretion that cannot be learned.

She told the congregation that Ramsey did more than pamper the presidents: "He made them laugh. He cheered them up. He brightened their days." On behalf of the entire Bush family, she said, "We thank God that James Ramsey was in our life."

For Ramsey, serving America's first families gave his life meaning and purpose. When I asked him how he felt when he first set foot in the residence decades ago, he said wistfully, "Oh my God, I was just so happy."

Acknowledgments

★

A few weeks after our daughter Charlotte was born, I went outside to get some fresh air and check the mail. I was surprised to find a crisp white envelope with a return address of 1600 Pennsylvania Avenue. In it was a note signed by the Obamas congratulating us on Charlie's birth. This kind of letter is sent to VIPs and friends and family of White House staff, and I couldn't think of *who* would have done such a thing for us. That's not because I didn't know anyone who would have gone to that kind of trouble; it's because there were simply too many people to choose from who *would* have been so thoughtful.

I've interviewed more than a hundred residence workers, presidential aides, and first family members during the course of my research, and so many of them were profoundly generous. Eventually, I narrowed it down to former storeroom manager Bill Hamilton, who started his career in the executive mansion when President Eisenhower was in office. When I called to thank him, Hamilton replied, "Sorry I didn't get it to you sooner." That's just the way these people are. They devoted their careers to taking care of the first family and they are far from the quintessential self-serving political operatives in this town. In fact, they seem to remain professional caretakers for the rest of their lives.

This book took me on a journey that began in October 2012 when I was taking care of our newborn son, Graham, at all hours of the day and night. Bleary-eyed, I started watching a marathon of *Downton Abbey* and became fascinated by the fraught relationship between two groups of people sharing a physical space so close in proximity but so far removed in every other way. It immediately took me back to an intimate reporter luncheon I attended with First Lady Michelle Obama. I remember the bright pink and green floral arrangements and champagne glasses clinking in the middle of the day—for a reporter used to eating sandwiches in a tiny office cubicle in the White House basement it was all so luxurious. But most of all, I remembered a butler who seemed to drift noiselessly in and out of the room.

I set out to meet these people who make the residence tick and it has been more eye-opening than I ever could have imagined. I've had the privilege of interviewing staffers who saw a playful side of Jackie Kennedy when she was relaxing in the family's private quarters, and I interviewed the White House electrician who accompanied President Richard Nixon on the emotional walk from the Oval Office to the residence after he announced his resignation.

None of that would have been possible without the generosity of the following residence workers, many of whom opened their homes and their hearts to me, including Christine Limerick, Lynwood Westray, Skip Allen, Betty Finney, Bob Scanlan, Bill Hamilton, James Jeffries, Roland Mesnier, Nelson Pierce, Frank Ruta, Cletus Clark, Stephen Rochon, Bill Cliber, Linsey Little, Wendy Elsasser, Chris Emery, Ronn Payne, James Hall, Wilson Jerman, Worthington White, Gary Walters, Betty Monkman, Mary Prince, Walter Scheib, Vincent Contee, Milton Frame, John

Moeller, Jim Ketchum, Tony Savoy, Ivaniz Silva, Nancy Mitchell, Providencia Paredes, Ann Amernick, Pierre Chambrin, Alvie Paschall, and Herman Thompson. Margaret Arrington shared stories about her deceased husband, Reds, and Charles Allen spoke lovingly of his father, Eugene. I especially want to thank James Ramsey whose smile lit up a room. I'm grateful for the time I spent with him.

Absolutely none of this would have been possible without my literary agent, Howard Yoon. Howard believed in me from the start and was there every step of the way. Beyond being an incredibly talented agent, he's also a good friend who's given me some wise parenting advice over the years. I'm also thankful to the remarkable Gail Ross, and to Dara Kaye, who is an integral part of the ace team at the Ross Yoon Agency. Their motto is "Books change lives." Well, they've certainly changed mine and I am so grateful for it.

I so enjoyed working with the very gifted Cal Morgan at HarperCollins whose edits helped bring life and clarity to the manuscript, and I'm thankful to the talented Emily Cunningham for bringing so much energy to this project and for working to make it the best it can be. I'm also grateful for the support of the visionary Jonathan Burnham and for the guidance of my first editor Tim Duggan, whose passion for the subject matter was contagious. And thank you to Robin Bilardello, who exceeded all of my expectations with her cover design, and Beth Silfin for her expert advice.

I'm so thankful to my husband, Brooke, whom I always want to see more and more of and who makes my life so much sweeter. And to our incredible children, Graham and Charlotte, who bring us so much happiness. Thank you to my mom, Valerie, the smartest and most loving woman I know. (She also happens to be a highly skilled editor who helped me organize these stories and find my voice.) And to my wonderful dad, Christopher, who is my role model and who has instilled so much confidence in my sister Kelly and me.

Kelly, it's fun watching you grow up into such a smart and kind woman. And thank you to Nancy Brower (aka Mom Mom), our entire extended family, and to Mini and Elizabeth. I'll always wish that we had more time with Bill Brower, who was a good man, a great father, and a loving Pop Pop.

The first ladies I interviewed wanted to help shine a light on the people who made their lives bearable in the White House. I appreciate their time and am grateful for their insights as ultimate White House insiders. Laura Bush told me about the horror of 9/11 and the healing process that she and the staff went through together. Barbara Bush recounted her playful friendships with the household workers. ("You don't tease people that you don't like. You tease people you like. . . . They teased back, and I deserved it.") Rosalynn Carter praised the staff for making her family feel more comfortable during the tense 444-day Iran hostage crisis. She seemed genuinely moved by the kindness they showed her. Tricia Nixon, Luci and Lynda Johnson, Steve and Susan Ford, and Ron Reagan all helped reveal what it's really like to live in the "great white jail."

I also greatly enjoyed talking with former social secretaries Amy Zantzinger, Desirée Rogers, Julianna Smoot, and Bess Abell, and am so appreciative for the help of Sally McDonough, Kaki Hockersmith, Melissa Montgomery, Deanna Congileo, and Wren Powell. Thank you to the presidential aides who provided an important perspective into the relationship between the political staff and the residence workers: Anita Dunn, Reggie Love, Katie Johnson, Katie McCormick Lelyveld, Reid Cherlin, Adam Frankel, Julianna Smoot, Andy Card, and Anita McBride. And thank you to Emmy Award winner Pete Williams, who very generously took my book jacket photo and made me laugh in the process. I'm also grateful to the White House Curator's Office, the White House Historical Association, and to the staffs at the John F. Kennedy Presidential Library and Museum, the Lyndon Baines Johnson Library and

Museum, the Nixon Presidential Library and Museum, the Richard Nixon Foundation, the Gerald R. Ford Presidential Library, the Jimmy Carter Presidential Library and Museum, the Ronald Reagan Presidential Library and Museum, the George Bush Presidential Library and Museum, the William J. Clinton Presidential Library and Museum, and the George W. Bush Presidential Library and Museum.

Gayle Tzemach Lemmon gave me this simple and necessary advice after months and months of interviews and research: "Sit down and start writing!" A bestselling author and accomplished journalist herself, Gayle was an important sounding board for me throughout this journey. And thank you to Christina Warner and Annie Kate Pons. Annie, I love "doing life with you" too, even if we are on opposite coasts.

I'm eternally grateful to Bloomberg's Al Hunt who gave me the chance of a lifetime when he assigned me to the White House beat, and to editors Joe Sobczyk, Steve Komarow, Jeanne Cummings, and Mark Silva who helped me discover the joys of reporting.

Sources and Chapter Notes

NOTE ON REPORTING

My research for *The Residence* included candid conversations with more than a hundred White House insiders. I interviewed three former first ladies and the children of four presidents, along with numerous presidential aides. But the most revealing details came from my conversations with roughly fifty former residence workers and a current staffer, most of whom had never spoken in such detail about their experiences working for America's first families. In fact, most had never even been approached by a reporter before. Many of these conversations were in person. In rare circumstances sources asked not to be named because of the sensitivity of the subject matter and I respected their wishes. These firsthand accounts of life in the residence were supplemented by extensive research from archival materials, including oral histories from presidential libraries, memoirs penned by residence staffers and political aides, and biographies.

INTRODUCTION

Interview subjects include Laura Bush, Rosalynn Carter, Barbara Bush, Reggie Love, Reid Cherlin, Susan Ford, Frank Ruta, Betty Finney, Amy Zantzinger, Stephen Rochon, Ron Reagan, Cletus Clark, Katie Johnson, Tricia Nixon, Julianna Smoot, Katie McCormick Lelyveld, Bob Scanlan, Tony Savoy, Nelson Pierce, Christine Limerick, Walter Scheib, Skip Allen, Ronn Payne, Roland Mesnier, and Worthington White. Published sources include Preston Bruce, *From the Door of the White House* (New York: Lothrop, Lee and Shepard Books, a division of William Morrow and Company, Inc., 1984); Lillian Rogers Parks with Frances Spatz Leighton, *My Thirty Years Backstairs at the White House* (New York: Ishi Press International, 1961); Faye Fiore, "Jacqueline Kennedy's Pink Hat Is a Missing Piece of History," *Los Angeles Times*, January 26, 2011; Dominique Mann, "In Wake of New Film 'The Butler,' Black Ex-White House Staffers Reflect,"

MSNBC.com, September 14, 2013; Hillary Rodham Clinton, interview of the first lady for *House Beautiful*, November 30, 1993, by Marian Burros, William J. Clinton Presidential Library; "Jacqueline Kennedy in the White House," John F. Kennedy Presidential Library and Museum; Sue Allison Massimiano, "Those Who Serve Those Who Serve," *Life*, *"The White House 1792–1992,"* October 30, 1992; (FY) 2014 Congressional Budget Submission—the White House; Preston Bruce's oral history is available at the John F. Kennedy Presidential Library and Museum; Liz McNeil, "Jackie Kennedy: New Details of Her Heartbreak," *People*, November 13, 2013; Carol D. Leonnig, "Secret Service Fumbled Response to 2011 Shooting," *Washington Post*, September 28, 2014; Carol D. Leonnig, "White House Intruder Was Tackled by Off-Duty Secret Service Agent," *Washington Post*, September 30, 2014; William Safire, "Inside the Bunker," *New York Times*, September 13, 2001; Laura Bush, *Spoken from the Heart* (New York: Scribner, 2010); Letitia Baldrige, *A Lady, First: My Life in the Kennedy White House and the American Embassies of Paris and Rome* (New York: Viking Penguin, 2001); James Bennet, "Testing of a President: The Overview; Clinton Admits Lewinsky Liaison to Jury; Tells Nation 'It Was Wrong,' but Private," *New York Times*, August 18, 1998; Courtney Thompson, "Obamas Called on Chicago Vendors for State Dinner Décor, Stage, and Lighting," *BizBash*, December 2, 2009; Abigail Adams, "Letter to Her Daughter from the New White House," White House Historical Association, November 21, 1800; White House Dimensions and Statistics, White House Historical Association; J. B. West with Mary Lynn Kotz, *Upstairs at the White House: My Life with the First Ladies* (New York: Warner Books, 1973); Carl Cannon, "November 21, 1963," *Real Clear Politics*, November 21, 2013; Claire Faulkner, "Ushers and Stewards Since 1800," *White House History: At Work in the White House: Journal of the White House Historical Association,* 26; Robert Klara, *The Hidden White House: Harry Truman and the Reconstruction of America's Most Famous Residence* (New York: Thomas Dunne Books, St. Martin's Press, 2013); William Seale, *The President's House*, Volumes I and II (Washington, D.C.: White House Historical Association with the cooperation of the National Geographic Society, 1986); Katherine Skiba, "Chicagoans at Forefront of White House Holiday Décor," *Chicago Tribune*, December 5, 2013; Walter Scheib and Andrew Friedman, *White House Chef: Eleven Years, Two Presidents, One Kitchen* (Hoboken, N.J.: John Wiley and Sons, Inc., 2007); Sheila Rabb Weidenfeld, *First Lady's Lady: With the Fords at the White House* (New York: G. P. Putnam's Sons, 1979); John and Claire Whitcomb, *Real Life at the White House: 200 Years of Daily Life at America's Most Famous Residence* (New York: Routledge, 2002); William Seale, "Secret Spaces at the White House?" *White House History: Special Spaces: Journal of the White House Historical Association*, 29 (2011).

CHAPTER I: CONTROLLED CHAOS

For this chapter the author drew on conversations with Desirée Rogers, Luci Baines Johnson, Rosalynn Carter, Stephen Rochon, Barbara Bush, Nelson Pierce, James Jeffries, Kaki Hockersmith, Bill Cliber, Betty Monkman, Laura Bush, Gary Walters, Bess Abell, Christine Limerick, Bob Scanlan, Tony Savoy, Skip Allen, Katie Johnson, Jim Ketchum, Chris Emery, Linsey Little, Ronn Payne, Walter Scheib, Michael "Rahni"

Flowers, Daryl Wells, David Hume Kennerly, Milton Frame, Roland Mesnier, Reggie Love, Ivaniz Silva, Cletus Clark, Susan Ford, Lynwood Westray, and Katie McCormick Lelyveld. Published sources include Michael Ruane and Aaron C. Davis, "D.C.'s Inauguration Head Count: 1.8 Million," *Washington Post*, January 22, 2009; Krissah Thompson and Juliet Eilperin, "The Elusive Mrs. R: Marion Robinson, the White House's Note-So-Typical Live-In Grandma," *Washington Post*, March 31, 2014; Kate Andersen, "Rogers Heats Up Obama Social Calendar That Economy Can't Chill," *Bloomberg*, April 10, 2009; Kate Andersen, "Obama Invites LeBron James to Play in White House Court Opener," *Bloomberg*, June 20, 2009; Letitia Baldrige, *A Lady, First: My Life in the Kennedy White House and the American Embassies of Paris and Rome* (New York: Viking Penguin, 2001); Laura Bush, *Spoken from the Heart* (New York: Scribner, 2010); interview with President Barack Obama, *The Tom Joyner Morning Show*, August 27, 2013; interview with First Lady Michelle Obama and Jill Biden, *The Gayle King Show,* April 19, 2011; Thom Patterson, "Special Ops: How to Move a President in a Few Hours," CNN, January 19, 2009; Traphes Bryant with Frances Spatz Leighton, *Dog Days at the White House* (New York: Macmillan Publishing Co., Inc., 1975); Preston Bruce, *From the Door of the White House* (New York: Lothrop, Lee and Shepard Books, a division of William Morrow and Company, Inc., 1984); Alonzo Fields, *My 21 Years in the White House* (New York: Crest Books, 1961); Anne Kornblut, "Reggie Love, Obama 'Body Man,' to Leave White House by Year's End," *Washington Post*, November 10, 2011; Carl Anthony, "Jackie Kennedy's Last White House Days & What She Found in JFK'S Desk," carlanthonyonline.com, December 6, 2013; Patricia Leigh Brown, "A Redecorated White House, the Way the Clintons Like It," *New York Times*, November 24, 1993; "Power Shifts Hands in Flurry of Activity," *USA TODAY*, January 22, 2001; Sally Bedell Smith, *For the Love of Politics: Inside the Clinton White House* (New York: Random House, 2007); Ann Devroy and Ruth Marcus, "Clinton Takes Oath as 42nd President Asking Sacrifice, Promising Renewal," *Washington Post*, January 21, 1993; Nancy Gibbs and Michael Duffy, *The President's Club: Inside the World's Most Exclusive Fraternity* (New York: Simon and Schuster, 2012); Lauren Collins, "The Other Obama: Michelle Obama and the Politics of Candor," *New Yorker*, March 10, 2008; Jodi Kantor, *The Obamas* (New York: Little, Brown and Company, 2012); Roland Mesnier with Christian Malard, *All the President's Pastries: Twenty-Five Years in the White House* (Paris: Flammarion, SA, 2006); Lady Bird Johnson, *A White House Diary* (New York: Holt, Rinehart and Winston, 1970); Nancy Mitchell interview by James Deutsch for the Ralph Rinzler Folklife Archives and Collections, Center for Folklife and Cultural Heritage, Smithsonian Institution, Washington, D.C., August 27, 2007; Henry Haller, interview for the Ralph Rinzler Folklife Archives and Collections, Center for Folklife and Cultural Heritage, Smithsonian Institution, Washington, D.C., August 27, 2007; Sheryl Gay Stolberg, "On Moving Day for 2 First Families, a Bit of Magic by 93 Pairs of Hands," *New York Times*, January 20, 2009; J. B. West with Mary Lynn Kotz, *Upstairs at the White House: My Life with the First Ladies* (New York: Warner Books, 1973); Tim Carman, "White House Memories: Chef John

Moeller on Pretzels, Maple Syrup and Calorie-Counting," *Washington Post*, February 18, 2014; Nancy Reagan and William Novak, *My Turn* (New York: Random House, 1989); Liz Carpenter, *Ruffles and Flourishes* (New York: Doubleday, 1970); John and Claire Whitcomb, *Real Life at the White House: 200 Years of Daily Life at America's Most Famous Residence* (New York: Routledge, 2002); Hillary Rodham Clinton, interview of the first lady for *House Beautiful*, November 30, 1993, by Marian Burros, William J. Clinton Presidential Library; President Bill Clinton and First Lady Hillary Rodham Clinton, interview for *National Geographic*, July 25, 1995, William J. Clinton Presidential Library; the Anne Lincoln and J. B. West Oral Histories are available at the John F. Kennedy Presidential Library and Museum; "Clinton Ok'd Using Lincoln Bedroom for Contributors," CNN, February 25, 1997; Jim Kuhnhenn, "Obama Returns to Chicago Home After Illinois Fundraiser," Associated Press, June 2, 2012; Barbara Bush, *Barbara Bush: A Memoir* (New York: Scribner, 1994); Andrew Rosenthal, "Bush Encounters the Supermarket, Amazed," *New York Times*, February 5, 1992.

CHAPTER II: DISCRETION

This chapter was based in part on interviews with Rosalynn Carter, James Ramsey, Stephen Rochon, Skip Allen, Jane Erkenbeck, Betty Monkman, Worthington White, Reggie Love, Cletus Clark, Laura Bush, Gary Walters, Bill Hamilton, Barbara Bush, Herman Thompson, Margaret Arrington, Frank Ruta, Walter Scheib, Roland Mesnier, Nelson Pierce, Ron Reagan, Steve Ford, Vincent Contee, Luci Baines Johnson, Ronn Payne, Ivaniz Silva, James Jeffries, Susan Ford, Bess Abell, Andy Card, Katie McCormick Lelyveld, Katie Johnson, Tony Savoy, Chris Emery, and Christine Limerick. Published material includes Gerald Boyd, "Nancy Reagan's Maid Is Accused of Helping to Export Ammunition," *New York Times*, August 14, 1986; Irwin "Ike" Hoover, "Who's Who, and Why, in the White House," *Saturday Evening Post*, February 10, 1934; Wilson Jerman, interview for the Ralph Rinzler Folklife Archives and Collections, Center for Folklife and Cultural Heritage, Smithsonian Institution, Washington, D.C., October 2, 2007; Walter Scheib and Andrew Friedman, *White House Chef: Eleven Years, Two Presidents, One Kitchen* (Hoboken, N.J.: John Wiley Sons, Inc., 2007); Roland Mesnier with Christian Malard, *All the President's Pastries: Twenty-Five Years in the White House* (Paris: Flammarion, SA, 2006); Alonzo Fields, *My 21 Years in the White House* (New York: Crest Books, 1961); Sheila Rabb Weidenfeld, *First Lady's Lady: With the Fords at the White House* (New York: G. P. Putnam's Sons, 1979); White House Historical Association, "The Working White House;" Douglas Jehl, "Chief White House Usher 'Grounded,'" *New York Times*, March 18, 1994; John and Claire Whitcomb, *Real Life at the White House: 200 Years of Daily Life at America's Most Famous Residence* (New York: Routledge, 2002); J. B. West with Mary Lynn Kotz, *Upstairs at the White House: My Life with the First Ladies* (New York: Warner Books, 1973); Traphes Bryant, *Dog Days at the White House* (New York: Macmillan Publishing Co., 1975); Betty Monkman's Oral History can be found at the Gerald R. Ford Presidential Library; Hillary Rodham Clinton, *An Invitation to the White House* (New York: Simon and Schuster, 2000); "Maid Cleared, Nancy Reagan Wants Her

Back," United Press International, November 4, 1986; and Betty Monkman interview for the Ralph Rinzler Folklife Archives and Collections, Center for Folklife and Cultural Heritage, Smithsonian Institution, Washington, D.C., August 27, 2007.

CHAPTER III: DEVOTION

Interview subjects include Barbara Bush, Cletus Clark, Rosalynn Carter, James Jeffries, Letitia Baldrige, Nelson Pierce, Roland Mesnier, Worthington White, Wendy Elsasser, Linsey Little, Christine Limerick, Chris Emery, Gary Walters, Skip Allen, Katie John-son, Luci Baines Johnson, Desirée Rogers, Stephen Rochon, Nancy Reagan through her assistant Wren Powell, and Tony Savoy. Published sources includes Barbara Bush, *Barbara Bush: A Memoir* (New York: Scribner, 1994); J. B. West with Mary Lynn Kotz, *Upstairs at the White House: My Life with the First Ladies* (New York: Warner Books, 1973); Sheila Rabb Weidenfeld, *First Lady's Lady: With the Fords at the White House* (New York: G. P. Putnam's Sons, 1979); Irwin Hoover, "Who's Who, and Why, in the White House," *Saturday Evening Post*, February 10, 1934; Zephyr Wright's Oral History can be found at the Lyndon Baines Johnson Library; Isaac Avery's Oral History can be found at the John F. Kennedy Presidential Library and Museum; Sue Allison Massimiano, "Those Who Serve Those Who Serve," *Life, The White House 1792–1992,* October 30, 1992; Carol D. Leon-nig, "Secret Service Fumbled Response to 2011 Shooting," *Washington Post*, September 28, 2014; Carol D. Leonnig, "White House Intruder Was Tackled by Off-Duty Secret Service Agent," *Washington Post*, September 30, 2014; Roland Mesnier with Christian Malard, *All the President's Pastries: Twenty-Five Years in the White House* (Paris: Flammarion, SA, 2006); Gerald Boyd, "Nancy Reagan's Maid Is Accused of Helping to Export Ammunition," *New York Times*, August 14, 1986; "Former White House Chief Usher Recalls Serving 7 Pres-ident at Oakland Town Hall," *Oakland Press News*, April 9, 2014; "Maid Cleared, Nancy Reagan Wants Her Back," United Press International, November 4, 1986.

CHAPTER IV: EXTRAORDINARY DEMANDS

For this chapter the author drew on conversations with Luci Baines Johnson, Barbara Bush, Skip Allen, Margaret Arrington, Bill Cliber, Herman Thompson, Christine Lim-erick, Frank Ruta, Wendy Elsasser, Roland Mesnier, Cletus Clark, Bess Abell, Ronn Payne, Lynda Bird Johnson Robb, and John Moeller. Published sources include Hillary Rodham Clinton, interview of the first lady for *House Beautiful*, November 30, 1993, by Marian Burros, William J. Clinton Presidential Library; President Bill Clinton and First Lady Hillary Rodham Clinton, interview for *National Geographic*, July 25, 1995, William J. Clinton Presidential Library; Sue Allison Massimiano, "Those Who Serve Those Who Serve," *Life, The White House 1792–1992,* October 30, 1992; Traphes Bryant, *Dog Days at the White House* (New York: Macmillan Publishing Co., 1975); Hillary Rodham Clinton, *An Invitation to the White House: At Home with History* (New York: Simon and Schuster, 2000); Adam Bernstein, "Rex Scouten, Longtime White House Chief Usher, Dies at 86," *Washington Post*, February 22, 2013; J. B. West with Mary Lynn Kotz, *Upstairs at the White House: My Life with the First Ladies* (New York: Warner Books, 1973); Preston Bruce, *From the*

Door of the White House (New York: Lothrop, Lee and Shepard Books, a division of William Morrow and Company, Inc., 1984); Sheila Rabb Weidenfeld, *First Lady's Lady: With the Fords at the White House* (New York: G. P. Putnam's Sons, 1979); Zephyr Wright's Oral History can be found at the Lyndon Baines Johnson Presidential Library; Wilson Jerman, interview for the Ralph Rinzler Folklife Archives and Collections, Center for Folklife and Cultural Heritage, Smithsonian Institution, Washington, D.C., October 2, 2007.

CHAPTER V: DARK DAYS
Interview subjects include Barbara Bush, Bill Cliber, Walter Scheib, Herman Thompson, Gary Walters, Laura Bush, Cletus Clark, Nelson Pierce, Jim Ketchum, Tricia Nixon, Roland Mesnier, Betty Monkman, Ron Reagan, James Hall, Linsey Little, Skip Allen, Chris Emery, Bill Hamilton, Worthington White, James Ramsey, Betty Finney, Ronn Payne, and Tony Savoy. Published sources include Sheila Rabb Weidenfeld, *First Lady's Lady: With the Fords at the White House* (New York: G. P. Putnam's Sons, 1979); Laura Bush, *Spoken from the Heart* (New York: Scribner, 2010); Preston Bruce, *From the Door of the White House* (New York: Lothrop, Lee and Shepard Books, a division of William Morrow and Company, Inc., 1984); Traphes Bryant with Frances Spatz Leighton, *Dog Days at the White House* (New York: Macmillan Publishing Co., Inc., 1975); Todd Purdum, "With Resolve, First Lady Lays Out Defense," *New York Times*, January 17, 1996; Hillary Rodham Clinton, interview of the first lady for *House Beautiful*, November 30, 1993, by Marian Burros, William J. Clinton Presidential Library; Susan Thomases interview, Miller Center, University of Virginia, William J. Clinton Presidential Oral History Project, January 6, 2006, Lady Bird Johnson, *A White House Diary* (New York: Holt, Rinehart and Winston, 1970); J. B. West with Mary Lynn Kotz, *Upstairs at the White House: My Life with the First Ladies* (New York: Warner Books, 1973); Monica Lewinsky Timeline, *Washington Post*, September 13, 1998; Roland Mesnier with Christian Malard, *All the President's Pastries: Twenty-Five Years in the White House* (Paris: Flammarion, SA, 2006); Douglas Jehl, "Chief White House Usher 'Grounded,'" *New York Times*, March 18, 1994; the Oral Histories of Maud Shaw and Lawrence J. Arata can be found at the John F. Kennedy Presidential Library and Museum; Jane Whitmore, "Mr. Nixon's Man Manolo Finds His Job Fetching," *Pittsburgh Post-Gazette*, May 21, 1969; Bill Cliber interview for the Ralph Rinzler Folklife Archives and Collections, Center for Folklife and Cultural Heritage, Smithsonian Institution, Washington, D.C., August 22, 2007; Henry Haller, interview for the Ralph Rinzler Folklife Archives and Collections, Center for Folklife and Cultural Heritage, Smithsonian Institution, Washington, D.C., August 27, 2007; Richard Nixon/Frank Gannon interview, University of Georgia Special Collections Libraries, The Walter J. Brown Media Archives and Peabody Awards Collection, June 10, 1983.

CHAPTER VI: SACRIFICE
The author drew on conversations with Nelson and Caroline Pierce, Desirée Rogers, Walter Scheib, Bess Abell, Charles Allen, Katie Johnson, Wendy Elsasser, Reid Cherlin,

Chris Emery, Worthington White, James Ramsey, James Jeffries, James Hall, Adam Frankel, Linsey Little, Skip Allen, Herman Thompson, Christine Limerick, Luci Baines Johnson, Nancy Reagan through her assistant Wren Powell, and Lynda Johnson Robb. Published material includes J. B. West with Mary Lynn Kotz, *Upstairs at the White House: My Life with the First Ladies* (New York: Warner Books, 1973); Isaac Avery's Oral History can be found at the John F. Kennedy Presidential Library and Museum; Jodi Kantor, *The Obamas* (New York: Little, Brown and Company, 2012); Associated Press "Frederick Mayfield, 58, Dies; Doorman at the White House," *New York Times*, May 16, 1984; Nancy Mitchell interview by James Deutsch for the Ralph Rinzler Folklife Archives and Collections, Center for Folklife and Cultural Heritage, Smithsonian Institution, Washington, D.C., August 27, 2007.

CHAPTER VII: RACE AND THE RESIDENCE

This chapter was based in part on conversations with Rosalynn Carter, Luci Baines Johnson, Bess Abell, Lonnie Bunch, Lynwood and Kay Westray, Gloria Nuckles, Alvie Paschall, Mary Prince, Charles Allen, Nelson Pierce, Bill Hamilton, James Jeffries, Chris Emery, Stephen Rochon, Otis Williams, Frank Ruta, Betty Monkman, Herman Thompson, Desirée Rogers, James Ramsey, and Tony Savoy. Published material includes Preston Bruce, *From the Door of the White House* (New York: Lothrop, Lee and Shepard Books, a division of William Morrow and Company, Inc., 1984); Jimmy Carter, *Keeping Faith* (New York: Bantam Books, 1982); Catherine Clinton, *Mrs. Lincoln: A Life* (New York: Harper Perennial, 2010); Clare Crawford, "A Story of Love and Rehabilitation: the Ex-Con in the White House," *People*, March 14, 1977; Alonzo Fields, *My 21 Years in the White House* (New York: Crest Books, 1961); William Seale, *The President's House, Volume I* (Washington, D.C.: White House Historical Association with the Cooperation of the National Geographic Society, 1986); John and Claire Whitcomb, *Real Life at the White House: 200 Years of Daily Life at America's Most Famous Residence* (New York: Routledge, 2002); White House Historical Association, *African Americans and the White House, 1790s–1840s*; "Michelle Obama's Ancestors: Purnell Shields," *Huffington Post*, February 24, 2012; interview with Michelle Obama on ABC News' *Good Morning America*, May 22, 2007; Nancy Tuckerman's and Pamela Turnure's Oral Histories can be found at the John F. Kennedy Presidential Library and Museum; Zephyr Wright's Oral History can be found at the Lyndon Baines Johnson Presidential Library; Traphes Bryant with Frances Spatz Leighton, *Dog Days at the White House* (New York: Macmillan Publishing Co., Inc., 1975); *Saturday Night Live*, March 12, 1977; Jodi Kantor, *The Obamas* (New York: Little, Brown and Company, 2012); Dahleen Glanton and Stacy St. Clair, "Michelle Obama's Family Tree Has Roots in a Carolina Slave Plantation," *Chicago Tribune*, December 1, 2008.

CHAPTER VIII: BACKSTAIRS GOSSIP AND MISCHIEF

Interview subjects for this chapter include Bess Abell, Bill Cliber, Lynda Johnson Robb, Christine Limerick, Bill Hamilton, Skip Allen, Ronn Payne, Roland Mesnier, Walter Scheib, Ivaniz Silva, Pierre Chambrin, Ron Reagan, John Moeller, and Margaret Arrington.

Published material includes Traphes Bryant with Frances Spatz Leighton, *Dog Days at the White House* (New York: Macmillan Publishing Co., Inc., 1975); Robert Rosenblatt, "Harassment at White House Alleged," *Los Angeles Times*, September 14, 2000; J. B. West with Mary Lynn Kotz, *Upstairs at the White House: My Life with the First Ladies* (New York: Warner Books, 1973); Anne Lincoln's Oral History can be found at the John F. Kennedy Presidential Library and Museum; Zephyr Wright's Oral History can be found at the Lyndon Baines Johnson Library; Reds Arrington, interview for the Ralph Rinzler Folklife Archives and Collections, Center for Folklife and Cultural Heritage, Smithsonian Institution, Washington, D.C.; Bill Cliber, interview for the Ralph Rinzler Folklife Archives and Collections, Center for Folklife and Cultural Heritage, Smithsonian Institution, Washington, D.C., August 22, 2007; Tyler Cabot, "White House Chefs," *Atlantic*, May 1, 2005.

CHAPTER IX: GROWING UP IN THE WHITE HOUSE

Information in this chapter was based in part on conversations with Rosalynn Carter, Lynda Johnson Robb, Luci Baines Johnson, Bob Scanlan, Roland Mesnier, Wendy Elsasser, Walter Scheib, Mary Prince, James Jeffries, Michael "Rahni" Flowers, Gary Walters, Susan Ford, Barbara Bush, Steve Ford, Tony Savoy, Nelson Pierce, Bill Hamilton, Amy Zantzinger, Betty Monkman, and Betty Finney. Published material includes Nancy Mitchell interview by James Deutsch for the Ralph Rinzler Folklife Archives and Collections, Center for Folklife and Cultural Heritage, Smithsonian Institution, Washington, D.C., August 27, 2007; Letitia Baldrige, *A Lady, First: My Life in the Kennedy White House and the American Embassies of Paris and Rome* (New York: Viking Penguin, 2001); Victorino Matus, "Notes from a White House Kitchen," *Weekly Standard*, March 5, 2014; Jose A. DelReal and Ed O'Keefe, "Hill Staffer Elizabeth Lauten Resigns After Remarks About Obama Daughters," *Washington Post*, December 1, 2014; Laura Bush, *Spoken from the Heart* (New York: Scribner, 2010); Traphes Bryant, *Dog Days at the White House* (New York: Macmillan Publishing Co., 1975); Roland Mesnier with Christian Malard, *All the President's Pastries: Twenty-Five Years in the White House* (Paris: Flammarion, SA, 2006); Doug Wead, *All the Presidents' Children: Triumph and Tragedy in the Lives of America's First Families* (New York: Atria Books, 2003); Sheila Rabb Weidenfeld, *First Lady's Lady: With the Fords at the White House* (New York: G. P. Putnam's Sons, 1979); Helena Andrews, "Jenna Bush Hager, Hanky-Panky, and the White House Roof," *Washington Post*, December 4, 2014; J. B. West with Mary Lynn Kotz, *Upstairs at the White House: My Life with the First Ladies* (New York: Warner Books, 1973); Betty Monkman interview for the Ralph Rinzler Folklife Archives and Collections, Center for Folklife and Cultural Heritage, Smithsonian Institution, Washington, D.C., August 27, 2007; C. W. Nevius, "Just Ask Chelsea, Jenna and Barbara: Escaping the Glare of the Spotlight Isn't Easy for Kids Whose Dads Work in the Oval Office," *San Francisco Gate*, January 22, 2004; Rachel Swarns, "First Chores," *New York Times*, February 22, 2009.

CHAPTER X: HEARTBREAK AND HOPE

Author drew on conversations with Laura Bush, Bill and Bea Cliber, Wendy Elsasser,

Betty Finney, Christine Limerick, Roland Mesnier, Nelson Pierce, Jim Ketchum, Gary Walters, Betty Monkman, Walter Scheib, Bob Scanlan, Ivaniz Silva, Skip Allen, John Moeller, and Lynwood Westray. Published material includes Lady Bird Johnson, *A White House Diary* (New York: Holt, Rinehart and Winston, 1970); Mimi Swartz, "Them's Fightin' Words!" *Texas Monthly*, July 2004; Letitia Baldrige, *A Lady, First: My Life in the Kennedy White House and the American Embassies of Paris and Rome* (New York: Viking Penguin, 2001); Preston Bruce, *From the Door of the White House* (New York: Lothrop, Lee and Shepard Books, a division of William Morrow and Company, Inc., 1984); Tom Wicker, "Kennedy Is Killed by Sniper as He Rides in Car in Dallas; Johnson Sworn In on Plane," *New York Times*, November 22, 1963; Laura Bush, *Spoken from the Heart* (New York: Scribner, 2010); Wilson Jerman, interview for the Ralph Rinzler Folklife Archives and Collections, Center for Folklife and Cultural Heritage, Smithsonian Institution, Washington, D.C., October 2, 2007; Transcript: Richard Nixon/Frank Gannon interview, University of Georgia Special Collections Libraries, The Walter J. Brown Media Archives and Peabody Awards Collection, June 10, 1983; Christopher Andersen, *Jackie After Jack* (New York: William Morrow and Company, 1998); J. B. West with Mary Lynn Kotz, *Upstairs at the White House: My Life with the First Ladies* (New York: Warner Books, 1973); interview with Luci Baines Johnson on CBS News' *Face the Nation*, November 17, 2013; the Oral Histories of Maud Shaw, Anne Lincoln, and Lawrence J. Arata can be found at the John F. Kennedy Presidential Library and Museum.

EPILOGUE
Interview subjects included Laura Bush, Rosalynn Carter, James Jeffries, Nelson Pierce, James Hall, Skip Allen, Reggie Love, Luci Baines Johnson, James and Valerie Ramsey, and Stephen Rochon. Published material used: Sheila Rabb Weidenfeld, *First Lady's Lady: With the Fords at the White House* (New York: G. P. Putnam's Sons, 1979).

PHOTO INSERT SOURCES AND CREDITS
Insert one: David Kennerly/White House, courtesy David Kennerly; Abbie Rowe/National Park Service, courtesy Margaret Arrington; Jack Rottier/National Park Service, courtesy Lynwood Westray; Robert Knudsen/White House, courtesy John F. Kennedy Presidential Library and Museum, Boston; Harold Sellers/White House, June 7, 1963, courtesy John F. Kennedy Presidential Library and Museum, Boston; Robert Knudsen/White House, December 6, 1963, courtesy John F. Kennedy Presidential Library and Museum, Boston; Robert Knudsen/White House, December 19, 1963, courtesy John F. Kennedy Presidential Library and Museum, Boston; Margaret Arrington, courtesy Margaret Arrington; official White House photograph, courtesy Lynwood Westray; Jack Kightlinger/White House, courtesy Richard Nixon Presidential Library and Museum; David Kennerly/White House, courtesy Gerald R. Ford Presidential Library and Museum; Bill Fitz-Patrick/White House, courtesy Jimmy Carter Presidental Library and Museum; Ricardo Thomas/White House, courtesy Gerald R. Ford Presidential Library and Museum; all four photos of President and

Selected Bibliography

Andersen, Kate. "Rogers Heats Up Obama Social Calendar That Economy Can't Chill." *Bloomberg*, April 10, 2009.

————. "Obama Invites LeBron James to Play in White House Court Opener." *Bloomberg*, June 20, 2009.

Baldrige, Letitia. *A Lady, First: My Life in the Kennedy White House and the American Embassies of Paris and Rome.* New York: Viking Penguin, 2001.

Bennet, James. "Testing of a President: The Overview; Clinton Admits Lewinsky Liaison to Jury; Tells Nation 'It Was Wrong,' but Private." *New York Times*, August 18, 1998.

Boyd, Gerald. "Nancy Reagan's Maid Is Accused of Helping to Export Ammunition." *New York Times*, August 14, 1986.

Brown, Patricia Leigh. "A Redecorated White House, the Way the Clintons Like It." *New York Times*, November 24, 1993.

Bruce, Preston. *From the Door of the White House.* New York: Lothrop, Lee and Shepard Books, a division of William Morrow and Company, Inc., 1984.

Bryant, Traphes with Frances Spatz Leighton. *Dog Days at the White House.* New York: Macmillan , 1975.

Bush, Barbara. *Barbara Bush: A Memoir.* New York: Scribner, 1994.

Bush, Laura. *Spoken from the Heart.* New York: Scribner, 2010.

Caro, Robert. *The Years of Lyndon Johnson: Master of the Senate.* New York: Alfred Knopf, 2002.

————. *The Years of Lyndon Johnson: The Passage of Power.* New York: Alfred Knopf, 2012.

Carpenter, Liz. *Ruffles and Flourishes.* New York: Doubleday, 1970.

Carter, Jimmy. *Keeping Faith: Memoirs of a President.* New York: Bantam Books, 1982.

Clinton, Catherine. *Mrs. Lincoln: A Life*. New York: Harper Perennial, 2010.

Clinton, Hillary Rodham. Interview of the first lady for *House Beautiful*, November 30, 1993, by Marian Burros, William J. Clinton Presidential Library.

———. *An Invitation to the White House: At Home with History*. New York: Simon and Schuster, 2000.

Clinton, William J., and Hillary Rodham Clinton. Interview for *National Geographic*, July 25, 1995, William J. Clinton Presidential Library.

Collins, Lauren. "The Other Obama: Michelle Obama and the Politics of Candor." *New Yorker*, March 10, 2008.

Coram, James. "A White House 'Fairy Tale' with No Happily Ever After." *Baltimore Sun*, March 25, 1994.

Crawford, Clare. "A Story of Love and Rehabilitation: The Ex-Con in the White House." *People*, March 14, 1977. http://www.people.com/people/archive/issue /0,,7566770314,00.html.

Faulkner, Claire. "Ushers and Stewards Since 1800." *White House History: At Work in the White House: Journal of the White House Historical Association* 26 (2009).

Fields, Alonzo. *My 21 Years in the White House*. New York: Crest Books, 1961.

Gibbs, Nancy, and Michael Duffy, *The President's Club: Inside the World's Most Exclusive Fraternity* (New York: Simon and Schuster, 2012).

Glanton, Dahleen, and Stacy St. Clair. "Michelle Obama's Family Tree Has Roots in a Carolina Slave Plantation." *Chicago Tribune*, December 1, 2008.

Hoover, Irwin "Ike." "Who's Who, and Why, in the White House." *Saturday Evening Post*, February 10, 1934.

Jehl, Douglas. "Chief White House Usher 'Grounded.'" *New York Times*, March 18, 1994.

Johnson, Lady Bird. *A White House Diary*. New York: Holt, Rinehart and Winston, 1970.

Kantor, Jodi. *The Obamas*. New York: Little, Brown and Company, 2012.

Klara, Robert. *The Hidden White House: Harry Truman and the Reconstruction of America's Most Famous Residence*. New York: Thomas Dunne Books, 2013.

Kornblut, Anne, "Reggie Love, Obama 'Body Man,' to Leave White House by Year's End." *Washington Post*, November 10, 2011.

Kuhnhenn, Jim. "Obama Returns to Chicago Home After Illinois Fundraiser." Associated Press, June 2, 2012.

Mann, Dominique. "In Wake of New Film 'The Butler,' Black Ex–White House Staffers Reflect." MSNBC, September 14, 2013. http://www.msnbc.com/melissa-harris-perry /wake-new-film-the-butler-black-ex.

Massimiano, Sue Allison. "Those Who Serve Those Who Serve." *Life, The White House 1792–1992*, October 30, 1992.

Mesnier, Roland with Christian Malard. *All the President's Pastries: Twenty-Five Years in the White House*. Paris: Flammarion, SA, 2006.

Nevius, C. W. "Just Ask Chelsea, Jenna and Barbara: Escaping the Glare of the Spotlight Isn't Easy for Kids Whose Dads Work in the Oval Office." *San Francisco Chronicle*, January 22, 2004. http://www.sfgate.com/bayarea/nevius/article /Just-ask-Chelsea-Jenna-and-Barbara-Escaping-the-2808210.php.

Parks, Lillian Rogers, with Frances SpatzLeighton. *My Thirty Years Backstairs at the White House*. New York: Ishi Press International, 1961.

Patterson, Thom. "Special Ops: How to Move a President in a Few Hours." CNN, January 19, 2009. http://www.cnn.com/2009/POLITICS/01/19/obama.move/.

Reagan, Nancy, and William Novak. *My Turn*. New York: Random House, 1989.

Rosenthal, Andrew. "Bush Encounters the Supermarket, Amazed." *New York Times*, February 5, 1992.

Ruane, Michael, and Aaron C. Davis. "D.C.'s Inauguration Head Count: 1.8 Million." *Washington Post*, January 22, 2009.

Scheib, Walter, and Andrew Friedman. *White House Chef: Eleven Years, Two Presidents, One Kitchen*. Hoboken, N.J.: John Wiley and Sons, Inc., 2007.

Schifando, Peter, and J. Jonathan Joseph. *Entertaining at the White House with Nancy Reagan*. New York: William Morrow, 2007.

Seale, William. *The President's House*, Volumes I and II. Washington, D.C.: White House Historical Association with the Cooperation of the National Geographic Society, 1986.

———. "Secret Spaces at the White House?" *White House History: Special Spaces: Journal of the White House Historical Association* 29 (2011).

Semeraz, Megan. "Former White House Chief Usher Recalls Serving 7 Presidents at Oakland Town Hall." *Oakland Press News*, April 9, 2014. http://www.theoaklandpress.com/general-news/20140409 /former-white-house-chief-usher-recalls-serving-7-presidents-at-oakland-town-hall.

Smolenyak, Megan. "Michelle Obama's Ancestors: Purnell Shields." *Huffington Post*, February 24, 2012.

Swarns, Rachel. "First Chores? You Bet." *New York Times*, February 22, 2009.

Swartz, Mimi. "Them's Fightin' Words!" *Texas Monthly*, July 2004.

Wead, Doug. *All the Presidents' Children: Triumph and Tragedy in the Lives of America's First Families*. New York: Atria Books, 2003.

Weidenfeld, Sheila Rabb. *First Lady's Lady: With the Fords at the White House*. New York: G. P. Putnam's Sons, 1979.

West, J. B., with Mary Lynn Kotz. *Upstairs at the White House: My Life with the First Ladies*. New York: Warner Books, 1973.

Whitcomb, John, and Claire Whitcomb. *Real Life at the White House: 200 Years of Daily Life at America's Most Famous Residence*. New York: Routledge, 2002.

Index

About the Author

★

KATE ANDERSEN BROWER spent four years covering the Obama administration for Bloomberg News. Previously, she worked at CBS News in New York and Fox News in Washington, D.C. She has written for the *Washington Post*, *Bloomberg Businessweek*, and the *Washingtonian*. She lives outside of Washington, D.C., with her husband and two young children. She can be followed on Twitter: @katebrower.